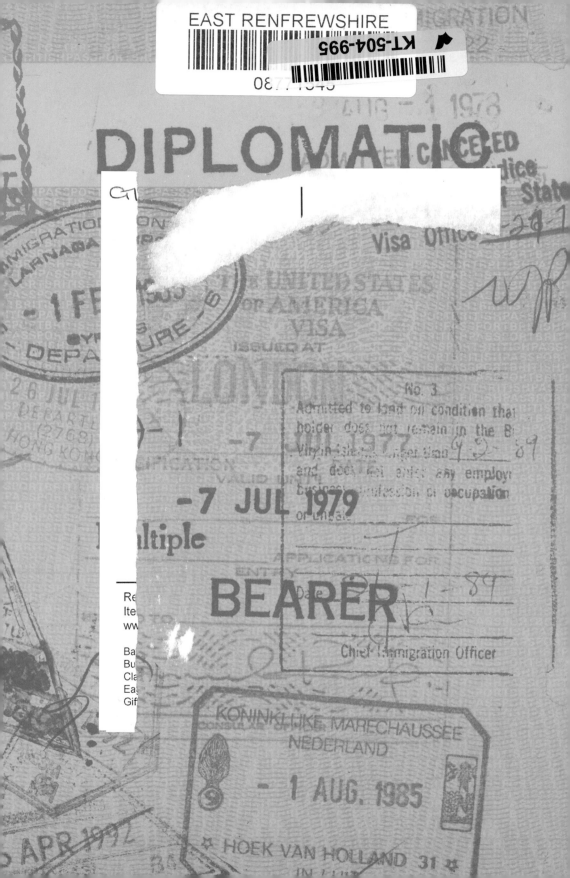

DIPLOMATIC ANECDOTAGE

AROUND THE WORLD IN 40 YEARS

Roger Carrick

First published 2012 by Elliott and Thompson Limited
27 John Street, London WC1N 2BX
www.eandtbooks.com

ISBN: 978-1-907642-55-5

The publisher would like to thank the following
individuals and organisations:

*New*Images, British Council (for the image of John Howard
and Sir Roger Carrick)

Sir Sam Falle (for the image of himself)

Colonel Ian Ker (for the images of Tommy Collins and Indonesian soldiers)

Harold Washington (for the image of himself and Sir Roger Carrick)

Every effort has been made to trace copyright holders for other images used
within this book. Where this has not been possible, the publisher will be happy
to credit them in future editions.

9 8 7 6 5 4 3 2 1

A CIP catalogue record for this book is available from the British Library.

Printed and bound in the UK by TJ International

Typeset by PDQ Media

This book is for Hilary, without whom the story would have been impossible, and with whom it has been a lasting joy; and for John and Charles, who contributed much and coped admirably with the drawbacks of our peripatetic life.

CONTENTS

INTRODUCTION

I thought I had invented the word 'Anecdotage' until I recently came across a quotation attributed to Disraeli: 'When a man falls into his anecdotage, it is a sign for him to retire from the world'. With respect, it is too early for me.

It was a Royal Marine officer, visiting my grammar school in late 1955 to explain National Service to the sixth form, who first caused me to realise how best to advance my ambition of joining the then Foreign Service. He explained that a small number of particularly fortunate young men were recruited each year into the Royal Navy for National Service. Five a year would become upper yardsmen – cadet officers. Others would learn Russian to a high standard and, if successful in examinations, would work for Naval Intelligence. Since two years' National Service was a requirement for all fit young men (and it had genuine appeal for me) this route, if it could be achieved, would be both a bargain and a help towards joining the Foreign Office. Despite emotional pleas from my mother, who had lost a Royal Navy submariner brother during the First World War, and with the helpful advice of my father that I had a rather distant cousin who was a naval officer, I duly registered for the Royal Navy. The Navy selected its Russian students before they were allowed to join, in contrast to the Royal Air Force and Army who selected theirs only after basic training; so with the Royal Navy, one could have some certainty about the following two years. The advance medical examinations, language aptitude tests and interviews went well, the last perhaps in particular because I could name a family connection – with the cousin so distant that we did not meet until over fifty years later, since when knowing Colin Harris has proved a real pleasure.

The examinations and interviews for my Diplomatic Service entry grade successfully behind me, the Foreign Office (FO) thoughtfully asked me to spend a very short time in the Office in September 1956 before I joined the Navy. This meant 11 days trying to help out in the Levant division, as the support staff for the Arabists in the Levant department was known. For those remarkable 11 days I was paid £11; the lowest salary point on the relevant entry grade pay-scale then being £365 p.a. After induction into the most basic procedures, I was allowed to certify the craziest of the huge quantity of letters to the Foreign Office about policy towards Suez as not worth the time and effort of replying: they then were filed in one of a long series of boxes marked LU (for 'lunatic', I supposed). My chief recollections, however, are of the demeanour and concern of the desperately worried but impressively calm Arabists as they laboured to advance their view of the deep folly of the Suez policy then being worked out at the highest level of government. It quickly became clear to me how inimical to real British interests it would be to take on Nasser in the way Eden planned, and alongside France and Israel. It was a privilege to be shown an historic document in the Levant department: a last-ditch attempt by senior officials to persuade the prime minister against his intent. This was a round robin, signed in a circle of senior names to demonstrate unanimity and to disguise hierarchy of signature. Among the mainly Foreign Office signatories were a few senior Treasury mandarins; a rare coalition indeed, and deeply impressive. Of course, the last-ditch effort was of no avail.

Basic training in the Royal Navy at Portsmouth was short and pleasant, evidently in contrast to the experience of many in the other two services. I recall playing rugby, enjoying coach drives to and from matches, learning a little of naval history and practice, very little drill and only two serious parades, or 'divisions'. We were trained to use a Bren gun in hot climates since, the demands of the Russian course notwithstanding, we were expected to go to Suez, arriving in landing craft to fight in pursuit of that so wrong-headed policy. Instead of Suez, there was, in the event, a short course in radio theory, and a few of us joined ships for a NATO exercise radar system. The system had been developed and fitted in three ships in time for the exercise, but no one had thought to train operators, and we National Service Russian students were thought able to learn quickly. Our brief training presented no problem. Three of us travelled to the Clyde to join HMS *Sheffield*, the Second World War veteran 'Shiny Sheff', predecessor of the *Sheffield* burned and sunk in the Falklands conflict. There was only one problem of which we were aware aboard the ship, but it was a serious problem. As mere probationary Coders (Special) we were unable to persuade the bridge that our (accurate) reports of positions of 'enemy' submarine periscopes briefly raised above sea level, and 'over the horizon', were credible. Officers of the midnight watch had not been briefed on the capabilities of the then highly classified new radar and, despite our protestations, did not believe the range we very junior ratings were reporting. Neither would they awaken the captain, whom we knew was 'cleared' and fully briefed. In consequence, our ship was 'sunk'. I should like to have been present at the post-exercise 'wash-up'.

Next came the Joint Services School for Linguists (JSSL) outside Crail in Fife, Scotland and an intensive and very well taught Russian course, whose length had been first reduced from 14 to 11 months, and then to the 7½ months we were allowed. That was my first experience of the power, influence and effectiveness of the 'bean counters' in the Treasury. I was awakened one night in the mess by a shower of naval boots hurled to stop me chanting Russian irregular verbs far too loudly in my sleep. I scraped through the Russian exams and, despite the collaboration in that ineffectual yet impressive round robin, have been prejudiced against HM Treasury ever since. Indeed I found throughout my Diplomatic Service career, little reason to alter my animus.

I much enjoyed the pure Royal Navy aspects of National Service, which were a sharp change from learning Russian. The naval staff at JSSL were all friendly, but the natural, swift and sometimes devastating sense of humour of the lower deck is especially memorable. Most weeks at JSSL, we Coders(Sp) broke away from linguistic endeavour to do something naval for some 40 minutes – seamanship, dismantling Bren guns, or a drill of some kind. Late one Sunday night before an early morning rifle drill, and after Russian homework was done, two of us were challenged to race down the long mess, hand-over-hand along two pipes suspended high against the ceiling. My competitor was David Fairhall, later a journalist, including as defence and shipping correspondent of the *Guardian*. Quite soon in the race we both learned that the pipes carried the hot water: they were unlagged and seemed (in those less energy-conscious days) to contain steam. Yet we carried on, but fast. I cannot recall who won (so it was probably David) but we both left large shreds of skin from our hands on the two pipes. Next morning we paraded before the drill instructor, a three-badge petty officer called Mangham, who told us he had been sent to JSSL as a punishment, and was still trying to work out what he had done quite so wrong. David and I showed PO Mangham our hands and explained that we were fit neither to drill with a rifle, nor to do justice to his 'power of command' – of which he was particularly proud. 'Ah,' said the good PO, 'I know what that is: that's a self-inflicted wound – and in this man's navy a self-inflicted wound is a chargeable offence.' 'Self-inflicted? Petty Officer,' we protested, 'we're not masochists!' The reply came instantly: 'I don't care if you're ruddy Greek Orthodox, it's a chargeable offence'.

Service outside Kiel in northern Germany followed JSSL, and featured many hours of listening on headphones, recording and transcribing Russian in a small contribution to the prosecution of the Cold War. There was the occasional real excitement, for example when well-guarded Russian 'trawlers' anchored in the Kiel Fjord, just off our base, to try to monitor what we were doing. (Three or four of us monitored them at dead of moonless night, using black-painted canoes and paddles, black clothes and our eyes and ears, the latter once pressed to the hull to surprisingly useful effect.) That tour of busy duty also permitted just a little time to see something of Germany and Austria. The British Kiel Yacht Club close by our base provided a first-class 13-week spare-time course in sailing with a rigorous qualifying examination at its end. Success in that both allowed me, as a 'Baltic Helmsman', to skipper former German Navy 'windfall' '30-square' yachts and sail them to such delightful ports as Sønderborg in Denmark. That happy experience engendered a lifelong love for sailing – a love later pursued and fulfilled in many parts of the world.

Curiously, I did not carry into civilian life the then Royal Navy practice, begun in 1655, of drinking rum. 'Up Spirits' was 'piped' at 1100hrs every morning. Senior rates and officers drank theirs neat if they wished. We on the lower deck had ours diluted – two of water to one of rum. That meant one-eighth of a pint of reputedly 95.5% Caribbean rum with a quarter of a pint of water. I was sure that it was the rum that kept me fit during a fierce winter in east Fife – where the icy wind evidently blew straight from Siberia in, some thought, a Soviet Russian plot. Oddly perhaps, I was not more than usually cross with the Treasury for having reduced the cost of the Russian course further by decreeing that we should be among the first Coders(Sp) not to be promoted to midshipmen on passing the interpreter examination near the end of the course – we became merely leading Coders(Sp). I was rather more moved by the Treasury conspiracy, as many believed it to be, to coerce the Admiralty to end the rum ration, which, despite a long-waged rearguard RN action, finally disappeared on 'Black Tot Day' some years later.

National Service for me was a bargain. There was high quality language instruction and practice, sailing, an educative variety of naval experiences, and a taste of naval intelligence and the business of the Cold War. Those two years in the RN were, even more than then conceivable, an ideal preparation for of the rest of my career.

In the autumn of 1958, I joined establishment and organisation (E&O) department of the Foreign Office, where a number of new entrants at my level had their first jobs. The head of department was the delightful, able and original Laurie Pumphrey, who had been a private secretary to Prime Minister Clement Attlee. I saw Laurie again a few years later when he was counsellor in Belgrade and I a third secretary in Sofia. His last job in a distinguished career was (as Sir Laurence) HM ambassador to Pakistan. In E&O department I learned something of the craft of diplomacy, and met the salvation of my career, Hilary. We married in 1962. In those days, and for another decade, lady members of the Foreign Service who married, thereupon resigned – and did so without fuss or complaint at the rule. Hilary duly resigned, though while I took my allotted seven days' marriage leave, she began to fulfil a written request sent by letter from the then foreign secretary, Sir Alec Douglas Home, to work on for a few weeks after her wedding. Such was the depth and breadth of Hilary's extra security clearance that it took time to identify, clear and induct a successor. Later, as a diplomatic wife, Hilary was again, and for much longer, to prove a most useful exception to Foreign Office rules.

For the academic year before our first posting, the Foreign Office sent me to London University to learn Bulgarian. That was an exercise in conversion from the (really useful) Russian I had brought from the Royal Navy. The two languages share most of the Cyrillic alphabet, which was developed by two Greek-born brothers and monks, Cyril and Methodius, who lived in Bulgaria. Bulgarian and Russian share the roots of many words, all but three letters of the Cyrillic alphabet (named for Cyril), but little grammar and less pronunciation, though Bulgarian has a wealth of words of Turkish origin not found in Russian. However, Slavic philology was a bond, and it was possible to read all the pre-communist and often philosophical and charming Bulgarian prose and poetry. Due to the deeply thoughtful, understanding and expert guidance of Dr Vivian Pinto at London University, I successfully read a degree course in the one academic year, and thoroughly enjoyed doing so. Dr Methodie Kussef, a Bulgarian émigré of extraordinary gifts and style, who happily provided in his warm and welcoming Islington home both evening conversation lessons in his native language and invaluable insights into the Bulgarian national character. The Bulgarian section of the BBC Overseas Service was also welcoming and helpful, and encouraged me to broadcast a number of times in Bulgarian, the broadcasts also being recorded on vinyl discs – then the best available method.

Language exams and wedding over, Hilary and I left England for our first posting, the real beginning of our diplomatic career, in which, rather like the Church of England, the employer in those days benefited from two for the price of one. It was a fortunate and happy career: one of extraordinary variety; of failure and success; of heartache and fulfilment; of diplomatic adventure; of only very occasional deep concern that either I or the United Kingdom were wrong in analysis or foreign policy; of involvement in momentous decisions and events – and of fun … please read on.

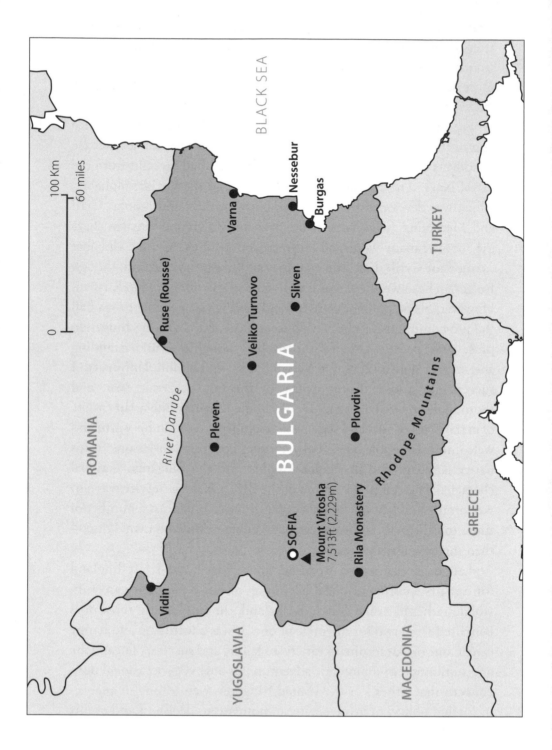

BLACK SEA

ROMANIA

River Danube

Vidin

Pleven

Ruse (Rousse)

Varna

Veliko Turnovo

Nessebur

Burgas

Sliven

BULGARIA

SOFIA

Mount Vitosha
7,513ft (2,229m)

Rila Monastery

Plovdiv

Rhodope Mountains

YUGOSLAVIA

MACEDONIA

GREECE

TURKEY

0   100 Km
     60 miles

CHAPTER 1

THE BEGINNING, IN BULGARIA:
LEGATION

The year is 1962. Hilary and I were junior Diplomatic Service officers. Hilary had served in London and Geneva. I had completed National Service in the Royal Navy, spent three years in the Foreign Office learning something – a little – about the business of diplomacy, and an academic year at university doing a degree course in Bulgarian studies. We were married in September. In November we left Britain for our first diplomatic posting, to the British legation in Sofia, Bulgaria. I was to be the third secretary in chancery – the political section, the information officer and the cultural attaché. Hilary was now to be a diplomatic wife.

1962: the very height – or perhaps depth – of the Cold War, shortly after the Cuban missile crisis. As I saw our national position, only a few years after Suez, the United Kingdom was still coming to terms with a bipolar world. We had declining but still substantial colonial responsibilities around the world. We had important military and intelligence, trading and diplomatic assets and skills. Following the hard long grind of economic recovery after the Second World War, we were doing quite well in international trade and investment. We were playing a key role in prosecuting the Cold War, and in preventing it becoming a hot war. A posting to Bulgaria (a small cog of a country in the massive machinery of the Soviet bloc) – to a small diplomatic mission but a comprehensive one, offered the chance for some front-line diplomacy, albeit in a junior job.

1962: the worst winter in Europe for decades. We drove to Dover. Well before the present access roads to the harbour were built, we stopped there in a complete traffic jam. While it persisted I had time to buy a hat in Dunn's and to have it steamed in the practice of the day to ensure a good fit and style. We boarded a car ferry to Calais and drove to our first post across a largely frozen Western Europe, through north-eastern France, Belgium, West Germany, over the Austrian alps, through Yugoslavia in worsening weather and over snowstorm-swept mountains on a pot-holed, even makeshift road to the Bulgarian border. In 1962 there were no road tunnels to help drivers through eastern Yugoslavia and modern Macedonia. Our proud new Morris Minor 1000, equipped with snow tyres and a snow shovel, and with most of our worldly possessions in the boot and on a roof-rack, carried us through the passes, once across fields for a few kilometres in preference to the road, and made it to Sofia in style. The conditions defeated other, bigger vehicles, including trains. Indeed, ours was the last motor vehicle into Bulgaria from the west until the following spring.

1962: the Bulgarians had not made a successful strategic decision for over 800 years. The centuries of oppression seemed to show in their demeanour. The Cold War raged and Bulgaria was now tied fast and close to the political apron strings of the Soviet Union. That, too, showed. At the first May Day parade we witnessed in Sofia, there was much mostly Soviet-made military hardware on display – for Western military attachés to count and analyse. The vehicles and endless squads of soldiers, members of communist youth organisations, schoolchildren and others paraded through the main square before the assembled party bosses, themselves dwarfed by huge pictures of Soviet and, in subordinate positions, Bulgarian party and government leaders. There were floats, amateurish constructions, including a crude and arrogant USSR display, indicating world dominance and adding, patronisingly, it seemed, and almost as an afterthought, 'Greetings to the Bulgarian Communist Party'.

Bulgarian loyalty to the USSR was apparently total, ingrained, indoctrinated into each generation, beginning in the crèches. Nevertheless, we hoped that the devotion to the false god of communism was only skin deep, or at least penetrable with time and effort. We hoped that by providing, through the British legation, a window on the West, to demonstrate the advantages of real, British style freedom and democracy, we might achieve something. We might at least offer some hope to those Bulgarians who knew there was a better way for their country. The much debated disadvantages of democracy are as naught compared to the gross inefficiencies, oppressions and other evils of communism in practice. Such painstaking Cold War work was hard sledding, and we measured our successes with a fine Vernier gauge of diplomacy. We were a legation because, put simply, relations with Bulgaria were not good enough then to rate an embassy – and there were only four British legations in the world at the time.

Yet there were real plusses. Bulgaria is a beautiful country, known in the region as the Switzerland of the Balkans. It also has some wonderful Eastern Orthodox Church architecture. It has a chequered history, some suppressed by the communist government, some exaggerated, some distorted. There were some interesting and challenging modern problems between our two countries. I was to be something of a diplomatic dogsbody, but the political and cultural work I did meant that for me it was the best job in the legation. And having the language, I could explore and enjoy the countryside and get to know the people far better than most. (Despite the Bulgarian ban against listening and the not infrequent jamming of the signal from London, I did later meet a number of people who had heard me broadcast in Bulgarian from London on the BBC's Overseas Service.)

And we had prepared. We had read everything on the approved reading list. There wasn't much in English. We had also read those most diverting two slim volumes by Lawrence Durrell, *Esprit de Corps* and *Stiff Upper Lip*. A decade or so before we went to Sofia, Durrell served as a temporary information officer at the British embassy in Belgrade and drew on his experiences in Yugoslavia to write those wonderfully amusing stories. We laughed a lot, aloud, as we read the two books, and concluded that for the sake of comic effect, Durrell must have exaggerated these experiences. After a few months of diplomatic life in the Balkans, however, we knew that on the contrary, he must, in the modern phrase, have 'dumbed down' the stories to achieve some degree of credibility. Sad and funny, tragi-comic country though it was in many ways, Bulgaria was also our honeymoon posting, and we welcomed the adventure it promised.

The minister (in this usage a diplomatic rank one below ambassador) in charge of the legation was a strict, correct, but hardly a warm boss. He was a stickler for diplomatic protocol, of the old school. We diplomats in Sofia followed the 'book' on such arcane but then useful practices as leaving visiting cards, inscribed with letters such as *p.r.* (*pour remercier*), and without a corner turned down, in nineteenth-century practice; and on how and when to arrive at and leave diplomatic gatherings. The British legation was a severe but useful school in the lubricant ways of the language of protocol.

The day after our arrival in Sofia, Hilary and I were summoned to call on the minister and his wife, who were known formally and with no hint of irony in the office as 'Leurs Excellences', and referred to in internal minutes (memos) by the abbreviation 'Ll Ee'. The summons was for sherry at 11am. During the interview (for that is how it felt), Their Excellencies' Siamese tom-cat strode purposefully into the small drawing room to join us. I naturally bent to greet it, whereupon it attacked my hand with a paw, claws to the fore. For some strange reason, Osric's words in *Hamlet* leapt to my mind as I attempted to draw back: 'A hit, a very palpable hit'. But the cat scored again, firmly sinking another set of claws into my hand. As I straightened to stand, the cat did not let go, but subtly eased the pressure a little so that the incisions in my hand were long and deep as he slowly, archly, descended by way of my hand to the carpet, and stalked off triumphantly into a neutral corner. Neither of Their Excellencies made any noise of comfort or regret. As I sought to staunch the flow of blood, they offered neither bathroom nor first aid. Rather, they maintained an apparently contented silence, each smirking with evident pleasure at the cat. As Hilary later remarked, 'No hand of friendship there'.

Some months later, early one morning in the office, I was summoned by the minister to be austerely and soundly censored for having sung American words to the British national anthem at a diplomatic musical evening the night before. I was guilty as charged, but what a silly charge: 'My Country 'tis of Thee' is an American song, admittedly patriotic, and a small gathering of Western diplomats were singing a number of songs around the piano being played after dinner in her residence by the American minister. (Eugenie Anderson, a fine public servant and noted concert pianist.) It would in my judgment, then and now, have been discourteous to have refused to sing the words we were given, even if the tune was derived from that of our own national anthem – via a German adaptation.

The British minister was also a stickler for correct British 'Diplomatic Practice' (the title of the Foreign Service's then 'bible' on the subject). He once instructed me to draft for him a despatch on the Stalinist or otherwise Soviet-influenced background of the members of the Bulgarian cabinet. One might nowadays question the value of such a piece of research and work, but for the minister it then made sense, and would help his conduct of relations with senior members of this difficult and pretty obtuse communist government, and perhaps inform the Office in London. When I had completed the draft, I submitted it to him, complete with flagged references and tied in the regulation red tape, via his PA. He soon appeared in my office, bearing the bundle, laid it on my desk and said that he would not accept work presented in this sloppy fashion. He left. I thought hard. I checked that the flags were in alphabetic order, and all pinned safely with the points of the pins buried in the cardboard of the flags, as officially prescribed. Eventually, I picked up the papers, and moved the bow securing the red tape from the front to the back of the bundle. I took the bundle back into his office, and laid it on his desk. He looked, paused, and silently nodded his acceptance.

As already exemplified in our snow-swept journey across Europe, we had good cause to feel confident in our Morris Minor 1000. Very early in the spring of 1963, the legation needed someone to cross Bulgaria from Sofia in the west to the east, the Black Sea coast, to attend to a consular emergency in Burgas. There were no aeroplanes flying, nor trains running; and no one had made that journey by road since before the winter. The consul was a lady, single, of course, and did not speak Bulgarian – so Hilary and I took on the task, by Morris 1000. There were very few cars in Bulgaria, so it was no surprise that there were only two operational petrol (as opposed to diesel) stations in the capital city, and perhaps three more in the rest of the country. Where, and when, one could buy petrol, it was of distinctly low octane. While our Morris Minor was being manufactured in England, its cylinder head and pistons had therefore been modified to lower the compression ratio. Sometimes, particularly when the petrol station's own tanks were low, water was present in the petrol pumped into our cars. The petrol naturally floated on top of the water, but from time to time water was drawn by the fuel pump out of the petrol tank, and, in winter, would freeze in the pumps or pipes overnight, or when waiting for the Queen's messenger at Sofia railway station. At least, when cars would not then start, we knew the likely problem. Another less frequent, but embarrassing problem occurred when the water slopping around the bottom of the Morris Minor's petrol tank mixed with air as the little car bounced along the bumpy roads; eventually a noticeable increase in the petrol consumption betrayed the fact that the petrol tank was rusting through. We had our perforated tank replaced in Denmark during a drive home for leave.

The day before we set off from Sofia for Burgas, we filled the tank with petrol. The weather was still wintry, and there was a lot of snow and ice about, so we also checked with the Bulgarian motoring organisation. This was a fledgling affair. The official said he was confident that we would have no difficulty driving across the country to Burgas. No doubt he, and the management of the hotel we booked, alerted our constant shadows, the so-called secret police, who followed Western diplomats everywhere in those days, and sometimes tried to ensure that we landed in trouble one way or another. That said, they could be helpful too, if, for example, we fell victim to a puncture, which, given the poor state of the roads, was not uncommon. This help was given on the implicit, unspoken, but clear understanding that if the secret police car had a puncture, then we would stop too, rather than drive off on our own having shed them and their pursuit. Given the state of their tyres, they had far more punctures than we, so if we stuck to the understanding, they had the better deal. This may be one reason why they often tailed us in pairs of cars. The secret police would vary from rear to front tail, and seek to confuse; but it was all too tempting for us to play tricks on them.

We set off early the following bitter cold morning and entered the broad central valley of Bulgaria. When we reached the Valley of

Roses, where attar of roses is grown for the French perfume trade, we stopped. I strolled across the uncultivated strip, through one of the regular access gaps and behind the thick hedge protecting the rows of roses – for purposes of relief that were obvious. The Bulgarian secret policemen in the cars behind were evidently pleased by my action, since they decided to emulate it. Their Russian-built cars then had no heating, so to try to keep warm their occupants wore regulation issue ground-length overcoats with a dozen or so buttons down the double-breasted front. They probably also drank quite copiously from hot flasks, or cold bottles, in the cars. Six large Bulgarian secret policemen scrambled out of two Volga cars and made for the gap in the hedge 50 metres back down the road from us, undoing their buttons as they ran. I stood behind the hedge, striking, as it were, an attitude.

The timing of my next action was critical. When the moment seemed propitious, I ran fast from behind the hedge back to the Morris Minor, jumped in and closed the passenger door as Hilary let in the clutch and we tore off down the road eastwards towards Plovdiv. Our stratagem was a success. The secret policemen were caught, mid-stream, and, quite evidently, were collectively unsure what to do for the best. Some continued to do what they (but, despite all appearances, not I) had begun. Others, with a more panicky cast of mind, or possibly with a more highly tuned sense of duty, ran back to their cars, mid-stream or no mid-stream. We much enjoyed the sight, receding in the driving mirror, of those people behaving like scalded cats, until, in something passing for charity, but out of sight round a bend, we stopped and waited for them to catch up.

Much later that day, our secret police shadows had unaccountably disappeared. We were to learn, or to surmise, why. Notwithstanding the motoring organisation's advice, driving conditions deteriorated sharply once we left Plovdiv. The road was frequently flooded – by muddy water: a couple of inches, then a few more, then less. We stopped and checked the map – a rudimentary and misleading map. The contours in particular, we later established, were inaccurate, whether for deliberate, if wildly overdone, military reasons, or due to simple incompetence, we could only guess. It looked from the map that we were at last beginning to climb into the hills, so we pressed on carefully. We were driving through some three inches of water (presumably from the Maritsa river, whose banks had not burst), when we noticed great chunks of ice floating in the floodwater. Before we knew it, we were propelled down into a huge hole, which the ice, swirling in a fierce local current, had gouged out right across the road. For years afterwards, I could still dream of the wave of yellow-brown water rolling up the bonnet of the Morris 1000 as we plunged down into the hole, some three or four feet deep.

I braked, of course. We graunched to a stop. The engine died. We were stuck in the bottom of the hole, with the little car's nose pointed down as if in a steep kamikaze dive into a flooded crater. Hilary, resourceful as ever, scrambled into the back of the car and hoisted up from the well onto the back seat the expensive BBC radio monitoring equipment we usually carried, and saved it. I climbed out through the driver's window, which I believe to be a practical impossibility, even in the two-door version Morris 1000 we had. I was certainly slimmer in early 1963, but to this day, I do not know how I managed it.

Landing in the icy water, I thought, initially, that it was not too bad. I had had the flu the week before, however, and by the time I reached the front of the car, the cold seemed to enter the marrow of my bones and I thought I might faint. I had had the idea of using the starting handle and reverse gear to wind the car out of the hole, but because the winding would have to be done under opaque water, I thought I should first try pushing. At such times, a reserve of energy seems to come from nowhere, and in the nick of time. I bent down and heaved the car – with Hilary aboard – back up out of the hole. I carried on pushing, and then winding, with Hilary steering, until we found some almost dry ground. After the no doubt medically unwise but uplifting action of taking some reviving nips – nay, slugs – from the bottle we carried in the boot, I changed out of wet clothes into something dry from the top suitcase. The same suitcase contained a dry towel that we had packed because Bulgarian hotels never then provided such luxuries: with it, I began the long process of swabbing and drying out the accessible parts of the engine and its electrics. There was, of course, no sign of our secret police shadows. They had presumably known what we had not known: that the Maritsa river, full but fairly gentle in summer, frozen through the winter, and now just threatening to melt, had been dynamited to prevent it from flooding Plovdiv; and that we would not make it along that road.

Some little time later, an ambulance especially equipped for floods, with a high raised body and engine, and long sharply sloping drive shaft and steering rod down to the axles, appeared from the other direction. I spoke to the ambulance driver. He readily accepted my advice to drive the ambulance into the field and widely to skirt the hole we had driven into. Before he continued his errand of mercy, I asked the driver to send a tractor or lorry and some help from the next village. Sure enough, a collective farm lorry soon arrived, full of chattering villagers. They jumped off the lorry and excitedly ran towards us, glad to have something to do, and possibly glad to be allowed to talk to a bourgeois capitalist Westerner. They rushed in a body for our little engine, and began to pull out all sorts of wires at once, upsetting my laborious but methodical work. I protested. They apologised, and helped more carefully. Then, suddenly, one pronounced the engine ready to fire, removed the oil cap, stuffed in a rag he had just before inserted into the fuel tank, and, pulling a box from his pocket, was about to put a match to the petrol-soaked rag. At this I shouted a swift and fierce negative. (Не моля, не! No, please, no!) He stopped, astonished. Did I not want the engine started? This was usually the way they started the collective farm lorries and tractors, he explained. I responded that they were fuelled by diesel, while this car had a petrol engine. Had he really meant to blow us all up? Petrol was clearly beyond their experience, but they backed away. We chatted a while, and later, when I thought the dangerous petrol had evaporated and we were ready, we returned to the car, turned it around with enthusiastic Bulgarian assistance, and the lorry gave us a tow to try to help the Morris 1000 start.

After half a mile or so, and several attempts, first one cylinder fired, then two. Eventually, after almost a mile, and via several lightly flooded areas, three cylinders fired, at which stage I cast off the tow and thanked our cheerful and successful saviours warmly. We drove several more miles before the fourth cylinder would fire (a good moment, that), and then fought our way the 150 miles or so back to Sofia through a snow and ice storm – and with our tails rather between our legs. Back at the legation, my failure to get through to the Black Sea coast and Burgas did not go down well. Next day, the car was taken into intensive care at the legation garage; the engine stripped down and overhauled, the carpets removed and cleaned, the whole vehicle refurbished – and a new hidden microphone and transmitter fitted so that the secret police could once again hear what was said in the car.

We did make it to Burgas shortly thereafter. The worst of the floods there subsided enough for the airport to reopen. We took the first, and dramatic, flight of the year. The early Tupolev aeroplane just scraped over the mountain tops. There were neither seat-belts, heating nor pressurisation. The aisle was full of extra passengers standing and hanging on to the luggage racks – giving the phrase 'strap hanging' a new meaning. Pigs and other livestock were crammed into the back few rows. Chickens flapped and tried to out-fly the aeroplane from inside it. Goats bleated. And the pigs made a loud squealing fuss about proving that they could fly. The flight culminated in a really soft landing, the wheels digging deep into the still very soggy ground, and mud plastering the underside of the fuselage. But we did reach Burgas and the consular emergency – just short of too late. The need was to help an old Bulgarian who had spent many years in the British Merchant Navy, and had acquired British nationality. He had had an accident, was seriously ill and the Bulgarian authorities were refusing free medical help because of his dual nationality. Only in Bulgaria, communist Bulgaria.

The fact that my earlier failure to reach Burgas did not go down well at the legation should not be thought to indicate that the British staff there were other than splendid people. The pressures, the peculiar difficulties and restrictions, and the extra care we had to take in all we did as diplomats working behind the Iron Curtain, could have been a real strain. Yet, for nearly all the time, far from lowering morale, those constraints operated as a stimulant to high morale and brought out the best in the fine people who were our colleagues.

Part of maintaining morale and enjoying life in communist Bulgaria was the fun we had at the expense of those Bulgarian secret police. On one occasion, Hilary and I and a colleague visiting from a Foreign Office research department were driving to Veliko Turnovo in our valiant Morris Minor. We stopped and changed drivers from time to time, sometimes in sight of our faithful followers in the Moskvitch behind, sometimes not. When it was Hilary's turn to sit in the back of the Morris, we changed drivers out of sight, and without a word, lest it be transmitted to the Moskvitch, Hilary lay down on the back seat and covered herself with a blanket. After a while, it must have dawned on the police behind that they could now count only two occupants of our car. Where was the third, and what dastardly deed was the missing Western diplomat up to? What dreadful fate would befall the policemen when they reported to base? The Moskvitch overtook us, and all four secret police occupants tried to peer into our car. We made it difficult for them, and they were evidently confirmed in their fear that we had dropped one of our number somewhere along the way. We now had a front tail. We, in turn, overtook, and, with the rather more powerful car, drew away and lost our no doubt now seriously worried tail. Hilary removed the blanket and sat up. We drove fast to Turnovo, parked outside the hotel, hurried into the restaurant, sat and ordered lunch. Sometime later, four policemen rushed in, saw us, and, as they saw that we were three again, changed their expressions from fear to relief, wonderment, then to bafflement. They marched up to the desk in the lobby and interrogated the manager for some five minutes. It seems doubtful that they ever solved their conundrum, and we wondered what they reported to base. Only in communist Bulgaria.

I mentioned the hidden microphone in the car. Counter-measures against Bulgarian spying, eavesdropping and action by agents provocateurs occupied some of our time and effort. The Bulgarians were mostly well trained, presumably by the Soviet KGB, yet were sometimes curiously inept, sometimes brutal, sometimes surprising. One day, under cover of a noisy working lunch gathering, our visiting experts found a hidden microphone in the plaster of our dining room wall, neatly obscured by the white distemper. Our experts instantly began to extract it with the most sophisticated counter-intelligence tools of the day – club hammer and cold chisel. They exposed, grabbed and pulled the business end of the microphone, together with its attached wire. From the other side of the party wall, someone (we knew that a colonel in the secret police lived there) yanked both the wire and our man hanging on to it, back to the wall. Our man hauled back in turn, and a tug of war ensued. The microphone and our length of the wire went to a classified museum, not far from Milton Keynes. I do hope they are still there.

Bulgarian bugging of our premises was often more amusing than irritating. Our military attaché's office was tapped via a hidden microphone and its wire concealed by the vertical weld in the drainpipe outside his window. I thought that one quite clever, but we found it – and our offices anyway had effective counter-measures. That military attaché's predecessor had been declared *persona non grata* (in effect deported from Bulgaria) for photographing parked military aircraft from under a coat draped over his arm. His successor, our colleague, used to have confidential conversations in his garden on a winding walk among the shrubbery, rather than in his house which was surely heavily bugged. In the garden, our visiting experts found hidden microphones at appropriate intervals in the ground either side of where the military attaché and his interlocutors walked.

Then there was the administration officer's wife. He was a former Army officer, on his second career; a good man. She was a classic loyal Army wife, and lovely. She was flabbergasted and deeply offended, not at the discovery of a microphone in their flat, but at its location – secreted in the bed-head. How could they?! (That discovery gave the phrase 'pillow talk' new meaning for us.)

Bulgarian plumbing was different, and in those days quite wonderful in its inefficiency. Our flat had been designed by a Swiss architect, who had ensured that the bathroom floor was tiled, sealed save only for the drain in the middle, and sunk three or four inches below the level of the rest of the flat. Thus when, as frequently happened, the complex valves on the water intake for the lavatory failed, and water under fierce (mains) pressure flooded the bathroom, little real damage was done – normally. However, late one Saturday night, when we returned from dinner exhausted by the effort of conversing for many hours in a couple of foreign languages, Hilary and I opened the door of the flat to find the carpets gently undulating and the entire flat under water. Ours was the first-floor apartment, and below us were garages and boiler room. Both had drains, so they could wait until morning. In rather less than good humour, we did what little we could in our flat to stop the flood and reduce the level of water. Just before giving up and splashing our way to a damp bed, I opened and addressed the rudimentary and crowded meter and fuse box in the roundest of lower-deck Bulgarian. I told the assembled fuses and other electrical paraphernalia in the cupboard precisely what I thought of Bulgarian plumbing under the People's Republic; of the bureaucracy; the government; and, at some length and with a good deal of Saturday night colour, of the whole system of communism and the Bulgarian Communist Party. Hardly an exercise in conventional diplomacy, I readily admit. Yet, next morning, the front door bell rang early – very early for a Sunday. There on the doorstep was a Bulgarian workman, complete with a wonderful moustache and a Gladstone bag. He said he was from the Bureau for the Service of the Diplomatic Corps, and that he had been ordered to come because we urgently needed a plumber – that was he. Hidden microphones do have their uses, perhaps especially in communist Bulgaria.

Hilary and I, well trained, conducted no conversations of any value to any others in our home, in hotels, restaurants or shops, or in cars, including, of course, our Morris Minor. Hilary took a driving test in Sofia, but, by force of regulation, not in our car but in a Moskvitch. Most of the few cars in Bulgaria were those two basic Russian models, the Volga or the smaller Moskvitch. Motorists were thus expected both to encounter mechanical problems and to be able to solve them. The driving test therefore included a 45-minute formal oral examination on what went on under the bonnet; on basic automotive electrics and how to repair common faults as well as the Bulgarian equivalent of our highway code. For foreigners, an interpreter was permitted if needed, but no one who possessed a driving licence was allowed to interpret.

Hilary had driven for a year on an international licence, but the time had come for a test. Her kitchen Bulgarian, while useful and effective, was insufficient for this purpose. We took along one of the British legation's best locally-engaged Bulgarian translators, Mrs Atanasova, whose job included this occasional duty. As a concession, I was allowed to sit in, but not to contribute – because I had a full licence. It soon became clear, in my view, that the rule about who was permitted to interpret was silly. Mrs Atanasova, skilled though she was in translating, simply had none of the Bulgarian vocabulary related to cars and driving – let alone the equivalent English words. I recall two simple examples. Poor Mrs Atanasova had no idea what the Bulgarian words for 'indicator' and 'steering wheel' – *putepokazatel* and *kormiloto* (пътепоказател and кормилото) – meant. Eventually I interceded and was allowed, under sufferance, to interpret. I soon learned that there was something in the rule after all. I was very tempted to translate an answer Hilary gave to one question about the minimum stopping distance for a car behind a stopped tram by giving in Bulgarian the figure of seven metres that I was sure was the answer. However, I just managed to resist the temptation and translated the figure Hilary had given – ten metres. 'Точно така' ('Correct'), said the examiner. I was not tempted again, and Hilary passed the oral with flying colours ('безпогрешно' – no mistakes). The practical part of the test included a short drive along a stony river bed and up a rough mountain road, normal enough for the outskirts of Sofia then. Hilary found no difficulty in passing a test a good deal more rigorous than any other test either of us has taken, before or since, anywhere around the world. Such were the scarcity of cars and motoring facilities in Bulgaria in the early sixties, that the rigour was more than justified. It has stood us in good stead ever since. So did our teaching ourselves how to skid on otherwise deserted, ice-bound cobbled roads in Sofia's severe winters. We could waltz our Morris Minor down a wide road called Oborishte (Улица Оборище) – the place of the byre – while singing the 'Blue Danube' or the 'Skater's Waltz'. Only in Bulgaria.

I used to think of the Iron Curtain as also a curtain of ironies. Despite their generally passive demeanour, ordinary Bulgarians in those generally unhappy days could occasionally surprise us, and lift the heart – usually only in private. The death of President Kennedy in 1963 was, of course, a great public shock throughout the world. The British Diplomatic Service abroad went into strict court mourning for a week. Hilary could not wear her only black indoor garment – a cocktail dress – all day and all evening, so had to buy some of the only available and very poor quality East German black cloth from a Bulgarian government-run shop, and to make a suit, overnight. The cloth was so shoddy that the suit lasted exactly the week of Court mourning. The day following the appalling shooting in Dallas, Texas, Hilary and I drove up into the hills, and spent some quiet time walking around the grounds of a monastery at Dragalevtsi. We were of the generation that, despite incipient, even growing cynicism, saw Jack Kennedy as a hope for the succeeding generations, the young people of the world, and not just the then Free World. We returned to Sofia to find a most welcome surprise. The queue to sign the American legation's book of condolence was huge, perhaps a kilometre long and three or four deep. The legation, entry to which for Bulgarians (as at the British Legation) was controlled by the Bulgarian militia on guard outside, was soberly yet warmly welcoming. Here was a window on the West indeed, but the terrible tragedy had so gripped the Bulgarians as they had heard the news on the radio, that they had flocked to express real grief and sympathy. To us this was an extraordinary sight and moment in the bitter Cold War. After the assassination, only hours earlier, we had felt hopeless. Now, the Bulgarians, of all repressed and depressed people, spontaneously, and in impressively large numbers, had made a singular and singularly important gesture and demonstration of genuine feeling. Out of the tragedy, they had conjured, for us, real hope: they renewed our confidence in what we were trying to achieve. Such a cheering and inspiring surprise could perhaps occur – only in Bulgaria.

British visitors to Bulgaria in the depths of the Cold War were very few. This was before the days of tourism, and visitors were either seriously misled 'fellow-travellers', or people we warmly welcomed: Queen's messengers, or the very occasional British minister trying, usually in vain, to persuade the Bulgarians, where we diplomats had failed, of some argument in foreign policy. Despite the paucity of our national commercial efforts in Bulgaria then, we also, from time to time, could welcome British businessmen. There were several reasons why we tried so little to foster trade with communist Bulgaria. The

Bulgarian economy was small, was constrained by its membership of the Soviet-dominated Council for Mutual Economic Assistance or 'Comecon', had little hard currency available for imports, was rarely interested in barter (nor, then, was nearly all of 'UK Ltd'); and the Bulgarian government was prejudiced against trading with the West. A few deals were done, for example by the fine British company, Molins, who supplied a cigarette-making factory in Bulgaria with their machine tools and expertise; but deals were few indeed, and with those few, there were frequent problems with payment. Another reason was the attitude in the early 1960s of many in the then Foreign Service to commercial diplomacy. At that time, while, as I recall with professional envy, the West German commercial office in Bulgaria having six West Germany-based people pursuing with some serious success their country's commercial interests, the British legation officially devoted only very limited time to commercial work in support of British companies. The British minister at the head of our legation, while explaining to me that I should stay away from anything like commercial diplomatic work, once actually used the infamous phrase, 'gentleman do not dirty their hands with trade'. He said it with a slight smile, but he meant it. Fortunately the attitude and practice in the Service later changed radically, often to very good effect. Unfortunately, the effort has not always been sustained. The Service must not lose this skill or practice, and must always regard it as a high priority, whatever the predatory attacks upon the Foreign and Commonwealth Office's resources.

Some of us did welcome and try to help visiting British businessmen. A rather inexperienced, jejune, but very decent and well brought-up young British salesman came to Sofia to try his luck with the communist government purchasing agencies – the only way a foreign company could then sell anything in Bulgaria. The secret police were only too willing to invest in the opportunities these trips provided to set up the visitors for later blackmail. We ensured that the young man was warned. After his first day's work, and dinner with one of us, he went back to his hotel room – to find a bright and beautiful blonde in his bed. Affronted, he threw her out. Next night, the Bulgarians tried a sultry brunette. Even crosser, our hero threw her out too, in something of a temper. So, on the third evening, he surely could not have been surprised when he found waiting for him a rampant red-head. As I recall his account, his rage as he threw her out must have been terrific to behold … unwise, but terrific. We warned him again. By his next and last night he really thought the Bulgarians would have given up. Not a bit of it. And when he found the fresh-faced young boy draped across his bed, he nearly committed murder. We had to rescue him and calm him down. Only in Bulgaria.

In late 1963, Hilary and I visited a Bulgarian vineyard and wine production plant. This was well before the days of the export to Western Europe of the Bulgarian wines enjoyed here today. But there were just a few aspirations in that direction, and, very much a believer in trying to stimulate two-way trade, though it was not, strictly speaking, my job, I was keen to see if I could offer any pointers. We knew already that such were the vine stock, the climate and the soil and other growing conditions, as well as many years of expertise, that there were some good Bulgarian wines. We also knew from experience that quality control then was weak: there was usually at least one bad bottle in every case, and Bulgaria in the early sixties was a good place to learn cork extraction the hard way.

In the communist system, marketing was almost unknown. Hilary and I were conducted through dowdy, factory-like processing rooms, not in any logical order, but finally to the bottling plant. There we watched two fairly basic machines bottle the wine and cork the bottles. We were mildly impressed to see that machines, not people, were doing this work. In the last of the production processes, Bulgarian female workers stuck the labels on the bottles. The labels were basic: rectangles of poor, rough, off-white paper with badly printed, smudgy words in the Cyrillic alphabet recording the type and sometimes the region of the wine, the name *Vinprom* [Винпром] – Wine Production Enterprise – and the year. The girls were using glue brushes to paste these labels onto the bottles. I wandered over to speak to the girls, and noticed that the labels, for *Gamza* (Гъмза) wine, had the wrong year on them – the previous year. I gently queried this. The answer was, quite cheerfully, 'Oh, we haven't yet used all the 1962 labels'. Only in Bulgaria.

Medical and surgical practice in communist Bulgaria in the 1960s left a good deal to be desired. When I needed an appendectomy, the Bulgarian surgeon was most reluctant to perform the operation, because, he said, of the uncleanliness of his operating theatre and its equipment. He spoke of rusty scalpels and no gloves. The British minister was also most concerned, primarily about his view that under anaesthetic, I might reveal British state secrets. He therefore instructed that a roster be established of so-called volunteers from the UK-based staff to attend the operation and when necessary to shout me down or silence me in whatever way they could. Volunteers were forthcoming only after Hilary led the way. Apparently unaware of these precautionary preparations, the surgeon then announced that the general anaesthetic at his disposal was of such poor quality that the risks of using it were too high; instead, a local anaesthetic would be administered.

The Treasury medical officer, who looked after British diplomats from London, took a third and different view: that if humanly possible, I should fly immediately to London for the operation. There was then one direct flight a week. I suppose the kindly Bulgarian GP to the Western diplomats, French-trained Dr Sarafov, came to my rescue. He prescribed many ice bags, and the condition was thereby calmed enough for me to be able to fly in a turbo-prop aeroplane the next day, via Belgrade and Amsterdam. The Treasury doctors advised that I be accompanied, so Hilary came too. Welfare section of personnel department were their usual kind and effective selves. As just one example, we were met at the foot of the aeroplane steps at Heathrow by a Foreign Office car and, to us, a huge advance of salary in sterling – 25 pounds. We were driven straight to Guy's hospital where the appendectomy was performed immediately.

Two postscripts: first, specifically medical events apart, throughout my career, I only once felt I had cause to be grateful to or to admire the Treasury as a body. That once was in their superintendence of what later became the Civil Service College (Chapter 9). Otherwise, personal liking and respect for individuals there notwithstanding, I had no cause for real respect of the Treasury. The institution seemed to me excessively devoted to the short-term and to the view of trees rather than the woods. The second postscript is far, far sadder, as well as more objective. Recent (post-communist) and credible research by the Bulgarian Medical Association shows that Dr Sarafov was arrested, imprisoned, accused of espionage, sentenced to death and executed. That tragic example of Cold War paranoia presumably reflects the communist government view of his connections with the West in general or possibly with a country other than the UK. I am confident, of course, that our British Foreign Service rules and practices would not have put Dr Sarafov at the least risk. And there was extensive, unjustified and cruel repression and persecution of intellectuals, including medical professionals, by the communist authorities in Bulgaria.

The case of the 'diplomatic dentist' may have been analogous. Dr Kirov's was the government-licensed practice for the diplomatic corps. His equipment included the best drill in Sofia, we were told. It was a treadle drill, which operated at speeds varying from slow to stop. Local anaesthetic was unavailable. I recall being present as interpreter when Dr Kirov and I together had to restrain Hilary, who in her pain at the drilling, seemed intent on climbing up the drill in an attempt to remove it from her mouth. I find it impossible to believe that the senior Bulgarian communist government officials did not have access to a dentist with an electric drill, and to anaesthetics. We in the British legation were always scrupulous in avoiding any action with regard to medical practitioners that might expose them to any real danger. We heard, a good deal later, a strong rumour that a fate not dissimilar to that of Dr Sarafov had befallen Dr Kirov.

One other much lighter medical history concerned a birth, to the wife of one of the British Diplomatic Wireless Service officers. There was in those days no question of the grateful British taxpayer providing a ticket home and a National Health Service delivery. Instead, the communist government-licensed Bulgarian gynaecologist, one Dr Mikhailovski, had everything prepared in his hospital. (As far as I know, he was not put to death; though, as I recall, he did try to offer more than medical services to the West). The moment of natal truth arrived, rather earlier than predicted, and the now very expectant young wife and her husband were driven to the hospital in the legation's Ford Consul estate car, complete with its diplomatic registration plates. Some while before they arrived there, the baby was born – in the luggage compartment of the estate car. Mother and child were fine, and Dr Mikhailovski declared himself relieved: as he put it, the back of the British legation estate car was a good deal cleaner that his labour ward. I think we declared the baby instantly a British citizen, having been born on British sovereign territory, even if mobile sovereign territory.

I have often wondered how Lawrence Durrell would have handled the strange and for my young bride Hilary, shocking and distressing event of 1963 that occurred within the privacy of our own legation. I have usually concluded that this was a true story Durrell would have been reluctant to write – or even to bowdlerise – when he was writing of the Balkans in the early 1950s. Times have changed.

The diplomatic wives at the legation naturally supported Her Excellency, the minister's wife, in many official ways. For example, some time before Hilary worked at the legation, I recall her being summoned to help cut roses in the residence garden. Hilary even donned the prescribed dress for such occasions, which included long gloves and a hat. This was an idiosyncratic exercise, rather silly, but quite normal in the diplomatic milieu of the day, and harmless. However, on one never-to-be-forgotten – or forgiven – winter's day, Hilary was summoned to the residence in the afternoon, presumably for tea. 'Her Excellency' sent her chauffeur and car to collect Hilary, who was welcomed by a smiling butler, and shown into the room where ladies would hang their heavy outdoor clothes, essential protection against the hard Bulgarian winter. She was then conducted, not into a downstairs drawing room, but upstairs, where Hilary had never been. The butler explained on the way up that the Spanish wife of the counsellor of another West European diplomatic mission was already with Her Excellency in the upstairs 'boudoir'. Hilary was shown in to the room – a bedroom – to be confronted with the sight of 'Her Excellency' and Spanish friend, lying on the bed, barely clothed, and to be invited to join them. Hilary fled. Remarkably soon after, she arrived in my office in the legation, in a state of alarm, fury and near rebellion, and announced that the next aeroplane home would carry her back to England. It was a source of considerable relief to me that flights to the United Kingdom were then weekly, and that one had just left. I had time to attempt calming, and other, action.

Serendipity helped. Like all legations and embassies we employed some locally engaged staff. They were paid in Bulgarian *leva*, an unconvertible soft currency. They had no access to any classified or sensitive British material or work: we presumed that however much we might enjoy their company and working with them, they were allowed by the Bulgarian communist government to work for the British in Sofia on the condition that they reported on and spied against us. That presumption was justified. There was a nice and in a particular way rather pleasant twist, however, when the story unfolded of one of our locally engaged staff members who took advantage of our scheme under which they could allot some of their salary to be saved for them by the legation. If the Bulgarian government ever gave our local staff an exit visa and allowed them to travel to the United Kingdom, we would give them their *leva* savings converted to sterling, so that they could spend money in Great Britain. Otherwise, the money could be returned to them in local currency whenever they wished. The scheme was clearly in British interests, in a number of ways, including in helping these staff members to see and feel the country for which they were working in their own land. The scheme seldom resulted in holidays in the United Kingdom. There were many difficulties in the way of the staff concerned, including in securing the essential exit visa from the Bulgarian authorities. On the rare occasions when such visas were granted, the authorities typically demanded a 'hostage' in the shape of a close relative. He or she would be prevented from leaving Bulgaria, as a surety against the return of the traveller.

After some years of such saving, and no doubt after some difficult negotiation with the communist authorities, the local staff member managed to secure an exit visa. His 'hostage', who stayed behind as a surety against his return, was his wife of just a year. However, he did not return to Bulgaria. To use the Cold War phrase, he defected to the West, complete, no doubt, with some valuable intelligence. I later became convinced that the year-long marriage had been carefully planned as a marriage of convenience only, and that our local staff member had fooled the Bulgarian security authorities. That said, it is a source of much sadness and some sad speculation, but I have no idea what happened to his courageous wife. We in the legation, of course, never saw her again.

In the immediate wake of the defection, penalties were imposed upon the British Legation, presumably because the authorities thought (wrongly, as far as I was concerned and aware) that we were complicit in this deception, or because they needed a scapegoat – or both. By way of reprisals, the Bulgarian authorities removed two of our key other local staff, upon whom we had relied to an important extent for arranging supplies and so on. The Bulgarian communist government also repeatedly refused to grant diplomatic entry visas to a number of UK-based diplomats who should have joined the legation as replacements for others who had come to the end of their posting, or, in one case, had to return to the United Kingdom on health grounds. This left us shorthanded, and eventually we had to do something about it.

Here was the distinctly pleasant twist. As I have mentioned, Hilary had had to resign from the Diplomatic Service on our marriage. She had served in the Foreign Office and abroad, in Geneva. She had the necessary skills and experience for diplomatic work abroad. She had a Bulgarian diplomatic visa. The legation's needs were considerable and rather urgent. Hilary was delighted to be employed as a 'locally engaged' pro-consul, very soon indeed after the 'upstairs boudoir' incident, and, indeed, for the rest of our time in Sofia. I rather think we won that little visa war, convincingly and satisfactorily.

CHAPTER 2

MORE COLD WAR DIPLOMACY

Communist Bulgaria's attempts to bribe or suborn, or by contrivance to 'set up' or 'frame' Western diplomatic staff for arrest and/or later blackmail, were generally rather amateur. We in the British legation nonetheless resented some of them. One of the underhand practices involved the secret police following the cars of younger, junior UK-based members of the staff when they were out for a summer drive at the weekend. Once well out in the country, the secret police would overtake, apparently to do a front tail. A little further on, the occupants of the British car would see the Bulgarian one parked, with police outside it, waving the British down. When they stopped, the British legation staff members would be accused of having driven into a forbidden zone. These zones, not too unreasonably forbidden for military reasons, were shown on an official map we all had, and marked at the side of the road by a special 'Forbidden' (*Zabraneno* – Забранэно) road sign we also knew well – and knew well never to pass. When our people denied having entered a forbidden zone, the Bulgarian secret police would invite them to drive back down the road the way they had come. After a couple of miles, there was the 'Forbidden' sign. While behind the British car earlier, the Bulgarians had, of course, stopped to plant the sign, which they kept in the boot of their car ready for the purpose. They had then caught up, overtaken, driven on for a while and then stopped our staff members. The next step was to ask our young people to sign a form – in Bulgarian, which uses the Cyrillic alphabet, and which most of our staff could not read or understand. They were told that if they had signed, they would be allowed to turn back the way they had come. Otherwise, immediate arrest would follow. Fortunately, our people knew better than to sign, but their next few hours at least before we could extract them would be most unpleasant and difficult, possibly harrowing.

Before they went to work in embassies behind the Iron Curtain, our people were well trained in defensive security, by the Foreign Office's own security department. When they arrived at post, they were given, in conditions under which no microphones could hear, tips on the latest local practices. Perhaps the principal area of attempted subornation that really caused us far more annoyance than detached amusement was any attempt to compromise any of our single lady UK-based staff members, who were allowed only limited diplomatic status. They had been carefully selected in London, of course. Necessarily, they led a restricted social life in communist Bulgaria, and the pressures on them were sometimes real and strong. We could take no risks where they were concerned for their, and the United Kingdom's, good. We did send one young lady home rather early, to avoid a possible problem.

That so popular dance of the sixties, the Twist, was banned in communist Bulgaria, as a lamentable example of the depravity, decadence and dissolution of the bourgeois imperialist West. It was a pleasant surprise to know that despite all the indoctrination and the less subtle pressures on the youth of Bulgaria, many wanted to dance the Twist. The effect of the ban, however, was to drive the Twist underground. Occasionally there would be raids on Twist parties supposed to be held in secret, but always vulnerable to informers. The guilty young people would be packed off to a kind of labour camp. As we understood it, the youngsters were awoken every other hour on the hour through the night, and, almost incredibly, made to dance the Twist for perhaps 20 or 30 minutes. I suppose this was designed as aversion therapy. However, the outcome was the reverse of that intended. The prisoners became expert and skilled in the dance; after release, they went back underground, trained others and increased the level and excitement of underground Twist dancing remarkably. Only in Bulgaria.

It was against this background that we paid an occasional visit at a weekend to a restaurant called Kopitoto [Копитото], which means the Hoof, the shape of the bluff on which the restaurant sat on Mount Vitosha, above and south of Sofia. It may have been the only restaurant in or near Sofia which had a band. One of our secretaries was an accomplished dancer, including of the Twist. The band played appropriate music, and she and I duly danced the Twist. The music then changed tempo, but later returned to the Twist rhythm, and we resumed dancing. Above the music came a loudspeaker announcement in the Bulgarian for 'Comrades, you are asked to dance with less abandon'. We two were the only ones dancing the Twist, and we were clearly not comrades. After one more set and, for us, one more dance of the Twist, the band stopped playing and were dispatched home early. As the leader of the band took a long way out through the restaurant to pass by our table, he whispered to me, also in Bulgarian, 'Thanks for the evening off'. Others in the restaurant quietly made it clear that they thoroughly approved our action, unobtrusively enjoyed it, and did not mind one bit the consequential absence of the band. Only in communist Bulgaria.

My immediate superior in the legation, Head of Chancery Mark Heath, and his wife Margaret, were splendid people, of the very best. Hilary and I greatly respected and liked them both, and they became good and enduring friends. Margaret is the elder daughter of Physics Nobel Prize-winner Sir Lawrence Bragg OBE MC. Among many gentlemanly pursuits, Mark Heath was a lay reader who took occasional services in the legation in Sofia, and was a caring, understanding, humorous and helpful boss, who inspired loyalty as well as liking. Among much else, he taught us to ski, a valuable series of lessons in a land blessed with wonderful natural ski fields, but not then with ski lifts. Having 'herring-boned' or trekked with skis on shoulders a long way upwards, we made every downhill run count. We also enjoyed cross-country skiing on many miles of fresh snow; this was spectacular skiing in fine scenery, with the mountains often to ourselves. Among the many good 'only in Bulgaria' memories to cherish, the spiced, mulled local wine, *toplo vino* (топло вино), in the simple but charming mountain village hostelry on the way back from skiing was wonderful. On a cold Western European winter's evening, I can taste it still.

Mark and Margaret's second car was a Mini, which, after inserting his elegant six feet and seven inches into the car with great skill and style, Mark would drive the long way down the Struma valley to Greece to join his family having a break there. Once he and the Mini had achieved top gear, it took a great deal to persuade either to change down: the gear stick was locked in by Mark's ankle, set at a determined if innovative angle, a little like that of his head, inevitably on one side.

That most colourful of Soviet leaders, first secretary of the Communist Party of the USSR, the diminutive, even squat Nikita Khrushchev, paid a grand visit from the USSR to Bulgaria while Mark Heath was acting as chargé d'affaires in Sofia. On arrival at the airport, Khrushchev shook hands with all the assembled heads of mission (mostly dressed in diplomatic uniform) in turn, but then walked back up the line to greet six feet and seven inches of Mark again, this time to attempt to give him a low bear hug and to say gleefully how much he admired tall diplomats: 'You will make a good communist', he added, inaccurately. The later cinema newsreel made amusing viewing indeed.

Crowning a distinguished diplomatic career as the first full ambassador to the Holy See, Sir Mark Heath KCVO CMG must have been among the best ever British representatives to the Vatican, at a time when Red Brigade terrorism was rife in Italy and Northern Ireland issues were especially sensitive, and for during a key state visit by the Queen. Mark later became chef de protocol in Hong Kong. He was certainly most effective in that role too, and must have been singularly impressive among the mostly relatively small Chinese. In retirement, Mark did much for Anglicanism and ecumenicalism, notably in and for Bath abbey, and, with Lady Heath, the Ammerdown ecumenical centre.

Among our diplomatic colleagues in Sofia, there were numerous colourful and interesting people. There was the Western European diplomat of Armenian extraction, who, when we arrived, had already spent seven long years in Sofia. He was desperately bored and pleaded repeatedly to be sent elsewhere. He had an enormous cheese plant in his drawing room that he had grown from a seed he planted on his arrival: it now occupied two-thirds of the room. His wife reputedly had an affair with a Bulgarian tennis coach, but (to our surprise) even that did not ensure his release from service behind the Iron Curtain. After twelve long years in Sofia, he was eventually posted in his same grade – to Tirana!

Then there was the countess wife of a Western European political counsellor. Late one Friday afternoon, the countess was dressing for a drive that evening with her husband down to Greece. She was in a hurry to be ready and begin the long journey as soon as her husband arrived home from work. She put on her best pearls, but as she was fastening them, the string broke. She caught all the pearls in her hands as they cascaded off the string, and carefully lowered them into the open dressing table drawer. She then gathered them into an envelope and left them in the drawer. On her return on the Sunday evening, she took the envelope from the drawer to show her husband and discuss where in the West to send the pearls for restringing. In the envelope, she found the pearl necklace whole, beautifully restrung! Taking advantage of the couple's absence, the Bulgarian secret police operatives had entered the house, no doubt to search for anything they might be able to use against the diplomats. This was a common practice, and the dressing table drawers would certainly be opened in case they contained useful handwritten notes, for example. Evidently, the secret police had rifled the drawer, opened the envelope, fingered the pearls, and concluded that they, the secret police, had broken the string. So, in an attempt to cover their presence in the diplomatic house, they had had the pearls restrung, and put them back in the drawer. However, by way of a change, this time, the string of pearls was carefully knotted. Only in Bulgaria!

That occasional drive to Greece became a joy – and a temporary escape to a free country – but only after Sofia and Athens finally came to diplomatic terms after a difficult chapter in their relations, established offices in each capital and opened the border. A weekend in Kavala (then but a small, gentle fishing harbour) became a rare and real treat. Later, if we had a few days' leave, a trip from Kavala by small ferry to the then unspoilt island of Thasos also became possible. Both became firm favourites for the Western diplomatic corps on leave. Our own first crossing of the newly opened border, however, was problematic. We must have been among the first Western diplomats to cross from Bulgaria into Greece. An image stays with me: the look of real fear on the face of a young Bulgarian soldier as he held his Kalashnikov rifle with the muzzle stuck in my stomach, and with a frightened finger trembling on the trigger. He could not have been more than 18 years of age. Hilary and I were clearly a dodgy, even alarming proposition for the apparently untrained, certainly unsure and resentful border guards. Our documents were being checked inside the border control office, and the young soldier was clearly under orders not to let me pass further. Hilary was behind me. It was that look of fear in his eyes, plus his finger on the trigger, his shaking finger, that made me grab and push the muzzle of the rifle firmly away from me and Hilary – and hold it there. We remained thus, at something of a stalemate. My knowledge of his language was a major asset: I suggested that he should relax; I was not about to go anywhere. Slowly, a little blood returned to his face. At last the border official turned up with the passports and other documents, and, rather more effectively than I had, told the soldier to stand down.

In summer in Bulgaria, we occasionally had reason to visit the Black Sea coast, usually accompanying a visiting MP or some such. Tourist resorts were then beginning to be constructed, and were pretty basic. Lifts rarely worked, and the minister could never have trusted my linguistic ability again after I translated for his wife the instructions on the shower above the brand new hotel bath. Her Excellency explained to me that on no account should she get her hair, her coiffure, wet; she wished to have a bath, not a shower. I translated the instructions. She later operated the controls. She, her hair first, I suppose, was drenched. I don't suppose she or her husband ever believed the truth, that the shower and bath controls and instructions had been assembled the wrong way round. Only in Bulgaria.

Back in Sofia, it was easy to detect that one's diplomatic flat or house had been searched in one's absence. There was always the unmistakable odour of Bulgarian tobacco mixed with Bulgarian garlic. There were the white footmarks under the thin rugs if one had bothered in advance to pull them back and sprinkle talcum powder underneath before replacing them. There were the displaced hairs we sometimes placed across doors – very simple indications. And there were always the disarranged photographs, slides, gramophone records – eventually we gave up rearranging them after these visits.

For some diplomats, there was worse. The secret police were evidently wary of dogs, and if entering diplomatic premises where a dog lived, would often first throw in a chunk of meat – poisoned meat. The dogs did not die, but were quickly tranquillised, and pretty sick. We had a small Bulgarian mongrel, rescued literally from the gutter. We named him Fergus. He was grateful, soft and friendly, but to keep him safe, when we went out, we would put him in a large glassed-in balcony, with his bed, water, toys and, if necessary, heater. The balcony was self-contained; there was no need at all for the Bulgarian operatives to open the sliding door. However, one day we returned to the flat, opened the front door, and immediately smelled the sickly odour of chloroform. We rushed to the balcony door and to Fergus, who was very unhappy and rather ill. Carefully, we gave him broth, brandy and tender loving care. His recovery was quick and complete – and his liking for brandy never left him.

Diplomatic life in Bulgaria could also be fun. Since I was one of the few Western diplomats who spoke Bulgarian, Hilary and I were invited to embassy dinner parties at which Bulgarians licensed by their government to attend would also be present. Those Bulgarians, by definition, were nearly always officials, and not often willing to talk frankly; they too knew about the microphones, and about their colleagues, and trusted no one. It was rare for us to be invited to a senior diplomatic party when Western diplomats were entertaining only other Western diplomats, in what we thought were sometimes rather incestuous and unprofitable evenings.

The protocol at such dinners was strict. At one, after the first course, the chargé d'affaires of a fairly small but rather self-important Western country rose to his feet, excused himself with formality bordering on the icy, and led his wife from the room and from the house. They left the dinner party and went home because he regarded himself as *mal placé*. He believed that he should have been seated higher up the table, and that he and his country had therefore been insulted.

As a matter mostly of amusement, but also of a little professional curiosity, I looked up the various dinner guests and their seniority next day. I found that the position he had occupied at the table was defensible, but that as a *chargé d'affaires en titre,* he could have had a small, esoteric protocol point in believing himself to be senior to another *chargé d'affaires ad interim.* That he was so concerned about such arcane matters illustrated the ridiculous nature of the incident; what worried some diplomats with nothing better to do; and how careful one had to be.

We were much privileged to be invited for dinner one dark Sofia evening to the French ambassador's residence, known traditionally as the *hôtel de ville.* The French ambassador was a strict, reserved, correct, ascetic, austere, *ancien siècle* bachelor. The dress for His Excellency's dinner was black tie. Well trained in the diplomatic protocol of the day, which was much stricter and more formal than today, we knew that as the most junior diplomats invited, we should arrive first, just one minute after the bidden time. The door opened and we were greeted, not by the butler we expected, but by the French ambassador's secretary, whom we knew well, and who sometimes was summoned to act as hostess for her elegant and rather distant boss. However, she hastened to tell us that she had been summoned that evening, in some ambassadorial embarrassment, to cook. The Parisian chef had had a tantrum, and had thrown pans and their contents over the kitchen walls. The secretary was starting from scratch. Would we please help out by chatting away and filling any awkward pauses while guests wondered if they were ever going to eat that evening? Having briefed us, she nobly headed for the kitchen. The butler appeared, and conducted us into the presence of *Son Excellence, Monsieur l'Ambassadeur de la France.*

In those days, French was the diplomatic language, and we were used to working in French. The ambassador was correct, polite, but unsurprisingly a little distracted. As the other guests arrived, a little English was heard to add to the French, but no Bulgarian. This was, except for us, a dinner of heads of diplomatic missions. Everyone was elegantly dressed. The new Ghanaian ambassador arrived. He was, I think, the first Ghanaian ambassador to anywhere. Ghana had become independent from Great Britain only a few years earlier (in 1957) and this diplomat, as ambassador to Bulgaria, after spending some time on secondment to the Foreign Office in London was now in effect training for a year before going to a really important new embassy, Moscow. He was a most intelligent and able man. However, he had made a mistake. He was not wearing a dinner jacket. Dark lounge suit; black tie, yes, but not bow tie. Normal diplomatic practice would have been for the host to welcome the guest warmly, to excuse himself and withdraw, to change down quickly to lounge suit and to reappear, saying nothing to draw attention to the change. However, *Son Excellence*, conscious of the delay to dinner and the problems in the kitchen, of which only Hilary and I among the 20-odd guests were aware, saw his chance. Politely but firmly, he sent the Ghanaian home to change. (I wondered, unworthily no doubt, whether the ambassador's action also said something about differences between the French and British approaches to Africa in the early 1960s: the phrase '*la mission civilatrice*' came to mind). The Ghanaian and his wife departed with grace, and we continued to converse with the other guests. I took an opportunity to whisper to Hilary as I was moving among the guests that I thought that would be the last we would see of the Ghanaians that evening.

How wrong I was. Sofia in the early sixties was a small capital city even by East European standards. The Ghanaians would have arrived home inside ten minutes. Forty-five minutes later, the Ghanaians returned, he in a dinner jacket. The Ghanaian ambassadress had also changed, into a stunning gold national dress, a sort of fine toga, but wrapped in a long spiral right around her, from shoulder to toe, and with a tall headdress to suit. The French ambassador must have been pleased with the timing, and with his ploy, for dinner was served soon thereafter, and in fine style. The ambassador's secretary had done an excellent job in the kitchen, though it was certainly by then a very late hour at which to dine.

The first course was served, and conversation flowed with the wine. When the third course was on the table, the Ghanaian ambassadress, seated near the French host, raised her hand and silently summoned from an anteroom the African nanny she had brought with her on her return to the dinner party, together with the Ghanaian couple's very young baby. The nanny entered at one end of the dining room, a *grand salon*, walked sedately down its length, and delivered the baby to its mother, at the table. Astonishing. Discomfiting, to say the least, to our bachelor host. But then, and unbelievably at any dinner table in the 1960s, let alone at this dinner table, the Ghanaian ambassadress unwound a few yards of her lovely dress and offered a bare breast to the hungry young baby. The silence at the table was as deep as we had ever experienced. The poor French ambassador's discomfiture was as deep and complete as the silence – and I knew it was my duty, as the junior diplomat present, to end the silence and to try to divert attention. At all events, the Ghanaians had won: game, set and match. Only in Bulgaria, Hilary and I once again concluded later that long night, despite that this time, the event was nothing to do with the Bulgarians.

They were strange times, during the Cold War, which was waged in many different ways and at many different levels, including beyond the military and the diplomatic spheres. Ideology played a large, sometimes, it seemed, a dominating role in Cold War warfare. We thought that while we were serving behind the Iron Curtain, in a country really a vassal of the Soviet Union, it would be interesting to have Hilary's portrait done – in pastels, by a lady called Elizaveta Gruncharova (Елизавета Грънчарова), which translates to Elizabeth Potter. She had exhibited at the Bulgarian National Academy of Art; was highly recommended; and was permitted by the regime to have Western diplomats as clients. I took Hilary to Madame Gruncharova's quarters, a basic, small and sparsely furnished flat, high in a Stalinist block, where at any rate the light was good. I was later invited – perhaps allowed – to attend, one morning, just one sitting. Madame Gruncharova served the customary strawberry jam and slivova (plum brandy) – whose cost was certainly included in the price of the portrait. I asked the artist her view of socialist realism in art. She switched a radio on and turned the volume to its maximum before answering – presumably to confuse the presumed, and likely, microphones in the wall.

We had a fascinating conversation about how she had compromised with the authorities, yet, as she saw it, also defeated them morally and intellectually. She would enter the competition every year for the national exhibition: a good artist, she averred, needed to be hung. But for her pictures to be accepted for the exhibition, they had first to be utterly socialist realist and thus politically correct; and second, artistically and technically very good, better than the others. Yet, she had 'fooled them'. Madame Gruncharova showed us examples. On every large canvas she exhibited, there was a broad swath of socialist realist tribute to some aspect or other of communist workers' endeavour and success. But at a deeper level, and invisible to the insensitive eye, there were woven small yet strangely powerful romantic images, which, if identified, would have been anathema to the official judges. I thought she was brave to the point of foolhardiness. She knew she was being faithful and true to genuine art, and offering herself and other sensitive souls, including, perhaps, Bulgarian artists of the future, some real hope. We saw later some of her work in national exhibitions. Having had the benefit of her tutelage, we could find and enjoy some of her 'hidden' little romantic scenes. The Iron Curtain was indeed, and in many ways, also a Curtain of Ironies.

It was certainly foolhardy of Mrs Gruncharova, and for us it was also depressing, when, showing us the scraps from her box of, once, the finest of Dutch pastels, she asked us to order a new box for her, to be sent to us through the diplomatic bag. We had watched, saddened, how she would use the scraps to draw Hilary's portrait, by holding them in tweezers. She could not import such materials, for lack of hard currency and permission. Her ration of pastels, obtainable via the Bulgarian National Academy of Art, but only if the Academy itself then had enough hard currency to pay against her Bulgarian *leva*, was one box every seven years. We guessed she probably needed at least one a year. It would have been easy for us to import a new supply for her. It would also have been illegal to use the diplomatic bag for such a purpose. But, even worse than this, we believed that had we done her that little service, it would have been discovered, either as a result of bugging, or more likely by a neighbour or so-called friend informing on her to the authorities, and she would have suffered greatly. No longer having her work included in the national exhibition would have been by far the least of her consequential deprivations. The dreadful and tragic deaths of Drs Sarafov and Kirov, with hindsight, are not irrelevant.

Our regretful refusal of Madame Gruncharova's request, made well out of range of the ears in the walls – or any other ears – seemed to cause no ill-will. Perhaps she too had an idea of the likely consequences. Perhaps she had been willing, unwisely, but out of desperation, to risk those consequences for the sake, as she saw it, of the continued and higher performance of her art.

When the portrait was complete, Madame Gruncharova insisted loudly – including to the walls of her flat – that not only would she have to supervise its framing, in the best quality frame, but she must also select the best place in our flat and hang it herself. Her ploy, together with overcoming whatever bureaucratic obstacles she had to face, evidently resulted in official permission to visit a Western diplomatic apartment. She duly came, bearing the picture and a large bag. The picture, she announced, again loudly, to our walls, was now framed to her taste and in the highest quality materials. To our minds the portrait was in the only frame available then in Bulgaria, and with the best People's Republic glass – that is to say, rather wavy and a little distorting. (The work has since been reframed.)

We three had tea. We offered a biscuit – Western, imported by lorry from Denmark. With a smile of gratitude and conspiracy, Madame Gruncharova took the plate of biscuits and silently emptied it into her capacious bag. We brought more biscuits, and smiled silently with her as she repeated the process. What a treat for her, and how pleased we were to provide it. In those days, one always offered cigarettes, and she quietly emptied the whole boxful into her bag. Then she took out of her bag a large hammer and a long, crude and rusty nail – a cut floor brad.

Mrs Gruncharova next walked around the flat, to choose the best place for the portrait. (Fortunately, she chose the spot we favoured.) We had other arrangements in mind for the hanging itself, but she insisted on banging the nail into the wall herself. Now one of the reasons why we had other arrangements in mind, and rather careful arrangements, was that the walls in the flat, unusually, contained a network of pipes containing hot water – for the central heating. I explained the need for care, but this was an artist, evidently delighted to be hanging her own work. The nail went in deep, where Mrs Gruncharova wanted it to be. To our relief, and mild surprise (because this was Bulgaria, after all), the nail missed the pipes, and the portrait was hung to the satisfaction of this fine, brave artist. Only in Bulgaria.

Another 'only in Bulgaria' episode took place at Kremikovtsi – some 15 kilometres to the north-east of Sofia. This was a huge steelworks, part of the Soviet bloc Comecon economic plan. Kremikovtsi, carefully sited above an iron ore mine, imported its coal from Poland and, wildly uneconomically, also from Brazil. The plan was for a vertically integrated operation, from the mining of the ore to the production of finished tractor parts for the Soviet bloc, the Comecon countries. Only two or three years late, the operation was ready to make its first steel, and the Bulgarians decided to make a big show of an opening ceremony.

Prime Minister Todor Zhivkov presided, and a raft of cabinet ministers were also present – the ministers of trade, of metallurgical industries, and of foreign affairs, one Gero Grozev, as I recall (the successor to Ivan Bashev, of whom more later). The press from Bulgaria, the USSR and the other Comecon countries were present in force. Their Excellencies, the chefs de mission of the *corps diplomatique*, were all invited, the Westerners in particular to admire and be impressed by this notable Bulgarian achievement. The Soviet ambassador, Nikolai Nikolaevich Organov, was there in a different capacity: dressed in an astrakhan-collared coat, he strode about with all the authority of a governor from the Roman Empire – appropriately enough, given the then dominance of Moscow over its vassal states in Eastern Europe. The American minister (same Eugenie Anderson, political appointee and concert pianist), dressed by a Parisian couturier in an elegant, fur-trimmed suit, was prominently placed next to the Russian, largely to ensure that she could see and be suitably awed by everything that happened in the ceremony. The French ambassador (the successor to His Excellency of the dinner party) and the British minister, Savile Row-suited (though how he managed that on a Foreign Office salary escapes me), were standing together, a row or two behind. I stood close behind my boss, to whisper interpretations of the speeches in his ear.

The speeches were, as ever in Bulgaria, long, very long, and full of highly suspect statistics illustrating the glorious achievements of the Bulgarian Communist Party and the fraternal assistance of the USSR. They were extremely boring, and I wondered if my attempt at simultaneous translation was even listened to. The speeches were delivered around a series of troughs made to form, eventually, large steel nuggets from the molten steel gurgling away in a huge crucible many feet high above the gathered dignitaries. Away across the hall were groaning tables of the richest of foods and the finest of wines, a post-ceremony feast for the gathered dignitaries – and that in one of the poorest of East European countries.

The Bulgarian prime minister's was the last in the long series of long speeches. He concluded with a ringing tribute to communism, to the USSR, to the Bulgarian Communist Party and to the Republic of Bulgaria where the miracles of modern technology that surrounded us had been created; and declared that the opening of the Kremikovtsi plant he was proud to perform would now be signalled and celebrated by the very first pouring of molten metal from the vast vessels high above us, into the troughs before us. He gave the signal. The first of the mighty crucibles began to swing. The molten steel teetered, swelled and pouted on the lip of the vessel, white hot and ready to do its duty to the party. With a hissing roar, the molten metal dived down towards the troughs.

Remember the venue: this was the Balkans – and Bulgaria. The white- and red-hot steel missed the troughs, and bounced off all other available surfaces in a thousand directions and a hundred times, spattering everything and everyone in its way. Their Excellencies scattered in almost as many directions, and at speeds unknown since their youths. The Russian ambassador's astrakhan collar was badly burned; I can still see it smouldering. The American minister's Parisian fur trimming was seriously singed, creating a new, charred look. Foreign Minister Grozev received a burn to his bald head and spent a week or two in hospital. Many others suffered minor damage from this disaster. Not Prime Minister Zhivkov. Perhaps he was lucky. Perhaps he was even nimbler and faster on his feet than he had appeared. He could, for example, dance a remarkably lively *'horo'* (xopo), as Hilary and I once found when duty bound to accompany him on a ballroom floor. Or perhaps a zealous or ambitious bodyguard protected Todor Zhivkov well that day; the prime minister certainly seemed to have suffered little beyond enormous embarrassment and heavy humiliation. The French ambassador and British minister together imitated the action of a couple of badly scared chickens with both fox and hounds baying behind them; they did not stop running until they reached the car park.

Imagine the press coverage if such an incompetence or misfortune had happened in the West. Next day, the Bulgarian press and radio, and those throughout Eastern Europe, each carried reports. They were all about the same. They read something like: 'Yesterday the glorious and historic achievement of the integrated metallurgy plant at Kremikovtsi was opened by the Bulgarian Prime Minister Todor Zhivkov, in the presence of the Soviet ambassador, His Excellency N.N. Organov, and cabinet members of the People's Republic of Bulgaria. Heads of diplomatic missions accredited to the People's Republic of Bulgaria were also present.' The sad aspect to me of that Kremikovtsi event was that both at the time and the next day, while there was shock around, even trauma, there was a palpable absence of surprise. That implicit ready acceptance of disaster and national humiliation seemed to be a paradigm or template for much of the modern history of Bulgaria under that disagreeable communist government that seemed to have abandoned integrity, good sense and decent values.

Less disagreeably, the Bulgarian government used to organise occasional events for the heads of missions of the diplomatic corps in Sofia. Some were mere propaganda events, but there were more genuine and enjoyable ones, such as a wild boar shoot. At one shoot, Their Excellencies of the corps were accompanied for the occasion by their military attachés – on the presumed grounds that if not all their heads of mission could shoot, at least they could. Ambassadors and military attachés spent some hours fruitlessly stalking. They became rather spread out in their search. The British military attaché spotted in a small clearing, the unmistakable grey hide and rounded form of a wild boar. He dropped to one knee, levelled his shot-gun, took careful aim, and fired. The bang was followed instantly by a high-pitched yelp, and a diminutive diplomat jumped up, down and around the clearing, complaining loudly. This head of mission was wearing a grey leather hunting suit, and had been bending down, peering through the undergrowth in search of his own prey. His trousers were peppered and perforated with shot. Only in Bulgaria.

That grey leather trousered diplomat was that same *chargé d'affaires en titre* who had left that dinner party after the soup, considering himself to have been badly seated – *mal placé*. I like to think of the military attaché's shot as particularly *bien placé* – well seated.

CHAPTER 3

BULGARIA: EMBASSY

Hilary and I were fortunate to be serving in Bulgaria when full diplomatic relations between the two countries were established, and our legation was promoted to embassy. It had been decided in London by ministers that it would be right to upgrade the legations in Sofia and Bucharest to embassies. This change was negotiated and agreed with the communist governments concerned: the upgrading was reciprocal, of course, occurring also in London. I saw this move not as a reward for effort, still less as a sign of a real thaw then in the Cold War, but as a sensible, regularising step that, with good fortune and careful handling, might be used to ease surface tensions and help our efforts in Bulgaria. It probably did some of that. It certainly offered us new hope and motivation, and it brought to Sofia Great Britain's first ambassador to Bulgaria, Bill Harpham (later Sir William, KBE). The ambassador's approach was new, positive, kindly to staff, thoughtful in all he did. Bill Harpham believed in commercial diplomacy, as well as its other forms – economic, political, cultural and the rest. His knighthood paid warm tribute to a singularly successful career. Astonishingly, justly, uniquely, his patient, determined yet gentle and equally successful work in Bulgaria was also, if three years later and still while the Cold War raged, recognised by the Bulgarian communist government, who honoured him with the iconic Order of the Madara Horseman. After retirement, Sir William took on new endeavours at the head of the Great Britain–East Europe Centre, which he established and led for 15 years, and where he achieved a great deal in cultural, person-to-person and other fields of diplomacy and mutual understanding against mighty difficulties; he was just the man quietly to make such a real and valuable contribution to the eventual end of the Cold War. In 1976, still well before the Cold War ended, Bulgaria honoured Bill a second time for this work, with the Order of Stara Planina.

Back to Sofia in late 1963. The minister was posted elsewhere, and, in January 1964, the British legation became history. The delightful ambassador Bill Harpham arrived, initially and temporarily, for protocol reasons, as minister plenipotentiary; he became ambassador very soon thereafter. Before he could begin his job in earnest, he had, as always for new ambassadors, to present his credentials to the president of Bulgaria. Credentials, or letters of credence, commend the ambassador to the country to which he or she is accredited, the receiving state, and seek his or her acceptance as the plenipotentiary representative of the sending state. These letters were signed by Her Majesty the Queen and addressed to the president of the Republic of Bulgaria. It is odd but interesting how some republics, including both Bulgaria and our subsequent posting, France, insist on elaborate ceremonial for the presentation of credentials, more elaborate ceremonial and dress than in many a monarchy. The Bulgarians required a full-dress ceremony, with their full-dress senior military guard, parade and band. It took some weeks to plan, negotiate and rehearse the event.

The ceremony was held later in that January 1964, in the depths of the Bulgarian winter. A large contingent of troops was drawn up as a guard of honour to be reviewed by the ambassador in the grand square outside the then presidential offices in the National Assembly (Народно Събрание) building. In this, the centre of the Communist Republic's capital city, under their long overcoats, the soldiers wore ceremonial uniforms dating from Bulgarian monarchical days and King Boris. The military band was also arrayed grandly, with frills and furbelows reminiscent of Gilbert and Sullivan.

The Bulgarian Republic's ceremony also required the ambassador and his staff to wear decorations and diplomatic uniform – elegant dark blues, with gold braid here and there, and a bicorn cocked hat worn fore and aft and with ostrich-feather plumes. The original plan and protocol also included an open carriage drive, as is the form in

London for ambassadors travelling to Buckingham Palace to present credentials. I never established why the Bulgarians changed this plan; perhaps they had not followed that practice for so many years that the logistics, whether equine or vehicular, were not up to the job. However, the new and first ever British ambassador must travel from the embassy to the grand square – perhaps a mile, but probably the coldest capital city mile then in Eastern Europe – in an open, coupé limousine, a vast maroon-and-chrome presidential Zil, from Soviet Russia, of course. These two requirements, uniform and open car, together with the thermometer stuck a very long way below zero, combined to persuade the ambassador's wife to intervene. She made it abundantly clear that the ambassador would not travel thus without being very well wrapped up; over his uniform, he could wear his full-length dark blue diplomatic uniform cloak, which was plain and unadorned. The ambassador politely demurred. The whole point of wearing the gold braided uniform and decorations would be lost, and it would not be right to represent the United Kingdom thus obviously cocooned and sheltered against the East European elements. The people lining the route, and the troops he was to inspect and address, should see the uniform and finery and recognise all it stood for. There was apparently domestic discussion of long johns – discussion quickly ended: diplomatic uniform trousers are very tight. The ambassador and his lady eventually reached a compromise – a classically British compromise. Those days, the early 1960s, were the days of the London *Times* airmail edition – very fine, thin, crinkly paper. The compromise was that as essential insulation against the bitter cold, the ambassador would wear a few layers of *The Times* airmail edition wrapped around him, lightly tacked together by the ambassadress, and hidden under his uniform jacket and trousers.

Thus he dressed, and thus he set off in procession, accompanied by the Bulgarian chief of protocol, he heavily overcoated and scarved. There was even some courageous applause along the route. The ambassador arrived in the square, descended from the open limousine and was joined by the diplomatic staff of the embassy. Those who had diplomatic uniform wore it. Others (such as I) wore lounge suit, with a good foundation of thermal underwear, and dark overcoats.

The ceremony proceeded. The ambassador mounted a dais and formally greeted the assembled guard and band with a couple of words shouted in rather old-fashioned formal Bulgarian, *'Zdravey, Voyneetsee!'* [Здравей Войници!], meaning: 'Greetings, Soldiers!' The several hundred soldiers bellowed out a response, a little updated for communism, and more or less together: *'Zdravey, Drugar Poslannik!'* [Здравей, Другар Посланик!] (Greetings, Comrade Ambassador!) After salutes, the ambassador walked the 60 or 70 yards of the ranks of soldiers, along and back, by way of inspection, while the band played marches. The ambassador returned to the dais for more salutes, and was then conducted, with his staff, into the National Assembly building, which also housed the presidential reception rooms. The Union Flag and the Bulgarian flag were flying above the entrance. Here the presentation of the letters was made, and mercifully (and for the Bulgarians most unusually), short speeches were exchanged. The ambassador, his head of chancery and his interpreter (that was I) were then received privately by the president and the prime minister in a separate salon. We sat in formal chairs around a low table talking and sipping Bulgarian champagne for half an hour while those outside in the square, all the soldiers and spectators, froze. Well, not quite all froze. Hilary, the ambassador's wife and a few others had thermos flasks of hot coffee; and the brass section of the band, having blown down their trumpets and other instruments, were thawing their frozen instruments with hot water in the kitchen of the restaurant on the square.

I had met those instruments before. The al fresco part of the ceremony was later to be resumed, and to conclude with fanfares and the British and Bulgarian national anthems. Some few weeks earlier, I had visited the band, given them the sheet music for 'God Save the Queen', and played the top line on the piano at the right speed and rhythm in an effort to help their rehearsals.

We were still inside, debating, perhaps unusually politely, some of the bilateral and international issues of the day; and toasting Anglo-Bulgarian friendship, greater East–West understanding – lots and lots of toasts. The glasses, set on a low coffee table, were topped up, frequently, on this historic if artificial occasion. The very tall, six-foot-four ambassador was constantly bending and leaning from the waist, downward to pick up his glass and forward and up to clink glasses with the Bulgarian president and prime minister. Exchanges of earnest diplomatic politesses abounded – interspersed with very many toasts and a few sharp, serious criticisms. As I tried to concentrate on my interpretation, I became increasingly diverted by a strange phenomenon. Each time my revered ambassador leaned politely forward and back, there appeared above his gold-braided stand-up collar at first a thin white line, then little by little, millimetre by millimetre, identifiably the airmail edition of the most internationally famous British newspaper – until I, and the president and prime minister of Bulgaria too, could read the unmistakable top halves of the words 'The Times'. I repressed the desire to laugh beneath my acute embarrassment and sympathy for my gentlemanly boss. Eventually, we stood; and the president conducted the ambassador through the halls and outside to the steps of the building, where they were to receive military salutes. I brought up nearly the rear, as was my junior place, and could not get near enough to His Excellency, as he took his place at the front, to render assistance by suppressing a British national newspaper.

Short salutes followed, and a fanfare of some sort; and then the full band played. But their brass instruments, aided by the restaurant's hot water for the fanfare, but now swiftly freezing, seized up again, and no one recognised the first few very faltering bars of 'God Save the Queen'. Knowing what should be happening, I hissed around the assembled dignitaries in English and Bulgarian, 'National anthems'. Fortunately, most were all already standing to attention. They remained thus, erect and still, the British diplomats in uniform or their best lounge suits, the military attaché in trews and bonnet, the Bulgarians in regulation dark grey formal suits; while the band shivered into silence and, in marked disarray, the brass section ran off once again to the restaurant to thaw their instruments while we waited. They straggled back, reformed after a fashion, and, severally seizing up again, struggled their way through both anthems, doing justice to neither. The president and the ambassador inspected the guard of honour together. The ambassador took his formal leave of the troops: *'Doveezhdaneh, Voyneetsee!'* [Довиждане, Войници!], 'Farewell, soldiers'; and, after their response, said goodbye less loudly to the president and prime minister; remounted the open limousine; and was played off the square and on his way home in the band's final unrecognisable but strangely memorable contribution to the historic event. Only in Bulgaria.

Back in the Embassy, the ambassador's relatively diminutive but loyal, loving and lovely wife Isabelle climbed on a chair by the grand piano and tucked *The Times* back where it belonged, out of sight below the ambassador's uniform collar. We had a warming glass. The ambassador said a few warming words. Soon, those in uniform changed into normal office wear, and we all returned to our diplomatic lasts with a will, in that beautiful, memorable, tragi-comic, but certainly then frustrating and so often disappointing country.

Bill and Isabelle Harpham worked well, hard and cheerily. They inspired much devotion among their staff. They brought fresh air and new endeavour to the embassy and to the bilateral diplomatic relationship, which continued to pose many problems but also now to offer a few more opportunities. We were renewed in our knowledge, or our trust, that it was well worth keeping open a window on the West, and in our case on Great Britain especially. It was indeed right to persist, despite – indeed in a real sense because of – the communist government's determined efforts to counter much of our work.

At one stage, when the United Kingdom was having some difficulties in Africa, the Bulgarians talked to, propagandised and, we strongly suspected, drugged a large number of Kenyan students at Sofia National University. The students then dutifully 'marched' and, accompanied by communist youth agitators and no doubt secret policemen, staged a so-called spontaneous demonstration against Britain outside our embassy. I had vaguely noticed the delivery of a large consignment of bricks early the previous day to the building next door to ours. I had assumed (as we were no doubt meant to assume, had any thought been given to that aspect) that some construction work was to be done there. Wrong. The bricks were ammunition for the students. They smashed the windows of the embassy. They overturned and badly damaged our cars parked outside. Inside, I telephoned the Bulgarian Ministry of Foreign Affairs to ask for the police protection to which every diplomatic mission in the world is entitled. There was a police station and barracks almost opposite the embassy. The answer was: 'Sorry, there's no one available at the moment. They'll come as soon as possible.' As I received this answer on the telephone, I was looking across the road at the police station and watching each window full of uniformed figures observing the demonstration. I even spotted the policeman who should have been on duty outside the embassy that morning – and had been there at his post, earlier.

Head of Chancery Mark Heath and I went outside, to try to talk to and to calm down the demonstrators, that mixed bunch of Kenyan students and Bulgarian agitators. I translated Mark's offer to talk with a representative or two inside the embassy. This overture was met with renewed volleys of bricks, and when one narrowly missed Mark's head by a close margin and from a great height, I persuaded him that we should retreat inside the office, where I rang the ministry again. This time, I angrily asked when the 'spontaneous' demonstration was going to end. After a pause long enough apparently to consult the office clock, came the answer 'In 14 minutes'. So the ministry failed properly to organise even its own propaganda. Sure enough, 14 minutes later, the demonstrators marched or rather straggled back to the university, with their minders, and all was quiet.

I have a number of memories of that day. Prominent among them is a face at one of our own embassy windows as I looked upwards from outside to watch the trajectory of the brick that nearly did for the head of chancery. My eyes captured a snapshot of one of the young secretaries sobbing as she watched her new and first car being smashed three storeys below her.

Mercifully, such physical attacks on Western embassies were not frequent. Rather less dramatic demonstrations were, however, rather regular in front of the American embassy, which was located in the centre of town and sported two very large shop windows. The US legation information section used to fill these windows, right on the busy street, with large captioned pictures portraying the American way of life or illustrating some message of democracy. Sometimes the Bulgarian Communist Party could not stomach this practice, and would retaliate in various ways. One was an atheistic exhibition nearby with the title 'Is There a God?' and pictures proclaiming the answer 'No'. One such I recall was, to our eyes a fairly obviously doctored picture of the pope or a bishop, blessing Nazi soldiers. Another, equally doctored, was a cartoon of the pope in front of an altar, with a gun, some armed monks and a well-ordered group of nuns with American rifles raised to their shoulders.

Quite regularly, there would be demonstrations at the US embassy, during which the embassy's huge windows would be smashed. The press would report these 'spontaneous' demonstrations next day. The press would not report that the Bulgarian government was obliged by international agreements to which it was a signatory, to replace the glass. This was a costly business, particularly because Bulgarian glass could not be made to the necessary size or quality. The glass was imported in advance of the demonstrations by train from Austria, and held in storage outside Sofia. I was to learn from an arguably indiscreet Bulgarian official that the foreign ministry had an annual budget for this replacement glass; and that once the budget was spent, there could be no more such anti-American demonstrations that financial year. Only in Bulgaria.

As a footnote to this account of 'spontaneous' demonstrations against the West behind the Iron Curtain, the American lady minister's husband, John Anderson, used to go out quietly with his camera during the attacks on the then US legation. He told me that he used the pictures to illustrate articles he sent through the diplomatic 'bag' (or 'pouch' as American diplomats call it) for publication in a newspaper in his home state in the United States. We rather admired that by-product of Cold War diplomacy, and probably envied his acquisition of pin-money. I don't think that we Brits would have been allowed (or wished) to do any such thing.

On the occasion of a Bulgarian Communist Party Congress in Sofia, selected heads of Western diplomatic missions were invited to attend the principal session. Towards the end of what had seemed an interminable address by the first secretary of the Party, Todor Zhivkov, he gratuitously attacked and insulted the Western powers,

NATO and 'Western bourgeois capitalism'. This was normal enough behaviour, and doubtless made Zhivkov and his party audience feel warm and comfortable. Early in this predictable tirade, and sitting in the balcony just behind my ambassador, I leaned forward to summarise Zhivkov's theme and advise that we should rise and walk out. Bill Harpham needed no persuasion. The Americans followed, in relief we shared.

The Bulgarian communist government behaved, in my view, in a thoroughly reprehensible way over the quatercentenary of the birth of Shakespeare in 1964. Those concerned in the United Kingdom organised a series of special performances and events, notably, of course, in Stratford-upon-Avon. At the University of Sofia, there was a professor of English, who was renowned throughout the international community of Shakespearean academics for his original and fine scholarship and for his serious and illuminating contributions over many distinguished years. Professor Minkov was among a small and select number of Shakespearean scholars from around the world to be invited to take part in the principal colloquium in Stratford that year.

Professor Minkov and his wife and daughter lived in a small flat in the attic of his family house. They had owned and occupied the whole house before the advent of communism and the associated appropriation of attractive houses of the intelligentsia for the use of party officials and apparatchiks. There was precious little room in the tiny flat. Many of the professor's remaining books lined the stairs up to the attic, behind wire mesh. The invitation to Stratford no doubt gave him much pleasure, professionally and personally.

In those days, Bulgarians had to have an exit visa to be allowed to leave the country at all. When the government believed that there was a good case for granting such a visa, which they occasionally did, there was usually a condition, to which I have referred in the case of the locally engaged staff member who defected to the West, that the person wishing to travel left behind a loved one, as a sort of hostage against his or her return. For us, of course, this practice demonstrated the government's lack of confidence in the devotion of its people to their country and its regime. The case for Professor Minkov to visit the United Kingdom to attend the colloquium was clear and sound.

The Western scholars would be saluting a distinguished Bulgarian academic at an important international event. His contribution to the colloquium would no doubt be published and do credit to his university and his country. The Bulgarian government would gain, not lose, in diplomatic terms, by issuing the visa. There would be no cost in hard currency to the Bulgarians: all expenses would be paid. Professor Minkov was a devoted husband and professional, about whose return to Bulgaria, to his wife, family, university and students there could be no reasonable doubt. If the government really required it, however, there could easily be a 'hostage' against the professor's return.

The Bulgarian Council of Ministers (cabinet), as I recall, addressed the question of Professor Minkov. They refused to issue the exit visa, and therefore prevented the professor from accepting the invitation. We in the embassy were saddened, regretful, and determined to try to reverse the decision, which we found unconscionable and absurd. The ambassador instructed me to accompany him on a call on the Bulgarian foreign minister, to lodge a protest and seek a reversal. The foreign minister was one Ivan Bashev (Иван Башев). He was the youngest member of the cabinet, and ambitious. As I recall the discussion, Bill Harpham argued well, in a gentle and politely persistent way, and Bashev attempted neither to defend the Bulgarian decision, nor to counter my ambassador's arguments for its reconsideration. He merely said, and reiterated, that this was a decision by the government and was immutable. Bashev was a fairly civilised, able and cultured man, and there was no bad temper, nor any raised voices. But there was a stony, to us bull-headed, refusal, for whatever reason, to entertain any view but the one the authorities had taken. I like to think that Ivan Bashev had at least argued in cabinet in favour of allowing Professor Minkov to go to Stratford, but had been defeated by a majority of obstinate anti-intellectuals, driven by a combination perhaps of their own anti-Western prejudice, philistinism, short-sightedness, habit and desire to repress intellectuals, and an inability objectively to assess the interests of their own country and government. Just possibly, the objections had also been to the fact that the proposal had been made or supported by this young, ambitious and able foreign minister.

Professor Minkov, I believe, took the rejection with quiet resignation and dignity. Ivan Bashev later died young, reportedly in a skiing accident when alone on the slopes, killed by an avalanche. Being communist Bulgaria, however, conspiracy theories abounded – and may still be heard – to explain his death in other ways.

One of my roles in the embassy was that of cultural attaché, and representative for the British Council. Fairly soon after he arrived, with good notice, well before the Shakespeare quatercentenary, our ambassador had instructed me to try to secure a visit by the Old Vic Theatre (to my mind, the precursor to Britain's National Theatre) to perform a Shakespeare play in Sofia, perhaps in the Bulgarian National Theatre. I tried, but found it a hopeless task. The Old Vic did perform abroad that quatercentenary year, and they did venture behind the Iron Curtain. But, reasonably enough, they went only to Moscow. I confessed my failure to the ambassador. Bill Harpham smiled kindly and, I hoped, sympathetically, but said that absent the Old Vic, Britain should nonetheless celebrate the quatercentenary in Bulgaria: he therefore still required a performance of Shakespeare. Since I was the cultural attaché and had failed to deliver the Old Vic, I had better do the job myself.

The ambassador's residence in Sofia was, and remains, a fine house, with many rooms, including a 'ballroom'. Like many ambassadorial residences around the world, it is an effective tool of diplomacy, or in the phrase of a former colleague, a theatre of diplomatic operations. The ambassador required a week of Shakespeare evening performances in the 'ballroom'. He would invite audiences from among a wide range of Bulgarians: government officials, academics and others whom he thought might be permitted to attend such an event in a Western embassy; and selected other diplomats.

This ambassadorial requirement posed a severe challenge. The UK-based staff at the embassy numbered only fifteen, of whom five were security staff. We then called them chancery guards. Their skills were vital to the embassy, but were rather different from those of the actor. The same applied to the three Diplomatic Wireless Service officers. There were, of course, some wives accompanying their husbands. Hilary and I thought very hard for a couple of evenings, and read some of my Shakespeare again. I concluded that we could neither credibly nor creditably perform an entire Shakespeare play: we simply hadn't the resources. Instead we would perform extracts, some extended, from five of the plays, and five speeches or soliloquies.

Embassy staff and wives rushed to be auditioned. There was more thespian talent in the embassy than I had supposed. The ambassador's personal assistant, Kay Lusmore, made both a wonderfully convincing Portia in the trial scene of *The Merchant of Venice* and a feisty and exciting Katharine in two splendid scenes from *The Taming of the Shrew*. The auditions for the witches in *Macbeth* took a long time, such was the clamour to be selected. None of the wives minded being made to look ugly, including by having some of their teeth blacked out for those parts. The few Diplomatic Wireless Service and Foreign Service technical maintenance service staff at the embassy built a stage in the ballroom, on two levels, and equipped it with most effective and flexible lighting. 'Macbeth' was the last of our five extracts, and the longest. We played five scenes, including an extended scene with witches crouched and circling a large steaming cauldron on the upper level of the stage. We borrowed *Macbeth* costumes from the Sofia National Opera. The administration officer, George Hinves, an Army officer on his second career, played Macbeth superbly and with great style. The head of chancery's wife, Margaret Heath, was a Lady Macbeth of a high standard, at least the equal of some of the best professional actresses I had seen play the part. Her sleepwalking scene was thrilling, and chilling. George Hinves also played a memorably effective Shylock. A British drama critic and academic, who happened to be a house guest of the ambassador at the time of the performances, could not tell that both roles were played by the same man. George Hinves also spoke John of Gaunt's patriotic soliloquy most eloquently. One of the younger wives, Ellen Titcombe, delivered Juliet's orchard soliloquy beautifully. The consul, Colin Nash, was a wonderfully camp Malvolio in the garden scene. The biggest surprise was Falstaff, played in a *Merry Wives* extract with excellent timing, fun and skill by Harry Brett, one of the Diplomatic Wireless Service officers. And to give the evening structure and continuity, I had asked Mark Heath to read connecting lines, as a kind of spoken recitative-cum-commentary. He did so perfectly.

Arguably the most pleasing feature of the week, however, was the presence at one of the performances of Professor and Mrs Minkov and their daughter, herself an accomplished student of English literature. The ambassador sat them in the front row. During one of the soliloquies, tears ran down the daughter's face. Only in Bulgaria.

By way of further illustration of life behind this curtain of ironies, the Bulgarians did celebrate the quatercentenary of Shakespeare's birth. Bill and Isabelle Harpham, Hilary, her sister Roz then visiting us, and I attended a memorable performance of *As You Like It*. The play was performed not in the capital city, which would have made rather too much of one of Britain's powerful and most enduring of 'invisible exports', but in the distant north-west corner of Bulgaria in the open air at a fine historic fortress, Baba Vida, in Vidin, by the River Danube. I recall fearing that the rather heavy Slavonic language would not render well such a light, fast-moving and romantic comedy, but an able and devoted troupe of actors and their director proved me largely wrong. The performance was distinguished by its faithfulness to Shakespeare's text in translation, and its rather unexpected sense of fun: it should have been performed in Sofia at the National Theatre, but that was indeed too much to expect. Vidin also sported a roadside design in coloured stones, recording '400 years of Shakespeare'. Bulgarian communist governmental duty was thus done to the principle of 'cultural exchange', on which subject we negotiated a bilateral treaty while I was serving in Sofia.

Margaret and Mark Heath left us in that year, 1964, for what must have been a welcome posting to Ottawa, but to the real regret of all of us. They were succeeded in Sofia by Lineke and Derek Thomas, who also became good and lasting friends. We served together again briefly in Paris, and, to our delight, for longer in Washington. Derek, too, was destined for greater things. Towards the end of his career, after a highly influential and successful term as political director in the Foreign Office, he should in my view certainly have been ambassador and UK permanent representative to the European Community in Brussels, for which he was uniquely qualified. I rather think he was the Foreign Office's choice, but at the highest level of government it was decided otherwise, and later, after further toiling in the vineyard of the political directorship, Sir Derek Thomas KCMG went to Rome as ambassador – where he served to great effect, but for less than 15 months, due to the absurdity of compulsory retirement at the age of 60. His subsequent career in and for British business was glittering and effective; so UK plc was served very well indeed overall.

The embassy's Shakespearean evenings encouraged further amateur productions, even once a farce, *Sailor Beware*, which George Hinves directed. Derek Thomas was splendidly funny in the part of Carnoustie Bligh, and Lineke played a commanding and successful Emma Hornet (the lead part made famous by Peggy Mount), spoken to great effect in the second of Lineke's several languages. That sort of self-help spare-time activity behind the Iron Curtain was good for morale in difficult professional circumstances, and did the reputation of Brits abroad no harm at all.

I was interested in the position of the Church, the Eastern Orthodox Church, in communist Bulgaria. I went to call on Patriarch Eftimi, in 1963. He told me of tough, difficult relations with the atheistic government, and how he had found it necessary to compromise in order that the Church might survive. I was young and idealistic, and asked the patriarch whether compromise might be seriously to diminish, if not to destroy, the faith. I asked whether resistance would not be the right and the nobler religious way. The patriarch gently explained his philosophy of survival in the face of all kinds of physical and psychological pressure and privation, in order to offer a glimmer of hope, however small, for the faithful. I don't think I was persuaded, then or for some years. He was, of course, right.

Shortly before Orthodox Eastertide in 1964, the Bulgarian government announced that for the first time since communism, the cathedral would be permitted to celebrate the religious festival in the traditional way. This announcement betokened a major departure, and followed some years of negotiation between the Bulgarian government and the oppressed Eastern Orthodox Church, whose religious treasures and freedom of worship the government had removed soon after coming to power. The thrill of anticipation in Sofia at this news was almost palpable. This was the major festival of the Eastern Orthodox year, much loved and much revered. We knew that the service would be long, and that it would be sung most beautifully by a large choir. We did not expect to see any of the precious chests of icons restored to the cathedral by the Communist Party, but we hoped that some of the splendid vestments and patriarchal accoutrements might have been returned, at least for this service and its patriarchal procession around the outside of the Alexander Nevski Cathedral. Hilary and I, and another couple, decided to try to witness this historic service and this apparently forward step in communist Bulgaria's life.

We arrived at the vast cathedral, which in the Orthodox tradition has no pews, nor any seats (except in the choir loft), to find it crammed full. There were thousands outside, too, all around the cathedral. There were also large numbers of uniformed and armed soldiers, and plenty of all-too-recognisable plain-clothed police and secret police, mostly also armed. We squeezed in near the back of the cathedral, close by the stairway to the choir loft. The atmosphere was heavy with excitement and devotion. The service proceeded, and the religious fervour was intense: not vocal but deep, and growing. But something else was happening too. There was movement among the packed congregation. People were trying to stand still, but not succeeding. There were waves of movement; lines of people surged forward and then back. We moved a few steps up the stairway, the better to see what was going on. From this vantage point we saw clearly gangs of communist youths spread among the congregation, perhaps twenty at a time with arms linked, pushing, heaving, forward and back, bent upon physical disruption of the service. Devout old ladies were being shoved and nearly crushed.

Then we spotted, near the altar, where the patriarch and other clergy were conducting the service, a few more communist youths. The altar bore huge candelabra with many tall candles, imported, no doubt, for this very special occasion and church festival. We watched two young men saunter slowly up the altar steps, and wander swaggeringly along its length. This almost surreal and crass scene was played out also against the starkly contrasting beauty of the service and the haunting a cappella singing of the excellent, even celestial choir. The scene at the altar came to a shocking, appalling end as the two youths each reached up and wrenched a long candle from the candelabra and with them, lit cigarettes. Those in the congregation who could see this ugly act gasped in fear and outrage at the sacrilege. The clergy, doggedly and even gracefully, continued to conduct the service, against even these extraordinary odds.

The loutish shoving in the congregation continued, even increased. We began to be concerned for our own as well as for others' safety. There was only one way to go: up. We ascended one of the two sets of stairs leading to the choir loft, where the choir was still singing superbly, and helping heroically to hold the service and the worship together. As I led the long climb up the stairs, I saw several youths swiftly mounting the parallel stairs on the other side of the choir loft. Their leader grabbed a chair, raised it high and brought it crashing down on the head of the choirmaster. The other youths followed suit and set about members of the choir. That was, of course, the end of the singing, and the service began to fall apart.

Resisting the strong temptation to go to the aid of the choir members (that would have been a fruitless and professionally stupid move), we waited awhile for the physical pressure to ease as some people left the cathedral, and then went outside ourselves. I spoke to the most senior military officer I could find, to protest that he and his men should stop the terrible and disruptive activities of the youths, and restore order to prevent further hurt to people and ensure that the service that had been authorised should continue. He responded that everyone was allowed to demonstrate against religion if they wished, and his orders were to allow that, and otherwise only to prevent riot. I felt the Bulgarian congregation were far too downtrodden for a riot to occur, whatever the provocation. So, I suspect, did the Bulgarian military and police authorities. The military presence was, as I saw it, an extra exercise in gratuitous intimidation and oppression.

The brave patriarch and his clergy determinedly proceeded with the tattered remains of the service. The climax of the long-banned Easter service was a procession around the square in the centre of which the cathedral stood. The cross in the lead, the procession tried manfully to form and to move off. It made a few struggling yards before being completely overcome, disrupted and forced to retreat in disarray. Slowly, sadly, the thousands who had formed the congregation dispersed, to walk home in the still of the early evening.

My last memory of that day, as we too walked sadly away, is the sight of an old bent lady, dressed in widow's weeds, performing a ritual practice denied to her for many years. She had a small lit candle in her hand, purchased at the cathedral, possibly with her remaining mite. The Easter practice was to take the candle home. If it arrived there still lit, this was a blessing, and brought good fortune during the succeeding year. The old lady clutched the candle in one wizened hand, and sheltered it with the other, cupped around it against the gentle movement of air she created as she walked slowly homewards. One of the communist youth walked up to her, leaned over and blew out the candle. The look of sorrowful resignation on her lined old face stays with me today.

However, however … the Bulgarian Church more than survived the Cold War, and today is accessible, is respected, and indeed thrives. And that brave and wise man, Patriarch Eftimi, who was proved so right after his death, recently had a boulevard and square named for him in Sofia, and a statue erected. Curtain of sad ironies.

To alleviate the sadness and tough times, there was fun for us in Bulgaria in the early 1960s. There was not much fun for the Bulgarians. As British diplomats, we certainly faced many problems. Some were difficult challenges to overcome, some were nasty, and some were insoluble. Yet, all in all, we had a marvellous time in Bulgaria. We learned a great deal, and usually enjoyed doing so. It was a testing and effective apprenticeship in diplomacy. Work was quite hard in a small post, but varied, and immensely worthwhile. Outside the office, we made our own fun, from amateur dramatics, via fancy dress treasure hunts through night-time Sofia confusing the secret police utterly, to summer boating and winter ice-skating at Pancharevo lake and winter skiing on Vitosha and the then always virgin slopes above the little mountain village retreat of Borovets, which then had almost no infrastructure. Its Turkish name, Tcham Kuria, still then survived, despite the efforts of the Bulgarian government.

So despite everything, we greatly enjoyed our honeymoon post; and despite everything, we were grateful to this beautiful if then sad and apparently godforsaken country. In practical ways, but so much more importantly in political and moral ways, thank goodness, things are so very much better in the Bulgaria of today, well after the Cold War was lost and won, communism was defeated, and our open window on the West had let in a great deal of fresh air. The Church in Bulgaria is respected and thrives. The government is generally a thoughtful, helpful one, working hard to improve the economy and society.

A Bulgarian we knew well used to tell us tales of the former royal family. She would become tearful at her stories of King Boris's sudden and mysterious death in 1943 (which evidently occurred soon after a less than warm and friendly meeting of the king with Adolf Hitler); the accession to the throne as King Simeon II of King Boris's then six-year-old son, Prince Simeon (Borisov) Saxe-Coburg Gotha (the surname, of course, of our own royal family before it was changed to Windsor); of the communist coup in 1944; the killing of the regents; and King Simeon's enforced exile in 1946. Sadly, our friend was not alive, 50 years after that exile, to see Simeon Saxe-Coburg Gotha return to his country, and, in the 2001 parliamentary elections, win a landslide victory and become prime minister – a role in which he served with distinction for four years. The earlier Balkan wars of the 1990s followed the end of the Cold War, when the strength of the political glue Tito had invented to hold his fissiparous Yugoslavia, neighbour to Bulgaria, together, finally gave out. These wars, among Bosnians, Serbs, Kosovans, constitute an appallingly dreadful and sobering story, but a separate story from that of Bulgaria. I for one was delighted at the welcome the European Union gave in 2007 to Bulgaria as, in her modern, helpful, genuinely friendly existence, she joined the rest of us in a Europe now so much less likely ever to return to the dark and bloody days of warring over internal European disputes.

There is often something engrossing, nostalgic and even magnetic about a diplomat's first post abroad, especially if he or she has learned the language. I have returned four times to Bulgaria. The first occasion was in the late 1980s; the Cold War had not ended, but the Iron Curtain showed some rust, and just a little fresh air was penetrating through the resultant perforations. As assistant under-secretary of state (economic) in the Foreign and Commonwealth Office (FCO) I thought it worth visiting selected East European countries in support of British companies and their exports. In Bulgaria there was a particular need to try to wrest from the Bulgarian state agencies payments well overdue to a number of British companies. One was a Welsh company whose unpaid bills were so large as to threaten the company's continued existence. Accompanied by the commercial diplomat from the embassy, I called on the relevant Bulgarian minister of foreign trade – a radical change from the level at which I could operate as a third secretary a quarter of a century earlier. I had done my homework, was briefed by the embassy, resurrected a little of my by then also rusted Bulgarian and deployed my case. It did not go down well. The interview was less well tempered than that with Ivan Bashev over the exit visa for Professor Minkov. I was treated to what I thought by then an old-fashioned anti-Western lecture, whose burden was sadly familiar. The Bulgarian minister also asked what I had expected: we British were experts in capitalism and must know that a key feature of that system was risk; the risk the British companies had run had been misjudged. I countered with a question about how well the Bulgarians were managing their currency risk management, and whether they were seriously short of hard currency; otherwise would not even they honour their debts? It was all just too soon before the Berlin Wall fell, I suppose, but I did secure payment of some, if certainly not all, of the debts.

I stayed at the ambassador's residence for that brief visit, and went for a walk through part of Sofia before returning home. At one familiar five-way cross-roads, there used to be a traffic policeman whose exhibitions of baton-twirling we had much enjoyed in the 1960s, particularly because he twirled away happily in the usual absence of traffic. He was now replaced by multiple traffic lights, and directions for pedestrians to use a new subway – a large affair rather like a rough concrete and empty version of that below Piccadilly Circus. To my astonishment and mild frisson, I saw painted on one of the concrete walls in large black letters and in English a graffito reading, 'Come back, Roger.' It must surely have referred to someone else, but the coincidence was extraordinary.

In 2009, Hilary suggested that we should try to repeat our honeymoon journey of 1962, but in our modern four-wheel drive car, and in October, well before winter. This we did, finding most of the old roads we had used 47 years before. A good number had been vastly improved; some had been replaced by tunnels through mountains; a few had been abandoned and could not be used at all. It was a delightful drive, followed by much new pleasure in exploring old Bulgarian haunts, for example finding the spot where our Morris Minor had dived down its icy hole, and marvelling at the international ski resort that Borovets had become. It was a particular joy to visit the many parts of beautiful Bulgaria denied to us in communist days for Cold War reasons. It was a delight to spend time in Plovdiv, perhaps especially in its vast Roman amphitheatre and other ruins, newly revealed in all their considerable and barely faded glory. We relished the multitude of changes for the better, visible and invisible, and the multiple indications of progress and movement towards democracy consequent on Bulgaria's cooperation with the West and her membership of NATO and the European Union. Many of the tangible signs of change, such as power stations and motorways, were declaredly financed wholly or largely from Brussels. It was sad to see the serious disrepair in parts of Varna, especially in and around the former Soviet naval base; but it was a further delight to find the British embassy in Sofia in new, smart, well-located and effective offices. It was a privilege and a treat to be taken over the ambassador's residence, scene of that Shakespearean quatercentenary week of performances and of many a professionally useful and personally most enjoyable discussion with the gentlemanly and wise Bill Harpham in his study.

In Sofia, many visible and symbolic changes caught our eyes. The mausoleum, which in the 1960s had housed the communist hero and former prime minister Georgi Dimitrov, in Lenin and Red Square style, had disappeared. In 1933, Dimitrov had been among the group indicted and tried for burning the Reichstag in Berlin: at the trial, he had argued with Göring to quite some effect. Evidently Dimitrov's remains were buried in the central cemetery in Sofia in 1990, though the mausoleum stayed in its square until 1999. The mausoleum had been built in 1949, ironically and doubtless deliberately opposite the former king's palace, and built reputedly to withstand nuclear attack: we heard that it took multiple blasts and much bulldozer work before it succumbed to the new national will. In its place in 2009 in the iconic square, was a charming children's playground. By August 2011, the playground had disappeared, the mausoleum site left empty yet clearly still delineated. The nearby and equally iconic square of the monument to the Tsar Liberator and of the National Assembly, the square where Bill Harpham had presented his credentials, then had dull grey cobble, which was replaced after the Cold War by the same fine gold-coloured pavé of the Dimitrov mausoleum and Vranya Palace Square. How many Bulgarians knew (or know) that that first golden pavé was a royal wedding present from the Habsburgs to King Boris? The National Assembly building's communist emblem in relief on the pediment has also been replaced, by a new and refreshingly historical coat of arms, bearing, in a reference to Bulgaria's past, a crown.

CHAPTER 4

SOME HIGHER DIPLOMACY: POSTING TO PARIS

A two-year posting to a political department in the Foreign Office followed Sofia (see Chapter 9). Then a 22-week (the long) course in economics and statistics at the Treasury Centre for Administrative Studies (later the Civil Service College), during which, to our complete surprise and delight, I learned that the powers that were had posted us to France, and to the British embassy in Paris. This was a plum posting, and I was the envy of my colleagues. I was to have two jobs: second (later first) secretary economic in the embassy; and the UK delegate to CoCom, the international committee that in Cold War days controlled the export of strategic goods, equipment and technologies from the industrialised countries to the Soviet bloc countries and China.

This was early 1967, so Britain's approach to the then Common Market was once again very much in the air. There was plenty of economic work to do in that context. As I saw it, Great Britain had missed an historic chance in 1957, when the Treaty of Rome was signed; and had failed again in 1962/63, with President de Gaulle's veto of January 1963, to become a member, on the best available terms, of what eventually became the European Union.

We did try again while we were in Paris. Our answer was President de Gaulle's famous – or notorious – veto late in 1967: a 'grand non' and a singularly sad moment for British diplomacy. We had laboured again, hard, and failed badly. I recall the moment on the steps of the Elysée Palace after President de Gaulle had delivered his negative answer inside the palace to Prime Minister Harold Wilson and

Foreign Secretary George Brown. The two of them faced, for those days, a vast array of microphones and eager journalists all asking the obvious question. The French journalists, naturally, were to the fore. The prime minister motioned the foreign secretary to say something. George drew himself up proudly and in a firm tone announced, in less than mellifluous (or accurate) French, '*Pas de comment*'. That infelicitous phrase seemed to sum up the day.

There was, of course, much comment on our national failure, by the press and academics. There was much analysis in the embassy. There was discussion of de Gaulle's history and his attitude to *Les Anglo-Saxons* in general, and to *Albion Perfide* in particular. Much has been written and argued to the effect that de Gaulle believed that the United Kingdom was interested only in the economic benefits of membership, and not in the construction of a politically new Europe. There may have been a little truth in that version (however misguided) of de Gaulle's perception, but I do not believe it was as important as other elements. For me, the reasons for his 'grand non' were many and complex. They included, as I saw it, at least three driving political or strategic forces. One was de Gaulle's belief that the safe and peaceful future of Western Europe had to be founded upon a union of states that gave the highest priority to defence and foreign policy, and the difficulties he presumably expected British membership to cause in precisely that context. For him, British foreign policy would be too independent, and her defence policy too Atlanticist for his vision of Europe. It followed for him that Europe with Britain might risk becoming too dependent on the United States. A second driving force was the resolution of the long and complex equation of French national interests in and indeed beyond Europe as de Gaulle saw and calculated them, including his wish to deepen rather than to expand continental European development – with France in the lead. A third was more domestic, and at least as influential: de Gaulle saw a threat to the heavily subsidised way of life of 'small farmers' in France from the effect British entry could have on the Common Agricultural Policy. These farmers were voters on whom de Gaulle depended and to whom he was loyal. Objectively, many of these small farms were uneconomic and unsustainable, and if market forces were to enter the equation significantly their continued individual existence would be threatened, but their owners voted Gaullist, and were, in de Gaulle's eyes, the backbone of France.

In some of this, de Gaulle was largely right, particularly given his view of the French national interest. NATO had recently moved its HQ from Paris to Brussels because of French unwillingness to integrate fully into the military side of that transatlantic organisation. There was no question for the United Kingdom of our compromising our independence or sacrificing our sovereignty in defence or foreign policy. And I believe that if the United Kingdom had entered the Common Market, the EEC, in the fifties or even the early sixties, the Common Agricultural Policy (CAP) would not now be the enormously expensive, and to me still indefensible, support system it is today. In Europe à Six, we would have pressed hard, and pressed with much more success than now seems to be possible, for radical change in the CAP. If that change had been achieved, there certainly would have been, as I think de Gaulle believed and would not countenance, serious effects on the French (and the German) agricultural scene. In a change with which we in the United Kingdom are not unfamiliar, but in a country five times our size, small farms would have been consolidated into large ones and the Gaullist vote might have declined – even if perhaps only marginally. On the other hand, with Great Britain in Europe, we would all have been able to make a much better fist of the arrangements for the new members later to join. The European Union would also have been in a much stronger and better negotiating position *vis à vis* the United States, for example, in the General Agreement on Tariffs and Trade and World Trade Organisation rounds, and recent meetings, for example those at Dubai and Cancun. That would certainly have meant a better deal for the third world, as well as freer trade all round.

The late sixties and early seventies were exciting times in the embassy in Paris. To add to the excitement, we had an unpredictable British foreign secretary in London, under whom I had served in my previous job in eastern department of the Foreign Office. Many were the stories of George's less than sober and sometimes unacceptable behaviour; and some of the stories were true. There was the ambassador's wife in London, possibly the French ambassadress, who reportedly responded to a remark from George as they walked in to a diplomatic dinner that that was the first time she had been propositioned 'even before the soup'.

Then there is the absolutely apocryphal but oft-repeated story of his appearance at a great gathering in a ballroom in a South American capital. The story insists that our foreign secretary, after a quick look around the room, advanced on a tall elegant vision resplendent in scarlet and requested the honour of the next dance. The reply was: 'No, I will not dance with you, Mr Brown, and for three reasons: you are drunk; the band is playing the Peruvian national anthem; and I am the cardinal archbishop of Lima'. I record this story to stress its inaccuracy: George Brown never visited South America.

On the other hand, it is true that I was one of four or five men who carried Secretary of State George Brown out the back way from a national day party in a foreign embassy in London. And in the Foreign Office, it was generally thought to be wise to ensure that any submission should arrive on George's desk for his sober consideration before eleven o'clock in the morning.

There was also the whispered tale of George, in opposition at the time, on his way back from President Nasser's funeral in Cairo aboard a Royal Air Force aeroplane as the guest of the then foreign secretary, the gentlemanly Sir Alec Douglas-Home. The story has it that instead of George's vastly preferred brandy to accompany the meal served during the return flight, he was served one of Sir Alec's reputedly favourite luncheon wines. Now whatever the reputation or quality of Mateus Rosé, George Brown's alleged action in hurling the bottle across the cabin in disgust does seem extreme.

If that story is true, it may reflect George's passionate nature; and it may even, in just one sense, be understandable. Some years, too many years, after the débâcle of Suez, George Brown was responsible for restoring British diplomatic relations with Egypt, which had, of course, been broken over Suez, restored in 1961 and ruptured again in 1965 (over Rhodesia). As I recall it, George initiated resumption talks very much in his own way (his autobiography is entitled *In My Way*) with a very senior Egyptian, in Leningrad and Moscow, arguably inappropriate venues, and in ways that conflicted with his official advice from Foreign Office Arabists. He then conducted a correspondence with Nasser, whom he also knew, and some 12 months later, diplomatic relations were resumed. For George to bring Egypt back, as it were, was an inspired achievement of diplomacy, driven by passion and reached eccentrically, rather than driven by analysis and reached with intellectual application. It was an achievement, too, of historic importance and very much to the benefit of the United Kingdom.

In a different vein was the way George Brown handled his own relations with a particularly fine and very able professional diplomat, the British ambassador in Paris, Sir Patrick Reilly, whom we in the embassy all admired tremendously. In our firm view, he was removed prematurely and unjustifiably: a scandal, really, and one of George Brown's emotional mistakes, as I saw it. I certainly was not privy to all the inside story, but during the tenure as ambassador of that very professional diplomat, I was at the same round table as George at a large embassy dinner at the residence on the rue du Faubourg St Honoré. It was Lady Reilly's table. George was rather the worse for wear, and getting worse still. I wondered whether I was going to have to repeat my London effort and help carry him out. But that evening, George Brown was not somnolent; rather, he became belligerent. He was deep in quiet conversation with the lady next to him, a distinguished French politician. Their conversation came to an end, and George looked across the table at his hostess, and suddenly told Lady Reilly, very loudly, in one of those near hushes from the other tables in the room, that she was not fit to be an ambassador's wife.

The astonishing rudeness, crassness and ignorance of the remark caused a deep silence among all the other guests. I imagine everyone present felt deeply for the ambassadress who was expected to put up with this extraordinary behaviour. Nor, I am sure, was I alone in being appalled and offended by the utter lack of justification for any such opinion that George Brown had uttered of this splendid and accomplished ambassadress. I should record that, sadly, Lady Reilly died rather young.

It was not long after this terrible evening that our ambassador left Paris, to retire prematurely from the Diplomatic Service. Before he left the embassy, Sir Patrick Reilly wrote a brilliant valedictory despatch, which dealt elegantly and effectively with the reasons for his departure. Soon after, he became a distinguished academic at All Souls, Oxford, and a captain of industry – including as president of the London Chamber of Commerce and Industry and chairman of the Banque Nationale de Paris. He was made a commander of the Légion d'Honneur.

The political appointee who became ambassador to France following those unedifying events of 1968 was Christopher Soames. Life in the embassy under him was very different. Christopher Soames was that unusual phenomenon in the British Diplomatic Service – a political appointee. He had been a Tory MP and cabinet minister and was appointed to Paris at the suggestion of the same George Brown, foreign secretary under Labour prime minister Harold Wilson.

Christopher Soames had also been a Coldstream Guards officer, who had served in the embassy before. He was assistant military attaché there when Winston Churchill visited soon after the Second World War, accompanied by his daughter, Mary. Christopher and Mary met. In 1947, they married, never imagining that one day they would return to Paris as ambassador and ambassadress.

Christopher Soames spent most of his first day as ambassador in Paris going round the offices in the embassy to meet everyone. When we later compared notes, it became clear that we had each reacted rather stiffly to his approach: that this was no longer to be a diplomatic embassy but a political one. He seemed also to have picked a quarrel about work with every senior diplomat in the embassy – perhaps to make the point, in a West Point Military College way, that he was the new boss and things would run his way; he implied almost that he did not need and would not heed our advice.

This was a bad start. Christopher made no friends that first day, and we felt professionally affronted. Christopher, however, quickly realised his mistake – or perhaps did accept the advice of one of us (not me) that his judgment that first day had been mistaken. Next day, Mary Soames visited each of us in our offices. She was, and is, a quite wonderful woman, with all the best of both her father and her mother combined in a brilliant, thoughtful, strong personality and a most attractive charm. We all fell instantly in love with her, and for her sake forgave Christopher – as they both had no doubt intended.

The Soames's first year in Paris was the tumultuous year of 1968, still a watershed for twentieth-century history, and in Paris the year of *Les Evénements*. That was a marvellous time to be a diplomat in Paris. Here was a country, for the first time since 1789, close to revolution. I do not exaggerate. There was an extraordinary and politically unprecedented alliance between students and unions. The students were, of course, at the Sorbonne and elsewhere, and the unionists, very powerful ones, were not far away, at Renault. They demonstrated together – and Sorbonne faculty members joined the protest. The Communist Party was very much involved. The *Compagnie Républicaine de Sécurité* (CRS) or Republican Guard turned out every day and every night in armed force. There were fierce clashes, many casualties, and some deaths.

On one memorable and strangely exciting day, President de Gaulle's whereabouts were unknown for several hours. As a well-placed French official said to an embassy colleague who asked him where the president was, '*Personne ne sait*' (no one knows). De Gaulle, we later learned, was with his generals, close to the border with Belgium. M Pompidou told some of us later in the embassy that there was a period of an hour or two that day, during which the government of France was so paralysed that had they but realised it, the Communist Party could have staged a successful takeover of the country.

Even before *Les Evénements* of May 1968 began, the atmosphere in Paris was heavy with foreboding and threat. It was clear to us in the embassy both that the disputes, industrial and educational, that preceded the Events were not going to be resolved quickly, and that tensions were being fomented to ensure they would not be. Walking about the centre of Paris, one was very aware of impending strife.

As strains increased and trouble began in earnest, there were shortages, for example of petrol. We used to drive without a right shoe, to try to conserve fuel. Yet cars seemed everywhere. One afternoon, the traffic at the Arc de Triomphe was entirely blocked, and Hilary was in our car in the middle of the Etoile. She had been on her way to collect our two-and-a-half-year-old son John from his nursery school. She simply abandoned the car, leaving the keys in the ignition in case it needed to be moved, walked to collect John and walked on with him to the embassy. Several hours later, in the dark, we three walked from the rue du Faubourg St Honoré up the Avenue des Champs Elysées to the Arc de Triomphe, strolled among the now moving traffic to our car in the middle, and drove home in the unscathed car. John, in his child seat in the back, enjoyed his usual practice of telling us the make and model of every car we passed often simply by reference to the rear lights. He loved cars.

One Sunday morning, very early, after a really rough night of angry demonstrations and some violence on the Left Bank, we drove, arguably unwisely, from Neuilly where we lived, to the Left Bank. There all was still and silent. Some of the pavé had been torn up the previous day for use as missiles; cobbles were now scattered around the roads. So were pieces of glass. Windows were smashed. So were some trees, which had been uprooted from the pavements. We drove on, slowly. We stopped when we came to lines of still, silent, still slowly smoking remains of burned barricades that had been formed of cars and vans, now blackened shells, barely recognisable. In the heavy silence, we heard quiet sobbing. We looked but could not see who was crying until we finally turned round in the car. It was John. He looked tragically at us and said in French, 'They've killed a Citroen 2 CV (*Ils ont tués une Deux Chevaux*)'. He really loved cars.

The fear of shortages of supplies was potent in Paris. Hilary and I refused to buy in bulk and to hoard, but many Parisians did just that. Quite early on, Hilary went to the local supermarket first thing one morning to buy a few things. The store was packed, and became more so, and more so. Eventually the doors were locked to prevent more people coming in. Hilary could not get out, and anyway could barely move for the crush, exacerbated by the phenomenon of Paris housewives pushing three, even four trolleys lashed together in a sort of crazy train, and loading them with whatever was on the shelves.

This extraordinary and deeply troubling time in the life of the capital of France eventually came to a stuttering end politically – with, if I remember aright, rather more of the students' demands met than those of the workers, whose political leaders had in the end missed their chance.

So, what a marvellous four years it was to be serving in France. De Gaulle's veto may have been among the saddest of post-war days for British diplomacy, yet overall, 1967–71 in Paris was an immensely stimulating time. The debate over United Kingdom membership was vital for British interests; it was also, we believed, of the highest importance for Europe.

The Anglo-French political atmosphere was often charged, to put it mildly. Mary Soames was very conscious of that. As Churchill's daughter, Mary, of course, had known de Gaulle during the Second World War, when, in England, and militarily and politically at bay, the general must have seemed aloof, grand and difficult. Mary recalled that while relations between Winston Churchill and Charles de Gaulle could be challenging, the general had a great deal of respect and liking for her mother, Clementine Churchill. This liking may have stemmed from, or even, perhaps, been brought about by, as Mary once put it, 'the time she flew at him for making an anti-British remark'. Winston had evidently missed it, being at the other end of the table, and, as Mary told it, 'Papa's French wasn't very good. But when the general insulted the British Fleet, Mama retaliated in perfect French. The next day there arrived the most enormous arrangement of flowers. For years after Winston died, Charles de Gaulle sent Clementine a personal letter on the anniversary of Churchill's death.

I rather like a story, of the truth of which Mary Soames and Churchill's then RAF staff officer have separately assured me. They had both been present one weekend at Chequers, one rare weekend during the war which Winston Churchill managed to spend at home. During dinner, the telephone had rung, in the booth far away at the end of a corridor. The butler came and bent down to Mr Churchill's ear to say that M de Gaulle would like to speak to him on the telephone from London. Churchill, far from best pleased, told the butler to tell M de Gaulle that he, Churchill, would telephone him 'when I have finished my dinner'. The butler left. Conversation resumed. A few minutes later the butler returned, to whisper in Mr Churchill's ear that M de Gaulle had insisted, saying that 'it was a matter of life and death'. Churchill, now furious, ripped his napkin from his collar and stormed out. Some ten minutes later, he returned, sat down with a thump, picked up his napkin and thrust it again under his collar. Clementine broke the silence to smile sweetly at him and say: 'Come on, Winnie, tell us what he said'. Churchill glowered around the table, removed his napkin again and said: 'Monsieur de Gaulle told me that I had to realise that his people regarded him as a second Joan of Arc. I had to remind him that we had to burn the first one.'

That recalls in turn an embassy Mardi Gras ball in the ambassadorial residence, always a white-tie-and-tails affair, and quite grand. One year, Hilary and I were asked to be the hosts at a table to include the ambassador and Mary Soames. During the evening, the embassy duty officer came in from the offices next door, and sought me out with a message. Would I please transmit some bad news to the ambassadress? I thought I would gain her uninterruptible attention only on the dance floor, so I asked Mary to dance. That is an interesting exercise. Dancing with Mary Soames is a bit like trying to drive an elegant and highly polished Churchill tank across bad terrain. She doesn't believe in being led, by anyone. Then I had to tell Mary the sad news that her by now rather frail mother had broken a hip and was in hospital. I advised against instantly dropping everything and rushing to the airport: the last flight that evening was about to leave Le Bourget; her mother was probably sedated; and the embassy courtyard and the street beyond were already full of eager, jostling journalists, whom she would wish to avoid but could not then escape. At the thought of journalists asking her personal questions, Mary stiffened and became even more difficult to lead in dance. I suggested we return to our table, tell the ambassador, go and telephone the hospital, book the first flight in the morning and be rid of the journalists. I am glad to say that we have remained friends since that evening, and Mary has stayed with Hilary and me half across the world.

Just to encourage the thought that diplomatic life in Paris in those days was all white tie, tails, dancing, quaffing and eating, at another Paris embassy Mardi Gras ball, with British royalty present, one of my colleagues arrived late, in full fig, with Beau Brummellesque frills at his cuffs, dragging behind him a willowy, pliant, and by contrast rather underdressed lady from the Moulin Rouge, or was it the Folies Bergères? The British diplomat later became a distinguished representative of the European Communities; and later still an equally distinguished British academic. All my colleagues in Paris, as almost everywhere else, were people of the highest professional and personal qualities. Some colleagues were a touch eccentric. I could only applaud that sort of eccentricity, and regret that there seems so little time and place for it in modern diplomacy.

In truth, the only other occasion for which I remember regularly wearing white tie and tails in Paris was the annual diplomatic soirée and ball given by the mayor of Paris at the Hôtel de Ville. This was a splendid affair indeed, with several orchestras playing in gilded halls, a rich plenitude of canapés and champagne, and a glittering gathering. I recall an elderly and evidently well-breeched comtesse draped over a chaise longue, her tiara, her dress and its train dripping with diamonds, and her manicured and bejewelled hand extended to a young suitor paying court to her on one knee, his tailcoat hanging perfectly to the floor. I recall doing just a little diplomatic business that evening with a colleague from the French Foreign Ministry. I recall dancing a Viennese waltz with Hilary until we were dizzy, and retired to catch our breath and enjoy the scene from behind a grand pillar. And I well recall the host, the mayor, a dashing, debonair, tall, handsome, confident, patriotic, ambitious, smooth and stylish young French politician called Jacques Chirac.

The colleague from the French Foreign Ministry, the Quai d'Orsay, with whom I had done a little business at the *Soirée de Paris* was a charming eccentric. He was the French delegate to CoCom and therefore my opposite number. A confirmed Parisian bachelor, he had served in the resistance during the Second World War. He took the cure every summer. He was devoted to his dachshund, whom he frequently brought to the rather formal CoCom meetings. One summer evening, he arrived at our apartment on the Avenue de Neuilly (now the Avenue Charles de Gaulle) dressed in a white suit and wearing a red rose in his buttonhole, exactly 24 hours early for a diplomatic cocktail party. Embarrassing, but also, for us, rather enjoyable. Always polite, he sent Hilary flowers the next morning, and slightly to our surprise, reappeared the following evening. A real professional, he was always fierce in his pursuit of French objectives at the CoCom table. He could also be difficult, and in consequence, his relations with the chairman of that organisation were not always of the smoothest.

Now there was a real eccentric. An Italian count from Rome, his name was Il Conte Massimo Casilli d'Aragona: an unforgettable name for an unforgettable character. One Saturday evening, early in our time in Paris, we were invited, with others of the CoCom delegates and their wives, to his apartment. The apartment was full of clocks, a fabulous collection, all showing different times, and all irregularly chiming, ringing or sounding off like demented cuckoos, and doing so, it seemed, very often. Casilli seemed oblivious to their presence as, flamboyantly dressed, he poured me, in answer to my request for a small whisky and soda, a very large whisky and, of all impossible mixers for whisky, tonic. There was, of course, no question of my making him lose face by pointing out his error, so a nearby aspidistra benefited (as did their cousin aspidistras in Moscow some years later when the Soviet delegation at some bilateral negotiations tried, classically, in the evenings, to ply me with excessive amounts of vodka). I remember the usual mixture of social and work-related conversation that evening *chez* Casilli d'Aragona over a buffet dinner, and then the after-dinner entertainment, a walk around the best Paris flea market, Le Marché aux Puces, a colourful and vibrant place on a Saturday evening, complete with its own generous share of eccentrics. Il Conte Massimo Casilli d'Aragona, in his element, dressed now even more flamboyantly, with a fine opera hat and a flowing cloak, was walking through the Marché with the Japanese delegate's wife, she beautifully attired in an exquisite kimono. The incongruity of the scene was given added spice when Il Conte spotted, I presumed, a fellow eccentric, a Parisian, smartly dressed, if in a velvet suit, and towing behind him on a chic dog lead decorated with diamanté, a fluffy white bedroom slipper. Casilli bent down, patted the slipper and said in fine French what a lovely little dog it was. The proud owner, affronted, even aghast, responded to the effect that Casilli must be mad: this was a carpet slipper, and the poor slipper mustn't feel insulted by the quite disgraceful comparison.

But it wasn't all madness by any means in Paris. Hilary and I were trying to bring up a very young family at the same time as my commuting to the embassy the other side of the Arc de Triomphe, and doing two diplomatic jobs, with Hilary's help every evening and more. Diplomacy for us was always a joint effort. Rather like the Church of England, the British Diplomatic Service we knew had the inestimable benefit of employing two for the price of one. Ours was, as was that of the vast majority of our colleagues, a team effort.

Our second son, Charles, was born in Paris – though he was emphatically not named for President Charles de Gaulle. We left Paris after four most fulfilling years, when our Charles was but 19 months old, briefly for London, then for a posting to Singapore. So Charles's knowledge of the French language was pretty limited. Our older son, John, was only six when we left France. His French had been acquired through the pores and was a delight. For example, when I had finished a telephone conversation at home, John would correct my subjunctives, without having the first idea what a subjunctive was. Later, at preparatory school in England, John quickly abandoned the natural advantage he had, and spoke French just like his peers at school – that is with an appalling English accent. A colleague in the British embassy in Paris left France after four years with a more fortunate son of 11 years. That young man's French stuck, and has remained perfect. Age and environment really do make a difference.

The principal function of the embassy was, of course, the conduct of a complex myriad of bilateral relations. This included the Anglo-French aspects of our negotiations to join the European Communities, to make the Europe of Six, but there was much else too, including, for example, the Anglo-French intergovernmental discussions about a Channel crossing – by tunnel or bridge. Those discussions were intense, but in the end led to only one really useful conclusion, as I saw it, that the private sector, not the governments, would have to do the job.

On the other hand and much more positively, there were the intergovernmental negotiations that led to the Anglo-French technological triumph that 'rolled out' in 1967 and 1968 – and came to a premature end in 2003: Concorde. As I recall, it took two or three meetings of the cabinet in Downing Street before Her Britannic Majesty's Government brought itself to agree to add the silent 'e' at the end of the name Concorde – the French spelling. In the embassy we worked on the speech that the then British minister of technology, Anthony Wedgwood Benn (formerly Lord Stansgate, now Tony Benn) would make to concede the addition of the 'e': 'e' for Entente, Europe, Endeavour, Excellence, and many more such obfuscations and rationalisations of the concession. It was, however, a very good moment when, in 1969, the first showing took place of the two prototypes, French and British, at Le Bourget Air Show. A short, sharp Anglo-French negotiation preceded that show, over which of the two prototypes when they crossed over Le Bourget's runway should fly the lower, and thus be closer to the gathered crowds. Brian Trubshaw was the British test pilot of our prototype, and kept threatening to come in even lower than the minimum height prescribed for the French prototype – prescribed, of course, by the French. But what a thrill it was when Hilary and I witnessed that first fly-past of the two supersonic and so beautiful aircraft.

While we were serving in Paris, the British economy went through a difficult period. There was much pressure on the pound sterling, which eventually was devalued, and general elections in the United Kingdom brought about a change of Government. Edward Heath, the new prime minister in 1970, had a number of key objectives, one of the principal of which was to succeed where his Labour predecessors had not, and take Great Britain into the European Community, the Common Market. Christopher Soames was still ambassador in Paris, had developed a close, good and effective relationship with the Elysée and played an important role in the careful, difficult negotiations to this end. His down-to-earth, intelligent and intensely political approach to diplomacy and his understanding of fellow politicians now paid dividends. I recall a letter Christopher wrote in April 1971 to the then head of the Foreign Office, Sir Denis (later Lord) Greenhill. The ambassador's letter argued that there should be a personal meeting between Edward Heath and the new president of France, Georges Pompidou. Our attempt to enter the European Community under arrangements that would serve the British as well as the European interest was heavy going indeed. Some leading Europeans even then, 41 years ago, were working for an eventual monetary union. We needed entry on very different terms.

The French seemed to block, or in other ways to cause to stall, almost every advance. Christopher Soames's letter is now released by the Public Records Office, so I can quote from it.

On the Anglo-French apparent – and real – stalemate, Christopher wrote: 'The French are waiting for us to make the first move.' He explained that the French, from President Pompidou downwards, did not believe that 'the centuries old hatchet of Anglo-French animosity can be buried by remote control from Brussels'.

This letter, and this advocacy of a personal, detailed discussion of the outstanding and thus far intractable issues in the negotiations for British entry, a discussion between the two heads of state, should be judged against the background of Pompidou's own attitude and approach to British entry. President de Gaulle's prime minister and successor, Gaullist Georges Pompidou, was not then, nor ever had been, enthusiastic about UK entry to the EEC. In reporting this, the British Embassy's view, Christopher Soames added parenthetically and penetratingly 'enthusiasm is anyway not part of his [Pompidou's] make-up'. The embassy analysis was that President Pompidou probably did not believe that the European Community would disintegrate, as opposed to stagnate for a while, if the United Kingdom did not join it. In Christopher Soames's words, 'He is not scared of German pressure and believes that the Italians always have their price.' Stagnation would not, in our view, have worried Pompidou. As the ambassador put it, 'Pompidou is no European visionary panting for political unification. He is a cautious, hard bargaining, reticent Auverngat with limited imagination and no talent for grandeur. He has got the all-important finance agreement under his belt and has reached agreement with Brandt on the beginnings of an economic and monetary union (including a useful medium-term support facility) without having had to pay for it in terms of supranationalism.' (This, in 1971.) 'Nevertheless,' Christopher continued, 'I remain convinced that he accepts that on balance it is right and necessary that we should come in: and he foresees a very unpleasant time ahead for him and for France if he can be blamed for keeping us out.'

The ambassador's advocacy was effective. Foreign Secretary Alec Douglas-Home and Prime Minister Ted Heath agreed. A meeting in Paris was duly arranged, but arranged with great care and confidentiality. The French Foreign Ministry, the Quai d'Orsay, to their later fury, was kept in ignorance of the plan and the planning. Ted Heath and Georges Pompidou had, exceptionally, eleven hours of discussions, just along the road from the embassy, at the Elysée Palace. These talks were a resounding success, and culminated in the historic press conference when Pompidou said, in effect, that he and Heath were two men convinced that Britain would join.

Some five months later, in October 1971, the House of Commons voted 356 to 244 in favour of the United Kingdom joining the European Community. Edward Heath has called that his finest hour. That night, Georges Pompidou's letter of congratulations to Ted Heath was generous and warm, and spoke of their May talks that year as having played an important role in the negotiations leading to UK membership, and seeing the promise of a friendly and close understanding (*une entente amicale et étroite*) between France and Great Britain.

I have one personal – and entirely ephemeral – memory of those Heath/Pompidou talks of May 1971. The registry at the British embassy along the road was asked to make a photocopy of a vital document to be put to President Pompidou by the prime minister during the morning at the talks at the Elysée Palace. Photocopying in those days was evolving rather slowly by modern technological standards. The chancery photocopier was the size of a small car, and about as reliable as a very early and inexpensive model. The duty registry officer operating this beast had the usual trouble with it. It was a weekend, and no service for the machine was available. The vital document, the only copy in existence, was apparently stuck somewhere in the depths of the huge machine – invisibly, irretrievably. I was the embassy duty officer, and thus in charge. In those days, one carried a toolkit in one's car. I used some of the heavier tools to take the machine apart so that the document could be extracted. I finally managed to put the machine back together again so that a copy could be made, just in time for it to be rushed along the rue du Faubourg St Honoré to the Elysée. Ted Heath, of course, never knew of this minor drama – nor of the fact that the grease and ink in the infernal machine had ruined my new white shirt. The embassy duty officer looked like a mechanic at the end of a bad day in the pit, and felt like one.

In such a busy embassy as Paris, the office was rarely empty out of normal hours, but the duty officer expected and dealt with the unexpected. An urgent message from London meant that as duty officer, I had to call on the Duke of Windsor to discuss a private matter. I was received most kindly by both the duke and duchess in their Paris residence. The matter at hand was dealt with efficiently. Unsurprisingly, perhaps, the duke and duchess were dressed most elegantly, as if they were on formal duty, rather than in retirement, yet the atmosphere was instantly friendly and informal. I sensed that keeping up standards was both natural and important to them. Everything about the call was stylish and, perhaps inevitably, also dated, as if time had not greatly advanced for them. This was well before the duke became ill, and both seemed in good form, if rather quiet. The experience was memorable, impressive, yet also saddening.

There was much fulfilment and enjoyment in being a member of the British embassy in Paris, and in living in France in the late sixties and early seventies. My work there as the UK delegate to CoCom was absorbing and, in those days of Cold War and Sino-Soviet schism, immensely worthwhile. I learned a great deal about multilateral as opposed to bilateral diplomacy. Because in important part my work depended upon it, I also learned something more of the commercial world. We achieved some advances for British companies. I developed an academic interest in the history and management of the strategic embargo against communist countries. Given the frequent divisions between the countries of Western Europe and the United States of America, I learned, too, something about how to manage the sometimes difficult relationship between Europe and the United States. Some of that learning occurred while visiting Washington in 1969 for discussions of contentious CoCom issues at the US State Department; but most memorably, those discussions were interrupted one afternoon by an invitation to break off and join a press conference down the corridor. That was when I met Neil Armstrong, 'Buzz' Aldrin and Michael Collins, recently returned from their stunningly successful Apollo 11 mission to land on the moon.

I learned a little, too, about crisis management, including, in a minor way, in the CoCom context. Very few times in my career did I have really serious doubts about important elements of British foreign policy. One such, though a disagreement on an individual and rather narrow policy matter, arose during an 18-month long intensive review of the strategic embargo operated through CoCom. This was a detailed policy review, often of very technical matters, conducted around the international table of CoCom members – the major European industrial countries plus the United States and Japan. We were sometimes at loggerheads with the Americans over the strategic embargo, on which, in pursuit of the British national, including commercial as well as strategic aims and interests, we frequently took a relatively more liberal position than they. The position we should take on one difficult and important embargo policy question for review, in which these two interests could reasonably be said to conflict, was put to the cabinet in London for decision. I was to table and argue the resulting British position at the next review meeting. I had, of course, contributed to the Whitehall-wide deliberations that preceded the cabinet decision. My instructions from the Foreign Office, following the cabinet decision, arrived two days or so before the next meeting.

I disagreed strongly with the instructions, believing that the cabinet had misunderstood the British interest and reached the wrong decision. I had earlier in effect argued for 'half a loaf rather than no bread', which I thought might well be the result unless we played our hand with care. My instructions seemed to me to lead us inexorably to 'no bread'. As the UK delegate to CoCom, I had no superior officer in Paris to consult who knew the subject matter or policy considerations. I telephoned the Foreign Office on a secure line, to receive short shrift: the cabinet had decided and there was no more to say. I said I would send a telegram overnight to seek reconsideration. That was my entitlement, I was told, but given no encouragement to think it would be taken seriously. I spoke to my boss on the economic side of my work in the embassy, John Galsworthy (later ambassador to Mexico), who recognised the importance of the issues; that he was unsighted on them; and that they were too complicated for quick understanding. He tested my resolve and encouraged me to draft and redraft until I was quite satisfied with the arguments in my proposed telegram, and judged that at least they ought to win the day. Some hours later, late at night, I completed the telegram and sent it for dispatch – we had 24-hour communications with London. Shortly before the next CoCom meeting, I received a telephone call from the Foreign Office, quickly followed by a telegram with new instructions reversing the original ones. I now regret that I forbore to ask quite how the U-turn had been achieved in London; but I was immensely relieved, and we secured rather more than half of that particular loaf, to the advantage of British industry, and as far as I (or, I believe, the Americans) could judge, without suffering any strategic disadvantage.

It was during that CoCom review that another good, and very different, moment occurred. Late one evening after dinner in our flat, we were trying to persuade the Japanese delegation to support a British proposal (against the United States). An animated debate reached a crucial moment of decision; a tense silence fell, while the Japanese delegation thought hard. Then a loud voice was heard from the nearby bedroom of our three-year-old John: 'Bloody CoCom again'. Heaven knows whom he was quoting!

The CoCom experience over four years was busy, testing, wonderfully enlightening about multilateral diplomacy, and intellectually stimulating. When we left Paris in 1970, I had no idea that I would pursue the intellectual interest I had developed in the subject some seven years later at the University of California at Berkeley.

In bilateral work in Paris, I learned something of the French economy, and a good deal about applied economics and economic analysis. All this learning was to prove most valuable in the years that followed. All in all, it was a marvellous posting for a middle ranking British diplomat, an excellent further education in the practice of diplomacy, a joy to be a member of one our most sought after embassies, and both a pleasure and a professional advantage to work in one of our finest diplomatic buildings, superbly located on one of the best, and operationally most effective, sites in Paris.

The Duke of Wellington – he of Waterloo and much other success – was appointed ambassador in 1814 to the restored Bourbon court.

He was the first occupant of the present residence, bought for Britain from Pauline Borghese, for whom Napoleon acquired this handsome property. There are some good embassy stories about how the purchase was made, including one of the duke overcoming Treasury objections (some things never change) by the simple expedient of sending a message directly to King George III, saying that only with this house, and for this sum of money, could His Majesty's and the nation's interests properly be represented and pursued in France. That may be a myth: the properly researched, true and fascinating story is well told in *Room for Diplomacy: Britain's Diplomatic Buildings Overseas 1800-2000* by Mark Bertram. The residence is an especially fine one, and ever since Wellington has had an envied reputation for both elegance and effectiveness. A later ambassador, Sir John Fretwell, aptly referred to the house as a theatre of diplomatic operations. It commands great respect among the Parisians who matter to British interests: it is a house of considerable architectural beauty and interest. Some of its furniture was purchased with the house, and still has labels and clear provenance from Napoleon's sister. Perhaps the most famous piece is a fine, canopied bed that belonged to Pauline Borghese.

There was, however, one ambassador who, embassy legend insisted in our time at least, was less than fully effective, well over a hundred years ago now. He was also a political appointee, but clearly not to be compared for skill and success with Christopher Soames. This Excellency's French left a good deal to be desired, and he did not impress the senior French at all. After two or three years in the embassy, and after many attempts, he finally persuaded the French foreign minister of the day to come to dinner: the residence may well have been the real attraction. After a pretty stiff evening at the table, the ladies left, in the custom of the day, and our ambassador moved to sit next to the foreign minister over the port. After an awkward silence, so the story goes, our hero, His Excellency, thought he should begin the conversation with something short of diplomatic business, and searching for some interesting small talk, said, in English-schoolboy French: '*Savez-vous, Monsieur le Ministre, que je dors dans le lit de Pauline?*' The instant but icy reply was, '*La vie privée de Votre Excellence ne m'interesse pas du tout*'.

We have returned several times to Paris since the end of our posting in December 1970, and have always concluded how different diplomatic life was in Paris in the sixties and seventies from the present day, or indeed than diplomatic life for us later and elsewhere. We had a splendid time in France, living and working in Paris and on holiday, notably a happy family holiday in Haute-Savoie. Perhaps, and it is probably also true of many busy Londoners, Parisians were hard to get to know. There were some good and honourable exceptions, of course, and we made some good friends. And we love Paris, of course. That said, the Parisians were often hard going – as opposed to the French outside Paris, whom we have always found to be most friendly, welcoming, charming and hospitable, in this huge and lovely neighbour country, five times the size of our own.

One among so many enduring memories is of a French family living in Paris, though originally from Brittany, who showed us real friendship. They had a delightful small restaurant on the Ile de la Cité: La Rose de France is still there, in the Place de la Justice, but under different ownership. In the late 1960s and early 1970s, the grandmother supervised and did much of the excellent Breton cooking for the simple room of perhaps a dozen tables. Her son-in-law was *le patron* and a charming man indeed. La Rose became one of our favourite Parisian restaurants. At the very end of a long evening during and after the *Evénements* of May 1968, when ours and perhaps one other were the only tables still occupied, *le patron* would join us and our guests for a chat and then stand at the street end of the room and call his dog, who would appear expectantly from the private quarters at the other end. *Le patron* would glare at the alert boxer and loudly utter one abbreviation: *'CRS!'* The boxer would leap on to the nearest table and charge down the room, bounding from table to table before lunging from the last table straight to his master's neck, as if going for the kill – of a policeman of the tough Republican Guard, whom most Parisians roundly disliked. The show would end with much friendly licking of his master and applause from the much amused, now few and indeed privileged diners. We revisit La Rose and relive those evenings to this day. That, too, was the Paris we loved.

CHAPTER 5

SINGAPORE: DIPLOMACY FOR CHANGE

We had expected another London posting after four years in Paris, so were pleased indeed to learn that I was to be appointed head of chancery in the British high commission, Singapore, after a short spell for briefing in, now, following the merger of the Foreign and the Commonwealth Relations Services and Offices, the Foreign and Commonwealth Office. To serve in a Commonwealth country and mission would be a new experience, as would a posting well outside Europe. The chancery is the political section in a diplomatic mission, and the head of it is also a glorified office and personnel manager. The timing, at the beginning of 1971, was particularly propitious from my point of view because, after economic work in Paris, there would be a real change of experience. British troops were to be withdrawn from east of Suez, and Prime Minister Lee Kwan Yew was not contented, so there would be much change as well as political and strategic challenge.

The British high commissioner in Singapore was Sam Falle DSC (later Sir Sam Falle KCMG KCVO DSC), also from the Foreign, rather than the Commonwealth Relations, Service. Sam has written his memoirs (*My Lucky Life: In War, Revolution, Peace and Diplomacy*), but it would be right here to include a brief account of one strand of Sam's Second World War experiences: in one or two respects, he does them a little less than justice in his very readable book.

My new boss was a former Royal Navy officer who spent three years in Japanese prisoner-of-war camps on Indonesian islands. In one, Sam was in charge of a group of other officer prisoners, whose interests he fearlessly pursued and in whose cause he was frequently in dispute with the Japanese military authorities. When he wasn't defending his co-prisoners, or suffering extra punishment for doing so, Sam Falle and Laurens van der Post, finding themselves in the same camp, taught each other foreign languages, tested each other, and developed and honed their superb linguistic skills, as Sam further did in other camps. Later, in the British Diplomatic Service, Sam studied still more, and there became the best linguist of his generation, and arguably of any post-war generation. He speaks a dozen languages, fluently. He loved learning and speaking languages, and in his nineties at the time of writing, he still does.

A Saudi Arabian scholar described Sam's classical Arabic to me as the best he had heard, from anyone, anywhere. In the Diplomatic Service, Sam's Russian was a joy to hear. He speaks all the Western and Northern European languages. Sam interpreted for the foreign secretary in French and several other languages. His Malay was much admired, and when I served with him in Singapore, he spent his spare time learning Mandarin. However, Sam would neither learn nor speak a word of Japanese. Nor would he visit Japan. I suppose that was his personal protest – protest against 1940s Japan and its military authorities that had made his colleagues and himself suffer so much physically and mentally.

Young Lieutenant Sam Falle RN was gunnery officer aboard HMS *Encounter*, a destroyer escort to the cruiser HMS *Exeter* at the battle of the Java Sea in February 1942. From 1 December 1941, *Encounter* was based in Singapore. As the Japanese Army advanced swiftly down the Malay Peninsula towards Singapore, Sam's ship was ordered to Tanjung Priok, the port of Batavia, now Jakarta. Immediately after that great British disaster of the Second World War, the fall of Singapore (the main military reason for which Sam had foreseen in 1938), the Japanese pressed home their strategic advantage. By land and sea attacks, they both defended and expanded the territories they held. At the beginning of 1942, Japanese naval power was formidable. By this time, Java was the only significant Dutch island remaining in Allied hands, and the small American, British, Dutch, Australian (ABDA) naval force was the sole Allied operational asset between the Japanese and their invasion of Java.

The battle of the Java Sea, the largest fleet engagement between the battles of Jutland in 1916 and Leyte Gulf in 1944, took place between 25 February and 1 March 1942. The ABDA force was fourteen ships strong. The Japanese had over twice as many warships and massive other advantages in weaponry, uninterrupted air reconnaissance and reserves.

The battle was fiercely fought. Smoke, storm, tactical skill, inspirational seamanship and raw courage all featured in the fearsome engagements. Sam's ship, HMS *Encounter*, fighting hard, rescued 115 allied survivors in the thick of battle. On the final day of the battle, another destroyer HMS *Electra*, together with *Encounter*, took on 2 Japanese cruisers and 14 destroyers. Both Royal Navy ships fought magnificently. *Electra* was sunk. Sam's guns scored hits on the enemy until the ammunition was exhausted. *Encounter* had fired all her torpedoes on the first day of the battle, not wastefully, but fighting hard. *Exeter* was at a critical stage so damaged that she could make only 12 knots instead of her normal 30. She fought heroically and courageously almost beyond belief, scored hits, and, despite the odds, avoided damage for an extraordinarily long time. Yet the eventual outcome was inevitable. *Exeter* finally took direct hits herself, was crippled and, perforce, abandoned. Before *Exeter* sank, *Encounter* defied *Exeter*'s instruction to seek escape – and instead began to close *Exeter* to rescue survivors. But *Encounter* was immediately then straddled by an 8-inch gun salvo: explosions lifted her clear out of the water – and stopped her dead. She would never recover. The captain ordered his ship to be abandoned, and sunk. Sam Falle and his naval gunnery colleagues laid the charges.

By one measure, this was the greatest Allied naval defeat of the Second World War. Eight of the 14 Allied ABDA ships were sunk. The remainder were mostly badly damaged. Not one was operational. The strategic outcome of the battle was the loss of Java. Yet the heroic sacrifice of the Allied naval forces merely delayed the Japanese invasion of Java – by only a couple of days.

When HMS *Encounter* was abandoned, there were not enough operational lifeboats for all her crew and the survivors she had rescued. As Sam's boat was being lowered, it was hit by a shell and a splinter took away Sam's binoculars from around his neck. He jumped into the Java sea. *Encounter* later rolled over and sank, as bidden. Sam and a number of his shipmates swam around and in turn hung on to floats. A Japanese destroyer, flying her battle ensign, came very close and trained her guns on the survivors. The captain of *Encounter* ordered: 'Close your eyes'. Sam could see little point. After a bit, the destroyer sailed away. The survivors, 150 miles from land, struggled on through the cool night and into the heat of the next day. The waters of the Java sea are warm, but they are also inhabited by sharks. However, the sharks may well have been more frightened by the noise of battle than attracted by the blood; and left the area. Sam did a great deal through the day and night to keep up spirits among the fatigued, oil-soaked, blackened and in some cases burned survivors.

In the afternoon, after some 24 hours in the water, a second Japanese Navy destroyer, the *Ikazuchi* (Thunder) appeared. In mid-Java sea, the *Ikazuchi* hove to). Instead of machine-gunning those in the water, as most again expected, she spent well over an hour picking up survivors. The Royal Navy personnel were welcomed, formally, politely, by the Japanese crew, treated for their burns and wounds, clothed, given food and drink, and made to feel as comfortable as possible. The following day, the *Ikazuchi* transferred the survivors to a captured Dutch hospital ship, which sailed to Japanese-held Makassar. There the survivors-prisoners were handed over to the Japanese Army. And that is when their real troubles and suffering began; though overall, Sam's PoW experience was mixed.

It was difficult, impossible really, for many years to persuade Sam to talk of any of this in any depth. However, in his retirement, Sam did some original research and thinking, about the Japanese view of the battle, its tactics and the wider strategic picture. He found that on the day after the battle had ended so disastrously for the Allies, Japanese naval intelligence had signalled the Japanese fleet to the effect that the Java sea was now full of British submarines – with the implication that the Royal Navy was bent on revenge. In fact, this intelligence (like much more recent intelligence reports we know of) was not correct: the nearest British submarine was a thousand miles away in Trincomalee. However, it occurred to Sam Falle that the Japanese fleet would have believed their own naval intelligence, and that therefore, the act of the captain of the Japanese destroyer in heaving to for over an hour to pick up British survivors in the middle of the Java sea, putting his ship and crew in – to him – evident grave danger from British submarines, was an act of charity, courage and honour, an act of the military code of virtue of the Samurai warrior – *bushido*.

Sam researched further and wrote a monograph, which argued that the rescue had been a demonstration of Japanese naval chivalry and decency that had now to be taken seriously; that, in effect, the Brits had misjudged the Japanese Navy. The memories in the United Kingdom of the real horrors of the Pacific war and of Japanese prisoner-of-war-camps were still too fresh, and Sam's monograph was rejected for publication in Britain. Eventually it was published in the American Naval Institute's publication, *Proceedings*.

The rest is happier history. The Japanese defence attaché in London, who read the monograph, intervened. Sam received a letter from a Japanese, one Shunzo Tagami, who had been the first lieutenant in the *Ikazuchi*, and who had also read Sam's monograph. His letter began a long and continuing correspondence, and Shunzo and his wife visited Sweden to stay with the Falles. That was the first of a series of visits. It led to the families, including grandchildren, meeting and holidaying in England and Japan. And in October 2003 Sam himself, by then in his mid-eighties, finally visited Japan. He was the guest of the Japanese government and of his rescuer, capturer and now friend, Shunzo-san. During long conversations, Shunzo told Sam of his view that the atomic bombs dropped on Hiroshima and Nagasaki had shortened the war, and saved lives – in effect the American and British position. Before he went to Japan, Sam taught himself some Japanese and spoke it during his visit. Five years later in 2008, Sam, now 89, was once again the honoured guest of the Japanese government. This time, at a Japanese government reception to honour Sam, the British ambassador in Tokyo made a speech in Japanese, a speech of tribute.

I believe this is a story about moral courage and the brotherhood of the sea. It illustrates how the British Diplomatic Service after the Second World War included real heroes.

In February 1971, a few days before the introduction of decimal currency in the United Kingdom, Hilary and I and our two sons sailed aboard the cargo ship MV *Glenogle* from London to Singapore. The good ship *Glenogle* of the long since disappeared Glen Line, whose business was chiefly cargo, also carried 12 passengers, and we were glad to have the time and the leave to make this memorable and thoroughly enjoyable voyage. We sailed down the Atlantic, around the Cape of Good Hope, across the Indian Ocean and down the Malacca Strait to Singapore. It was a fine way to go to a new posting and a new job, with plenty of preparatory reading time thrown in. Between Tilbury Dock and Singapore we had only one port of call: we spent just six hours for bunkering at Dakar, Senegal. Once beyond the Bay of Biscay, the weather was kind. Hilary was delighted with the accommodation and hospitality and our two young boys had a wonderful time with deck games with the officers. They were spoiled by the Chinese crew, who even rigged a canvas swimming pool for them on deck.

Hilary had lived in Singapore as a child. Her father was the first post-war adjutant at RAF Changi in Singapore. She looked forward to the fun of bringing up children for a few years there, and to being a diplomatic wife in a busy post in the warmth close to the Equator. Hilary had also lived in Malaysia in her late teens, but South-East Asia was then new to me. I was entranced by the varied and importantly British history of Singapore and the region. But I was to work on the present and the future. Her Majesty's Government had made the difficult and much disputed decision to remove the British troops from their bases east of Suez by 1971. The largest concentration of these bases by far was in Singapore. The bases, Navy, Army and Air Force, were dotted all over Singapore Island: for example, Terror, Seletar, Tengah, Nee Soon, Changi, Phoenix Park, and the busy and impressive dockyard at Sembawang with its Royal Navy and Royal Fleet Auxiliary ships. There was also a string of British forces schools, churches and clubs, and a sailors' rest, Aggie Weston's.

At the prospect of the removal of Far East Command and its bases, the then prime minister of Singapore, Lee Kuan Yew, was not best pleased. The contribution our forces made to the economy of

Singapore was then huge. As I recall it, this bilateral financial problem had largely been resolved before I was posted to Singapore: resolved by an agreement between the two then prime ministers Harold Wilson and Lee Kuan Yew, shortly before the general election of 1970. The final terms of the agreement were evidently reached on the nine-hole golf course in the grounds of the Istana, the presidential palace: British government aid, then still given to Singapore, would have a massive new injection of an extra 50 million pounds over five years – worth many more millions in today's terms, of course. The British high commission administered the aid. It does seem strange now that the United Kingdom gave such generous aid to that later great economic success story, Singapore. However, I believe that we, the UK, contributed directly and importantly to that success. As a consequence our trade and diplomatic relations with a successful Singapore have been valuable to us ever since.

Chief among the political and diplomatic problems was Lee's expressed view that by withdrawing, the British were letting Singapore and him down. Lee appeared to believe that British ministers had promised him no withdrawal, or at least not then. Certainly he had been closely, directly, almost unprecedentedly consulted by British cabinet ministers, notably the then secretary of state for defence, Denis Healey. Although this part of the argument was largely over by the time I joined the High Commission, Lee Kuan Yew remained disgruntled. He seemed genuinely to worry about the political vacuum in the Far East that he declared our withdrawal would create. He evidently believed – and both his memoirs and a lecture he gave in New York suggest that he still believes – that the disbandment with no replacement of the British Far East Command would bring about the resurgence of a communist threat from the north and another threat from the south. Lee also felt threatened by the Malays. And he knew that the Indonesians would never forget that during Confrontation, while he was prime minister, five Indonesian marines were hanged in Singapore.

Far East Command certainly was a major British garrison and strategic defensive operation, the ultimate product of the fall of Singapore in 1942; of the Allied victory in the Far East and Pacific in 1945; and of all that had followed in the region. There was the Malayan emergency and the defeat of the communist terrorists in the peninsula from 1947 through the fifties; and the challenge, also successfully overcome, of Confrontation, Soekarno's bid for expansion northwards from Indonesia between 1962 and 1966. The military contribution of the British armed services, in support of and in conjunction with Malaysian, Singaporean and Australian and New Zealand forces, was dominant in each of these extended military actions.

So complex and well dug in were the British military assets that the withdrawal from east of Suez in 1971 would be a massive and complicated logistic exercise. Far East Command was a huge operation and establishment. There was the Royal Navy's Far East Fleet, to which by 1971 a good deal more than those 14 ABDA ships were assigned. I recall aircraft carriers and other large ships visiting frequently to fulfil their commitments to the Far East Fleet. There were all the support systems and accommodation ashore associated with the large naval base at Sembawang, and those quite splendid shore establishments – such as HMS *Terror*. There was the Army, FARELF (Far East Land Forces), with their extensive fighting equipment, based in a string of barracks across Singapore Island. There was the Royal Air Force, FEAF (Far East Air Force), with all necessary logistic support, an impressive flying and fighting capability based at two major air stations, including the historically sensitive and very fine RAF Changi. And there was the considerable command headquarters, based at Phoenix Park in the south of the island, with all its communications, its planning and operations directing capability, its own joint intelligence committee and capability, and much more.

By then there was a new government in office in the United Kingdom, under Edward Heath. Whatever the objective validity of Lee Kuan Yew's concerns, and they were much debated, they constituted a political problem for the United Kingdom. Yet we had decided to withdraw. Much as it was debated again in the election of 1970 that had changed the British government and brought Edward Heath to power, that decision held. Ted Heath, with Alec Douglas-Home, then foreign and commonwealth secretary, went to Singapore for the Commonwealth Heads of Government Meeting (CHOGM) in January 1971. They doubtless also had serious talks with Lee Kuan Yew. Thereafter, diplomacy at the professional level took a hand. Other regional powers were consulted, and for me the culmination of a good deal of diplomatic negotiation and work came when three diplomats, one each from the Australian, the New Zealand and the British high commissions sat around a table in Singapore later in 1971. We had a blank sheet of paper before us, and the task of refining and giving effect to that which had been agreed in principle by the three governments.

We wrote 'ANZUK Force' at the top, for Australia, New Zealand and United Kingdom. Below we wrote 'Two-Star'. Those stars became Rear Admiral David Wells of the Royal Australian Navy. We took further expert military advice, thought hard, and constructed an organogram of a viable, trilateral force – a small force, bespoke for the unusual and largely political circumstances, yet capable of commanding real respect. We proposed some 7,500 service personnel from the three ANZUK countries. Importantly for the effect on Singaporean employment and economy, we also proposed a civilian component, almost all Singaporeans, of around 4,750 people. For the naval element, COMANZUKNAV, we decided on two Royal Navy frigates, and one from each of Australia and New Zealand, plus a submarine from alternately the United Kingdom and Australia. On land, there would be a brigade of three infantry battalions; an ANZUK support group of two field batteries; a signals regiment; and support bases at just two of the previous Far East Command locations in Singapore. In the air support group, the Royal Air Force would have Shackletons (later Nimrods) and helicopters, at a third base. Malaysia also agreed to become involved. The Australians would have two squadrons of Mirages integrated into the ANZUK Force but based in Malaysia as part of the Five Power Defence Arrangements (FDPA). The force even had an intelligence group based in Singapore – ANZUKIG(S).

All this came about in 1971/72. The first British battalion was from the Royal Highland Fusiliers, who came fresh from difficult duties in troubled Northern Ireland. I well recall the thrill and the danger of taking part, by invitation (or was it challenge?) of their commanding officer, in their rough and realistic war games with the Kiwis and Aussies in the jungles across the causeway in Malaysia. The ANZUK Force was real and realistic, but, in historical terms designedly short-lived and, by intent, importantly political.

However, the Five Power Defence Arrangements, established well before the ANZUK Force as part of the 1957 independence agreements, have grown, been modernised and live on today, quietly and effectively. The Five Powers are Australia, New Zealand, Malaysia, Singapore and the United Kingdom. The FPDA is an agreement to consult in the event of a threat to the territories of Singapore or Malaysia. In practice it also operates an integrated area defence system, and holds joint defence exercises – when, these days for the UK, funds permit.

While the controversy over post-withdrawal arrangements was still raging, an FPDA exercise was mounted – in large part to demonstrate to the sceptics that we could commit forces to the region from the United Kingdom in time of real need, and do so quickly and effectively. The exercise involved ships from the United Kingdom (including the carrier HMS *Bulwark*) as well as from Australia, New Zealand, Malaysia and Singapore. In total, over 50 ships, 200 aircraft and 20,000 men took part. Very large troop numbers were deployed from Britain to Singapore by air in this notably successful exercise named Bersatu Padu ('to form a solid unit' in the Malay language – with a connotation of togetherness, indeed unity).

The detailed negotiations over the withdrawal of British service personnel and assets from Singapore were long and surprisingly emotional. The original broad plan meant that the United Kingdom should leave behind for the Singaporeans all the real estate we owned together with all fixed assets in the various establishments. A commonly quoted statistic still taught, I understand, in Singapore schools, was that this amounted to 10% of Singapore. The devil, as ever, was in the detail. Which assets were fixed, and which removable, back to the UK? As I recall it, the devil was also in some of our own military officers and civilians, with whom our own private negotiations were every bit as difficult as, and certainly more passionate than the formal ones with the Singapore government. For some time, a real sticking point was the amount of real estate, buildings and other fixed assets that would need to be retained for the ANZUK Force. I recall the chief of staff at the Far East command headquarters, the gentlemanly and able Major-General Patrick Howard-Dobson with whom I had many negotiations, making a speech at a mess dinner one night in which he informed all present that when he died, the words HMS *Terror* would be found graven upon his heart.

A deal was eventually done, tolerable to each side, British and Singaporean, and workable (just) by the withdrawing force and (readily) by the incoming and much smaller ANZUK Force. The British Diplomatic Service gained a useful practical advantage during the negotiations: the use of some of the former British military housing on the island. In accordance with our agreement with the Singaporean government, the houses, undoubtedly fixed assets, were duly transferred to the Singaporeans. The side arrangement we in the high commission made was that for a peppercorn rent, the Singaporean government would grant us use of the houses for as long as we required them for diplomatic purposes. This arrangement saved the British taxpayer a great deal of rent for the houses and flats we had previously occupied.

We also had to build a new British high commission on land granted by Singapore as part of the withdrawal arrangements, to replace our offices in the Phoenix Park Far East Command Headquarters complex. After transfer, Phoenix Park became the Singaporean Ministry of Defence. The new high commission building was designed by a particularly fine British government architect, Ken Campbell (whose work I came to appreciate even more years later in the FCO – see Chapter 9). His generous, elegant and efficient building with its 'floating' roof was and still is greatly and widely admired. It is well described (as is so much else) in Mark Bertram's *Room for Diplomacy*. A complementary wing for the British Council was later, sensibly, added. (I had wanted the British Council to have a wing and to join us in 1972, but there was then effective, if, in my view, ill-judged opposition in the governing body of the Council to such close association with the practice of diplomacy, and a preference to stand alone and separate in the purer pursuit of international cultural exchange.)

The new building was indeed another effective tool of diplomacy. So, too, was Eden Hall, the fine 'colonial' residence of the high commissioner. Eden Hall already had an interesting history: the Japanese military had occupied it after the fall of Singapore, and reputedly used it as a senior mess or HQ. There was a story, popular among knowledgeable expatriate British, that it had served as a hotel for single gentlemen before the war; rumour had it that it was then really a high-class brothel. At all events, Eden Hall worked very well as a residence, as a fine hotel for senior British visitors, as an admired venue for diplomatic receptions, and as the place where some serious and important foreign policy and diplomatic work was done. I believed that we should retain the house and its useful garden both for all those purposes, and, after the withdrawal of British forces, to demonstrate the United Kingdom's continuing interest in and diplomatic and foreign policy commitment to Singapore. The high commissioner was much less persuaded. He believed that the house was rather 'over-the-top'; he saw a case for selling it and moving to a flat or town house. I argued with Sam Falle. Eventually, with good grace and to my great personal and professional relief, he conceded. There were sequels to this debate. The residence was later saved again from sale in 1983 when the then permanent under-secretary, Sir Antony Acland, strongly and effectively defended the FCO before the Public Accounts Committee (PAC) of the House of Commons. It was saved again some years later when part of Eden Hall's garden was sold – instead, I imagine, of the whole property. This later change was made to no good effect, as far as I could see on a later visit, and the boundary line looked a metre or so too close to the house. Mark Bertram records in *Room for Diplomacy* that when Her Majesty's Government bought Eden Hall in 1955, the vendor insisted on a plaque at the foot of the flagpole declaring 'May the Union Jack fly here forever'. So far, so good, just: I am certainly not alone in sharing the sentiment. I have some reason to think Lee Kuan Yew would also agree. I hope the present Singapore prime minister (whom my predecessor as head of chancery, Richard Samuel taught Russian), Lee's son Hsien Loong, does too.

The formal British military withdrawal from Singapore in 1971 was a series of historic and moving events. At the mammoth, disciplined and poignant parade and march-past of the withdrawing troops of Far East Land Forces, there could not have been a dry military moustache on the island. To a man all were conscious that there had been British troops on Singapore Island since Raffles landed in 1819.

Perhaps even more impressive was the steam-past to mark the departure of the Far East Fleet. In the straits of Singapore, south of the Island, a long line astern of ships passed the Royal Fleet Auxiliary vessel *Stromness*. Aboard *Stromness*, Air Chief Marshal Sir Brian Burnett, the Far East commander-in-chief (who died recently at 98), took the salute in the presence of the high commissioner Sam Falle, who surely enjoyed the naval splendour and efficiency of the event. Hilary and I were also aboard, and we certainly did so. Perhaps the star of the steam-past was HMS *Albion* with her plenteous helicopters. HMS *Albion* was also known in the Far East in those days as the Grey Ghost of the Borneo Coast, from her successful operations during Confrontation. It was said that day that this was the largest assemblage of naval vessels since King George VI had reviewed the Fleet at Spithead. It was a particular pleasure that visiting Australian and New Zealand vessels also took part: HMAS *Derwent*, HMAS *Swan* and HMNZS *Otago*.

The following year, 1972, with excellent but carefully planned timing as we in the high commission saw it, there was a state visit by Her Majesty The Queen. The Queen was accompanied by His Royal Highness The Prince Philip, Duke of Edinburgh; Her Royal Highness The Princess Anne; and the Queen's uncle, Admiral of the Fleet Lord Louis Mountbatten, who had been supreme commander, South-East Asia from 1942 until the defeat of Japan in 1945. He had taken the surrender of Japanese regional forces in Singapore and was greatly respected there.

Sam Falle, who steered his high commission ship with a light and friendly hand, delegated the planning of the state visit to me. Sam inspired us, and inspired the results he required, along with a great deal of respect and liking, including by the high commission defence staff, who also helped with the state visit. A colleague in the chancery, Martin Hall, and I did the necessary detailed planning, and the necessary negotiation with the Singapore chief of protocol, the cabinet secretary and others; and I worked to Philip Moore, deputy private secretary to the Queen. Philip later became Her Majesty's private secretary, and was knighted, and later still became Lord Moore of Wolvercote. He was marvellous to work with. He had been deputy commissioner and deputy high commissioner in Singapore not long before, and knew everyone who counted there; yet throughout the three months of our working closely together, Philip always guided, never imposed, suggested rather than ordered, and accepted the high commission's thoughts and advice.

Philip Moore and others paid the usual reconnaissance visit to Singapore to agree the broad lines of the forthcoming state visit, and then left the detail to us on the ground. Negotiating among interests competing for the Queen's time was educational. It was useful for Martin and me to be a step ahead of our interlocutors. One of us always walked the ground before beginning a negotiation, and we used a stop-watch. This was unusual, but fascinating diplomacy and negotiation, in unusual and often emotional circumstances.

Indeed, there was enormous and fierce competition for royal time, especially, of course, for that of the Queen. The eventual programme was pretty well balanced, and acceptable both to Buckingham Palace and to the royal family's Singaporean hosts, though there were some last-minute adjustments to be made too: we settled some of these by radio-telephone with Philip Moore aboard HMY *Britannia* as she sailed southwards from Bangkok after a successful state visit to Thailand.

Where to berth the royal yacht in Singapore had been a contentious question. Lee Kuan Yew was clear that he wanted her to be in a stunning location alongside Queen Elizabeth Walk, just across the Padang from the cricket club, the supreme court, other major government buildings and St Andrew's Cathedral, and close to the then mouth of the Singapore river. But there was no berth there, and I also knew that there was not enough depth of water for HMY *Britannia*. (Since land reclamation, Queen Elizabeth Walk, like Raffles Hotel, is now well inland.) The rear admiral commanding the royal yacht, Richard Trowbridge (the first boy seaman to rise to command the royal yacht), had made it absolutely clear to me that this would not do. Sam Falle and I were at lunch with the Singapore foreign minister, Lee Kuan Yew and his cabinet secretary. Lee insisted. At Sam's request, sensibly keeping himself in reserve, I explained. Lee insisted again. I explained again. Lee said he would have the water, fuel, shore power and so on laid on, and the quayside so-called 'berth' dredged to make room for *Britannia*. As an amateur yachtsman who sailed off Singapore, I knew this would not do. I had no real faith in the dredging plan: any dredged berth would quickly be silted up by the outflow from the Singapore river. Further, in contrast to today, the Singapore river was a long way from sweet-smelling. The thought of *Britannia* aground on Singapore river mud was unappealing. We debated and argued. Eventually, at the end of lunch, to my relief and rather to my surprise, Lee conceded, and the royal yacht was allocated a berth in the then new, fresh container port – nowadays, the old, small container port. East Lagoon, Berth No. 48 would provide much less impressive a backdrop, but was immensely more practical. Singapore, of course, made a stunning job of the berth, the berthing procedures and everything necessary for a smooth and happy visit.

The Queen's routes on Singapore Island were meticulously planned – in some cases challenged and debated in negotiation. I recall being keen for Her Majesty to drive by some of the Indian and Chinatown shop-houses: they were the real old Singapore, full of character. This route was eventually agreed by the Singaporeans: we won the minor argument. But when the day arrived, the scruffy shop-houses were obscured by tall, pristine canvas hoardings, erected the night before. A pity, but, I suppose, I should have foreseen the instant 'make-over' in Lee Kwan Yew's Singapore.

There were a few tense moments, for example when the Rolls-Royce bearing the Queen nudged a concrete bollard with its rear wing on the way to a housing estate, lifting car and Her Majesty a few inches into the air. No lasting harm, save to the pride of the poor driver, who had practised the manoeuvre many times, but was carried away by the moment and by the cheering crowds.

One of the more exciting events of the state visit was a trip to Pagoda Street as part of what the official programme listed as 'night tour of City'. Pagoda Street, a bustling, narrow road, full of Chinese market stalls and the noise of cheerful bargaining, was put on its best behaviour that evening, for the one 'walkabout' of the state visit. At 10.20pm, the programme directed, laconically: 'Walk through Pagoda Street'. The reality was very different. The welcome for the Queen and Prince Philip was quite extraordinarily warm, happy: almost overwhelming. The number of people in Pagoda Street far exceeded the expectations of the Singapore police; the atmosphere was electric and noisy with squeals and laughter as Singaporeans, mostly Chinese, in their eagerness to see the royal couple at close quarters, jostled and, uncharacteristically, shoved. The Queen did stop and shop at market stalls. Every time, the throng pressed closer. The police could not keep them back. Pagoda Street now had more people in it than it could reasonably contain, and more, many hundreds more, were trying to join them. I found myself in the front row of a rugby formation. With Philip Moore, Martin Hall from chancery, and even the Singapore chief of protocol in the second row, scrum down, heads down and heaving, we pushed the crowd back slowly in front of the Queen and the Duke of Edinburgh so that they could proceed with the plan in the official programme and reach the royal motorcade that was waiting at the other end of the street. As I muttered to Philip something about the ball at our feet, I recalled his sporting prowess, and asked whether it was an essential requirement for a private secretary to the Queen to have a rugby blue from Oxford. He made the quick response that it helped, smiled determinedly and heaved again. We, and Her Majesty and Prince Philip, made it to the end of the street, the Hindu temple and the cars. We even made it on time – 10.40pm – as the programme prescribed. That was probably the toughest ten minutes of the state visit.

There were other good moments. Lord Mountbatten returned from his own, separate trip to the then Singapore crocodile farm, the proud owner of a young beast (presumably made safe), some five feet long. His high commission escort, First Secretary (Commercial) George Stansfield, bravely tucked the crocodile under his arm, and bore it from the large limousine into which it had squashed, up the royal yacht's brow. With, no doubt, some relief, he then handed the reptile to waiting sailors. Where could they put it? We heard that the next morning, Lord Mountbatten found it – as he stepped into his ready drawn bath!

Britannia was also the venue for HM The Queen's dinner for the Singapore government and after dinner reception, a splendid affair. The day before, the master of the royal household told me that, try as he could, he could not wrap his tongue around the Chinese and other Singaporean names: could I therefore deputise for him and present the guests for both dinner and reception to the Queen and the Duke of Edinburgh? I could and would, of course, but because of the protocol, this meant that Hilary could not be presented to the Queen at Her Majesty's reception, to which we had been invited. This was a disappointment for Hilary: the Queen would be wearing a tiara and a fabulous gown. The master of the royal household went away and quietly sought the Queen's permission to break a royal yacht rule: that while Her Majesty was aboard, the officers might not invite ladies to any function in the wardroom. That evening, while I was doing my duty, Hilary was the sole guest of the wardroom at dinner, was much fêted, and had a marvellous time. Later, when I had presented 200 reception guests to Her Majesty and Prince Philip, I joined Hilary, who had been conducted from the wardroom to the veranda deck aft. The master of the royal household found us and took us to a quiet spot at the forward end of the deck. He then brought the Queen to us. We had a long private conversation with Her Majesty, who was looking radiant. Honour was far more than even, and Hilary was justly thrilled.

The evening was completed by the Royal Marines band from *Britannia* beating Retreat on the quayside while we lined the rails of the royal yacht. Soon after we all took our leave of the state visitors and the yacht, and stood on the quayside – as *Britannia* eased her way gently, quietly, apparently effortlessly (the tug on the seaward side invisible from the quayside), so impressively, away from the berth and into the night. The Royal Marines band, now aboard and stationed right aft, were playing alternately with the Singapore band ashore as the royal family and all those ashore waved their farewells. The atmosphere on the quayside that tropical night was emotional, in many cases tearful, but certainly happy.

The state visit set the seal very happily on an unprecedented, difficult, sometimes tense but ultimately satisfactory period in British relations with this former colony, this occasionally resentful and often autocratic, but distinctly successful young country.

Around this time, Lee Kuan Yew called his country, for the benefit of anyone who cared to listen, but especially Singapore's neighbours, a 'poisonous shrimp'. Apt – at least for the time and for Lee Kuan Yew's then political stance. There was a lot to admire in Singapore's management and efficiency of government; but the practice and pursuit of real democracy never seemed high in the national priority list. Yet Lee complained, in conversation with Sam Falle, that there was no effective opposition in Singapore's parliament. True. When we arrived, there were no opposition MPs. When one, J. B. (Ben) Jeyaretnam, a good man, lawyer and patriot, was elected and criticised the government, he was sued and jailed. After release, Ben stood again and was re-elected. Further complex legal processes ensued. Ben appealed his disbarment to the Privy Council, who found that he had suffered a grievous injustice, but the Council's powers were limited. Hilary and I exchanged Christmas cards and messages with Ben and his English wife, and later with widower Ben until he died in 2008. Interestingly, I learn from a Singaporean academic friend that Singapore over the years has graduated from 'poisonous shrimp' to 'porcupine' and, more attractively, to 'dolphin'.

Yet no one could gainsay Singapore's developing economic and national success; and once all the business of withdrawing our military resources, human and physical movables, and setting up the ANZUK Force was done, Singapore was, in my time there and since, a good ally with whom to work and do much diplomatic business.

The ANZUK Force, the creation of politicians and diplomats, was in our eyes always rather more a temporary and political device than a military necessity. Its objective, 'to promote stability and confidence of the area', was, I believe, fulfilled: in part because the ANZUK Force did indeed fill Lee Kuan Yew's perceived 'power vacuum'; in part because it provided valuable and valued training opportunities for British, Australian and New Zealand forces; and importantly for Singapore and the region, simply because it was there. The politics

– international, bilateral and national – changed over time. Britain warmly welcomed the then new Association of South East Asian Nations (ASEAN) in a statement we drafted in Eden Hall and was issued thence by a visiting FCO minister. ASEAN developed and became respected regionally and beyond. The Integrated Air Defence System and the Five Power Defence Arrangements (United Kingdom, Australia, New Zealand, Singapore and Malaysia) matured. Australian and New Zealand approaches to the provision of the military assets and personnel altered. UK defence cuts played their part. Both Singaporean and Malaysian troop and other military capabilities and equipment were modernised and improved, partly as a result of training and other help provided by the ANZUK Force and its contributing countries. These developments steadily removed the need for the ANZUK Force itself. So it was disbanded, without serious dissension, by the end of 1974, a year after we left for our next posting to London.

As a small ANZUK Force footnote, after the British high commission occupied its fine new building, the Royal Highland Fusiliers (RHF) pipe and drum band played at the annual Queen's birthday party reception. The RHF also helped us greatly with the move, including our classified materials, to the new office building. They mounted guard there in unusual circumstances. This was the first British diplomatic building to be equipped with bullet-proof glass instead of bars across the windows. The innovative and expensive glass was especially made in Britain to withstand shots by high-velocity rifles. It arrived by sea exactly to plan, just in time to be installed as one of the last construction operations. When the packing cases were undone, however, the glass was seen to have been shattered into many millions of pieces. Much later, after much investigation, many tests, and a fair amount of recrimination following our refusal to pay a penny, it was accepted that once mounted vertically in its special frames, the glass worked perfectly. However, if travelling by sea in containers, and lying flat, ship movement in a seaway could evidently result in the glass shattering. Whatever the physics, we had a security problem until new bullet-proof glass could be manufactured and delivered safely.

The solution was to fit ordinary glass in the windows temporarily and to have our splendid soldiers of the Royal Highland Fusiliers mount guard around the perimeter and on the roof of the new building. As head of chancery, I feared that after a time, the soldiers would become bored and not want to continue with this extra duty. Not a bit of it. They were soon queuing up for the job, especially, to my initial surprise, for the night duty. I went to see them one night, late, unannounced, and found them happily and industriously engaged, notably on the roof, peering in turns through (for the time) remarkably powerful night-vision binoculars. It did not take too long to discover that the Royal Highland Fusiliers had found a unique view of the back wing of a hotel across the way. Through lit, if dimly lit windows, the Fusiliers could clearly see the most remarkable of exciting, tropical, even torrid goings-on among unclad young Asian lovelies and their athletic clients.

There is another security footnote, and a serious one; an early lesson, looking forward to today's global terrorism. The high commissioner, Sam Falle, was among other things, an accomplished Arabist. As his book reveals, he was an active and influential diplomat in a number of seminal, even revolutionary, events in the Middle East. While Sam was serving in Singapore, we had intelligence, good and reliable intelligence, of a specific and serious threat against his life from terrorists in the Middle East. We had to lay on extra security precautions, including a 24-hour armed guard, efficiently provided by British Military Police from the ANZUK Force. I also recall Sam's understandable frustration at the imposition of these necessary precautions. They worked, and we were all most grateful. Forty years later armed guards for British and other diplomats are, sadly, surprisingly widespread around the world.

It seems to me logical to suppose that the increased personal protection for some presumed higher risk targets results, inevitably, in softer, less protected and so easier targets being hit instead. Tragic examples and victims may well include a deputy British high commissioner in (then) Bombay, and the British consul-general and staff, as well as a British bank, in Istanbul. With all the global progress in technology and in international understanding, to strengthen personal security, to combat increasing terrorist attacks and to remove their underlying motivation are among the most important and difficult challenges for modern diplomacy and its allies, and need at least adequate resources devoted to them.

I was most grateful for the posting to Singapore. It was then a fine place in which to bring up our two young boys. And I could sail. We sailed over many square miles of sea that is today reclaimed land, including Changi International Airport, reclaimed by using the tops of hills in Singapore and from Indonesian islands. In a round the island race, I sailed a Dragon yacht through water that is now Singapore's cruise ship terminal and new land forming part of the modern Sentosa Island resort.

Towards the end of our posting in Singapore, John, our elder son, went to boarding school in the United Kingdom. That was a heartrending time. We had decided that the boys should board. In my view they should be equipped to compete in the British economy, if that were to be their wish. Experience in Bulgaria had taught me that education available abroad was patchy to say the least. That said, education in Singapore is admirable (and the boys gained much from their brief early schooling there). More important than my view was Hilary's. As the daughter of an RAF officer, she had moved very frequently and had attended many different schools. It was no surprise that her views on the disadvantages of discontinuity on education were commensurately strong. Stable education would also, we agreed, allow the boys to grow roots in their own country and to make lasting friends. Though there could be no controlled experiment, and the judgment is subjective, we believe that heartbreaking decision was the right one. It was harder to bear for Hilary than for me, since I could bury my worries in work. Hilary had rather less opportunity to do that, but bore up very well.

My work in Singapore broadened my understanding of diplomacy. The subjects of our negotiations ranged from the future of military assets via aid administration and international politics to the tough world of commercial aviation, where we had a good deal of bargaining to do in the interests of British companies. I well recall sitting once a month in the office of the relevant Singapore cabinet minister until very close to the midnight deadline, just before which he would sign the renewal document that allowed British Caledonian Airways to continue to fly to and from Singapore, and then rushing to the high commission to let British Caledonian know. All this provided the invaluable experience of negotiating with some of the cleverest and toughest of negotiators in the region, the Singaporeans. Many, but not all the senior officials and politicians were sharp, able Chinese. All were bright, finely educated, pretty single-minded patriots, who knew how to drive a good hard bargain and drive it well, but who also respected good arguments and debate. Singapore, and Britain's relations with Singapore, went through considerable changes while Hilary and I served there. I believe those changes have stood the test of time, and have no doubt the senior officials are just as able and tough as ever. Arguably the toughest and most effective of them all, Lee Kuan Yew, yet owed a great deal to his most able and impressive wife, Kwa Geok Choo, who died in 2010. Lee himself was the world's longest-serving prime minister. He resigned his latest position in the cabinet as minister mentor in May 2011, in his eighty-eighth year. It is hard to believe his influence will not last at least another few generations.

One change made in our time in Singapore seemed to me at the time draconian: it was a considerable, sharp increase in the compulsory levy on workers to fund the Central Provident Fund, a social security savings plan for old age dating from 1955, some eight years before Independence. I thought the extra levy imposed in the early 1970s (at 16% of income if I remember aright) hurt the ability, particularly but not only of the lower paid, to manage their finances and to choose how, when and for what they saved. Now, nearly four decades later, the Central Provident Fund of Singapore funds medical and other insurance, education, housing and retirement-related finance schemes as well as some withdrawals. It now collects some 20% of salary from Singaporeans and another 15.5% from the employer. The fund does not provide all the answers, locking up some money the better paid might prefer to invest elsewhere, and enforcing one of the highest savings rates in the world. Its interest rate doubtless reflects the economy, so is to some extent vulnerable to external influences.

However, on balance, I think I was wrong in my 1970s judgment. With its few drawbacks, the Singapore Central Provident Fund is a success, its levies are generally accepted by Singaporeans, and it is a more effective system than that of many Western countries, including, I believe, our own. It would not be practical politics for the United Kingdom: for Singapore, it has worked, and works, well.

Another Singaporean feature that seemed draconian when introduced, that works, and this time, the United Kingdom has belatedly copied, is traffic congestion charging. London's system was based on Singapore's, including much of its technology. Another of the requirements of life introduced by Lee Kuan Yew as prime minister in our time was short hair for men, young or old. The long-haired, for example, were sent to the back of the always long post office queues – repeatedly. The best example of tonsorial autocracy was the long line of barber's chairs at the international airport past which no male visitor (or returnee) to Singapore could pass with long hair without sitting and being shorn. This policy and practice gave endless and deep satisfaction to expatriate fathers awaiting their sons' holiday visits from boarding schools – at a time when long hair for males in the West was so fashionable that the young deemed it compulsory.

More seriously, one way to judge the maturity and sensitivity of a nation may be in the amount and quality of its current literature and perhaps especially poetry. We knew some of the rather few published authors in Singapore. Professor Nalla Tan's thoughtful and tender short stories and her collected poems were a good example. The later writings of Ben Jeyaretnam's younger son, Philip, were another. But there were sadly few examples: I hope there are more now.

Among Hilary's and my countless personal memories of Singapore is a moonflower of a kind that reputedly flowers for only one night once every seven years: our moonflower did so on our patio one magic night. Other memories are of orchids in our garden; HMY *Britannia*; torrid tropical days and nights; cars with no air-conditioning; playing squash in the heat at the Singapore Cricket Club; watching a 'test match' on the cricket ground between Singapore and Hong Kong in which a bright and able member of chancery, Simon Fuller (later permanent representative to the United Nations at Geneva), played; really fine Chinese food in the delightful company of Diana and George Wong, also of the chancery. George was an invaluable member of the Diplomatic Service – I wish he had stayed in it longer, but he did do great work later also for UK plc and the Rothschilds. There are many other memories of an astonishing variety of political, management, representational and other work at the desk and on our feet; and of friends made and kept – in many walks of Singaporean and diplomatic life.

The time flew by. We were very sorry to leave an island state we were confident would grow and prosper, in some genuine part because of the way the United Kingdom implemented her decision to withdraw troops east of Suez, and helped Singapore; in part because of the roles played by Singapore's other allies; and in important part, of course, because of Singapore's own extraordinary efforts and drive to succeed. The Singapore of today is very different, physically flatter and bigger, so changed in so many ways and, despite the recent global economic downturn, relatively prosperous. It is, however, also worth remembering that Britain founded Singapore in 1824, principally as a trading centre, and helped her, both towards and after independence, to become known and admired today not as a 'poisonous shrimp' but as the Switzerland of Asia, a leading 'economic tiger' and a singularly successful trading and financial centre and a base for business, notably British business.

CHAPTER 6

SABBATICAL AT UNIVERSITY OF CALIFORNIA, BERKELEY

After a four-year stint in the Foreign and Commonwealth Office (see Chapter 9), I was fortunate to be selected for a sabbatical academic year in 1977–78. The University of California Berkeley accepted me as a visiting fellow. This was a welcome mid-career refresher and intellectual stimulant. I went to California a touch jaded: I left reinvigorated, richer in mind and spirit, and thinking and working more effectively.

The Institute of International Studies at Berkeley, then headed by Professor Carl Rosberg, could not have been more helpful. I was invited to join a number of interesting and influential East–West and other international policy seminars and colloquia at Berkeley, and down the coast at Stanford University in Palo Alto. I lectured at both, and at another University of California campus, Davis. Defending the UK position on a wide variety of international political subjects to able and challenging senior academic groups was good further diplomatic experience. To lecture to eager and bright young undergraduates was flattering, even heady – but also instructive.

However, my primary task at Berkeley, where I spent most time, was to write a monograph which might be of some help to the British national interest. The Foreign Office rightly required a serious and useful piece of policy work as the product of a sabbatical, and I used the Californian opportunity and extensive research facilities to think and write about the transfer of technology from the Western world to the communist world of the then USSR and Eastern Europe. My own Cold War experience behind the Iron Curtain, and that of representing the United Kingdom in Paris at CoCom, had stimulated an interest in the longer, earlier history of the subject, in trying to set right some international misconceptions, and in offering some policy prescriptions. To do this work in Berkeley seemed particularly appropriate. There was in those days a division, one which quite often led to sharp disputes, between the harder-line United States on the one hand and the more liberal United Kingdom and other West European countries on the other hand, and about the policies of the embargo. A fine, internationally renowned Berkeley professor, Gregory Grossman, took a firm view of East–West trade with which I disagreed. And the standard, and voluminous, history of East–West trade was an American publication – with chunks of which I also took issue. So there was plenty of opportunity for challenge, debate and self-discipline to try to ensure that the opposing views I was arguing in the draft monograph were tolerably well argued.

Other things happened at Berkeley while we were so happily ensconced there. Hilary and I rented a wonderful house (built in the Berkeley hills by an eccentric English architect) from a charming and brilliant American professor of government who, serendipitously, was taking a sabbatical in London. This was the distinguished and brilliant Nelson Polsby, the much published author and authority on government and the politics of government. We also took care of his and his wife Linda's well-tempered dog: all three became our good, much valued and lasting friends. Nelson and Linda later stayed with us in England and in Australia. Nelson's last and fifteenth book, 'How Congress Evolves', published before his untimely death, may yet prove his finest, possibly even outranking his seminal 'Presidential Elections' (with Aaron Wildavsky), now in its thirteenth edition.

The view from the Polsby house was of San Francisco Bay, including the Golden Gate Bridge, through whose piers we frequently watched the sun set. I sailed occasionally at weekends in and from San Francisco Bay with a neighbour George Becker, and with another friendly professor, vulcanologist Bruce Bolt. Bruce lived next door but one, also, determinedly and appropriately, slap bang on the Hayward fault. We learned a little about Californian wines, then so different and so differently produced from French wines. Our two boys, by then at preparatory school in England, had a couple of wonderful Californian holidays. There were British visitors, academic, official and political. The British consul-general, Tim Kinnear, and his wife Rosemary invited us to interesting events, including a visit by HRH The Prince of Wales, who spoke at Berkeley. I was asked to brief him. During that briefing, I tried hard to persuade Prince Charles of the authenticity of the American pronunciation of Berkeley (Burrkley). I failed: I squirmed the next day when, in his successful speech on the campus, he made it sound like London's Berkeley Square. The Prince of Wales was much applauded, so must have been forgiven.

Life at Berkeley was by no means only a temporary excursion into the groves of academe, but rather a much appreciated mind-broadening and sharpening exercise. By UK standards, the campus was vast. It included some 28,000 undergraduates, around 8,000 faculty members and eight Nobel laureates. It was an extra and an enjoyable privilege to be both part of the Berkeley faculty scene and an observer of it. Hilary and I were very warmly welcomed. Perhaps because, not seeking the grail of tenure, we were seen as no professional threat, we were confided in a good deal and at every opportunity by warring factions among professors. The hope of securing us as campus allies was evident. This was great fun, and I concluded that perhaps I wrote the wrong book while on sabbatical. The raw material for a rich and entertaining novel (aspiring to a C.P. Snow of California) about academic life at this huge and hugely impressive campus was all around us, in great abundance. To try my hand at that, however, would certainly not have been in accordance with the properly strict precepts of a Diplomatic Service sabbatical year.

Stanford seminars were exciting, sometimes almost overwhelming in their esoteric, abstruse quality and intellectual power. At one such seminar, on politico-military matters of the day and in particular highly technical Cold War 'anti-missile missile' calculations and strategy, I found myself seated at a table with some of the world's leading experts and Nobel Prize-winning minds, bent on a deep debate on the most arcane aspects of these subjects. I was also sitting next to an American who had been an ambassador in Africa and chief of protocol at the White House, and was now spending some time at Stanford pursuing, as the US State Department called it, public diplomacy. This was the former and much loved film star Shirley Temple (Black). As the debate became so recondite that it threatened to go over both our heads, Shirley Temple and I made common cause – and indeed briefly held hands. I later gained considerable kudos with our sons, who had already fallen heavily for the lovely star of almost countless films.

There was another surprise for me, when in this then generally mellow California, I opened a hotel front door and held it for one who proved to live in a ferment of feminism: she harangued me for many minutes in a fury at my patronising presumption that she was incapable of opening a door herself. She used many and colourful epithets to describe me and my unconscionably chauvinistic attitude just made so blatantly evident. She spoke or shouted so fluently and for so long that I had plenty of time to think of and frame my eventual response – of which, had I not been on sabbatical, I should not have dreamed of using. I replied, 'Madam, I do apologise: I mistook you for a lady'. I have never again been presented with an opportunity to use this riposte.

The chancellor of the university, Albert Bowker, gave rather splendid, interesting and stimulating black tie dinners. After debate over the food one evening, the after-dinner entertainment for the men consisted in a then cutting-edge piece of computer technology: we played American football online against Stanford University. That was more intimidating than the vastly well-informed discussion over dinner had been, including the extra challenges to me as the sole European at the table. Generously, and riskily – the game was taken very seriously – I was encouraged to act as coach and decide upon some key 'plays'. My ignorance was considerable, but Berkeley won the game: my 'plays' had worked well. It was a small victory for Great Britain as well as a larger one for Berkeley: in the minds of my US academic colleagues it was at least as important as winning the Oxford and Cambridge boat race. Hilary recalls vividly her surprise that in Berkeley, California, of all places, while the men played computer football, the ladies sat on hard chairs and supped coffee.

The FCO and cabinet office cleared my book for publication, and the Institute of International Studies and the University of California kindly published it. The institute director, the good Professor Carl Rosberg, pronounced it 'very well written' – perhaps, I wondered, to avoid having to offer any political comment on the book's content that might have been thought un-American. The very able Professor Grossman was kind and polite too, but, unsurprisingly, seemed less than convinced by my arguments. A senior political scientist and White House policy adviser in the East–West field, Sam Huntington, reviewed the publication positively, and I was later told by an interested and interesting US academic that my work had made some difference to US policy. I hope so, but however that may be, the subject became a mere footnote in diplomatic and international business history when, *mirabile dictu*, the Cold War ended so decisively a decade or so after the publication.

I did feel it was a pity that my carefully constructed research and writing plan had to be truncated when my sabbatical academic year was itself truncated by my next posting. I had planned a supplementary chapter on the separate and fascinating story of technology transfer to China, with some rather different policy conclusions. The chapter was abandoned; I regret that because it might have been of different and to an extent more enduring interest.

I wonder if sabbaticals are now in the least affordable in the modern Diplomatic Service. The very few there were in the 1970s were valuable as inputs into the capabilities and later effectiveness of the officers concerned. Sabbaticals were usually quite hard work, rewarding personally, but, more importantly, professionally – and they provided an extra and enduring network of diplomatically useful contacts and credentials. Their name was changed later to 'career development attachments' following, I understand, some scepticism from Prime Minister Margaret Thatcher, and perhaps a pause. Politicians may well be sceptical as they often seek shorter rather than longer term value for the taxpayers' money.

We had arrived in Berkeley in September 1977 and left in May 1978 to drive across the United States when I was posted to the embassy in Washington. It was a wrench to leave Berkeley a couple of months earlier than we had expected; to leave a refreshing and stimulating and productive study period; good friends; Californian wines; Californian national parks; sailing in San Francisco Bay and on into the Pacific. We had an interesting and instructive drive across the US, during which Hilary and I learned something of the great diversity of the nation; of the equally great contrasts of politics around the nation; and of the gulf of political and economic understanding and caring between the cognoscenti and most Americans – a greater gulf even than in the United Kingdom. That said, we also learned something of the positive tolerance of bankruptcy that stems from the second chance syndrome which lies at the root of much of America's history, philosophy and economic success over the years; and of the enormous size and resilience of the US economy. Indeed, it is a surprise now to see the signs of strain rather than of bouncing back which that resilience has allowed so often, so effectively and for so long.

California had started, for Hilary and me, as a colossal cultural shock, bigger by far than that occasioned by any other move to a new country. The capital, Washington, barely signified to most Californians. Europe might well not have existed. East Asia, however, did exist for California, even in the 1970s – perhaps part of the Vietnam effect, but also of the increasing consciousness of China's development. News of the east coast of the United States or of Europe, however, was entirely obscured by the thrill of the chase of local state politics. Indeed that chase was quite thrilling in the late 1970s, under the classically educated, modest-living Democrat, Governor Jerry Brown, himself the son of a governor.

California's state politics were also exciting so much later and so differently under Governor Arnold Schwarzenegger, who was himself succeeded by a resurrected and rejuvenated Governor Jerry Brown – at a young 72. There are lessons there for the modern United Kingdom, including its Diplomatic Service, of which more later.

We learned much in California and enjoyed doing so. Our boys greatly enjoyed holidays there. Diplomatic life is nomadic: to join the British embassy in Washington now held new and immediate promise ...

CHAPTER 7

COUNSELLOR AND JIC REPRESENTATIVE, BRITISH EMBASSY, WASHINGTON

Though we had less time than we would have wished, Hilary and I much enjoyed the 3,500-mile drive in mid-1978, on not quite the straightest route across the United States from Berkeley to Washington. We savoured the physical, cultural and political differences among states, and the changes from west to east, evident as we stayed in towns, small and large. We progressed via Sacramento from mellow yet exciting California eastwards through Nevada (paying our motel bill with a modest and unique win at one of the countless casinos on Winnemucca's main street). Our Ford Maverick and we enjoyed the glistening Bonneville salt flats of Utah as we thought of Sir Malcolm Campbell's successful 1960 land speed record run there in *Bluebird* and his son Donald's high speed, but not fatal, crash on the same flats a quarter of a century later. The Salt Lake Temple is extraordinary, and the pervading Mormon cultural influence in the city seemed to reflect both the building and the strong beliefs and practices it symbolises. Tourist sites, some with historical associations, followed apace – we came to call the many roadside 'historical markers' 'hysterical markers', so intense was the devotion to and exploitation of, to us, a short but nonetheless rather thrilling US story. Wyoming's majestic scenery included Yellowstone National Park (fortunately for us then lacking other visitors). On to Cody, Bighorn, Buffalo, Sundance, Custer, Keystone, and the almost chilling Badlands of South Dakota with Mount Rushmore, the national monument to four US presidents, their heads 60 feet high and carved in the

Black Hills. We drove on to Kadoka and Sioux Falls and into Nebraska at Omaha.

Eschewing the freeways as much as possible, we drove south through the Great Plains of Nebraska (the 'Cornhusker State', with huge beef herds too). The capital, Lincoln, has a commensurately huge capitol building, and the only unicameral legislature in the United States. On through much more corn (maize) and strongly Republican and Protestant Kansas via the fine city of St Louis and across the Mississippi river into southern Illinois and Indiana (having no idea that these last three states would one day form part of my ten-state consular district – see Chapter 8). On we drove further east, sensing again easily and strongly the changing demographic, political and cultural scenes, notably as we found charming, rural and evidently pretty happy Kentucky. We found one or two interlocutors in deepest Kentucky (near the battlefield of Perryville) more difficult to understand than any Americans we had met – or, surprisingly, ever were to meet. We traversed the Cumberland Gap, and drove into Tennessee and lovely West Virginia with its Allegheny mountains, forests, coal mining, and its fascinating Civil War history. Last came Virginia with the Appalachians, the Shenandoah valley and the spectacular Blue Ridge parkway, and Arlington before we crossed the 14th Street Bridge (scene of the later, dreadful aeroplane crash in icy mid-winter) and into Washington DC.

The posting to the embassy began in August 1978. The US administration I was to work with was then led by President Carter, and Jim Callaghan, former foreign secretary, was our Prime Minister.

My job was to be a demanding and wonderful one: Joint Intelligence Committee (JIC) representative, and a political counsellor in the chancery.

The British ambassador in Washington at the time was a political appointee, the Hon. Peter Jay, former Treasury official and later broadcaster and economics editor of *The Times*. Such appointments are rare in the British, as opposed, say, to the American diplomatic service. I happened to have worked for two political appointees (Soames and Jay), but throughout my career there was usually one or none among all our diplomatic posts abroad. The most I recall at any one time is three, a tiny number compared with that in the American service – variously 40% or more of head of mission posts – and most of the major ones.

Peter Jay's appointment to Washington was controversial, and has largely remained so. He was the then 40-year-old son-in-law of Prime Minister James Callaghan. The press and public mostly believed that the appointment was made because of that relationship. In fact, as I knew from my personnel department days and from acting as secretary to the No. 1 Board that met to recommend the appointment, it was the personal wish of the new foreign secretary, David Owen, who knew, liked and admired Peter Jay, and who wanted to replace the professional ambassador in Washington, the (very able) Hon. Sir Peter Ramsbotham, who had served there for over three successful and effective years. When Jim Callaghan moved to No. 10 Downing Street to succeed Harold Wilson in 1976, the new prime minister appointed David (now Lord) Owen to succeed him as secretary of state for foreign and commonwealth affairs – in a controversial promotion to the cabinet and to one of the great offices of state. Jim Callaghan had withstood the consequential criticism. When, soon after the papers recommending his son-in-law as ambassador to the United States appeared in No. 10, the prime minister received wise advice from then Tom (now Lord) McNally, who had been Jim Callaghan's political adviser in the FCO, and went with him in a similar capacity to No. 10. There, as I understood it, Tom McNally warned the prime minister that there would be hostile press and other reaction and advised against endorsing the proposed appointment. Jim Callaghan nonetheless decided not to oppose David Owen's first official recommendation to him, so it went on to the palace for formal approval. There was an immediate and considerable fuss in the press as the predicted accusations of nepotism were widely and loudly made.

Once in post, Peter Jay insisted on interviewing every proposed new member of his staff above a certain rank. He interviewed me during a visit he made to Berkeley. We are exact contemporaries, and when he discovered that we had been in the Royal Navy for National Service at the same time (though he as a rare upper yardsman and I as a mere leading Coder(Special) – a Russian linguist), the interview went well and enjoyably. I later also enjoyed working to Peter Jay on the intelligence assessment front: he was interested in this work, supportive and understanding, including when there were transatlantic differences of interpretation of shared intelligence – much of the meat of the JIC representative job, and often important for the conduct of the Cold War. There were, perhaps unsurprisingly, rather more frequent, even stark and hotly debated differences of view within the embassy, for example of President Carter's approach to US policies, and some Anglo-US matters. These debates further heightened the atmosphere in this hothouse of a chancery with its political appointee as ambassador and the fiercely professional John Robinson as his No. 2. Jimmy Carter was facing tough challenges abroad, in some of which the United Kingdom was involved. He laid much stress on human rights, on energy saving and on managing difficult economic problems (including 'stagflation') at home – though not nearly as difficult as those besetting fellow-Democrat Barack Obama later. Neither did Carter face quite such implacable opposition from Republicans on Capitol Hill.

Before I could become JIC representative in Washington, however, and most unusually for Diplomatic Service postings at the time, I also had to survive another job interview, this time with the intelligence coordinator in London. In those days, senior diplomats typically performed the necessary function of holding the ring among the intelligence agencies, and settling or managing any differences. Hence, for example, the useful and effective practice for many years, and until fairly recently, of the chairman of the JIC in London being a Diplomatic Service officer. Similar considerations applied to the posts of intelligence coordinator in London and JIC representative in Washington. The late, great Sir Brooks Richards, former ambassador to Greece, distinguished in Special Operations Executive operations in the Second World War and much else, was the coordinator who interviewed me. I had had some direct Diplomatic Service experience of the different world of the intelligence agencies, but when Brooks discovered that in the Royal Navy I had in effect worked for GCHQ, I was home and dry. Brooks and his also genuinely great successor,

Sir Antony Duff (former legendary submarine commander, wise and accomplished diplomat and later, at Margaret Thatcher's request, head of MI5), became most welcome and effective official visitors to Washington, house guests and friends. Brooks and Tony were further examples of that rich vein of war heroes the Foreign Service was so fortunate to secure. In retirement, both did good works: Brooks presided at the Special Forces Club (which among much else looks after widows and dependents), and Tony worked for London's homeless.

Prime Minister Jim Callaghan and his wife Audrey used to find the time for an occasional weekend away from No. 10, and would fly to Washington privately to spend a little time with their grandchildren and the Jays. Hilary and I thought their efforts as grandparents most admirable.

In the embassy, I also had regional responsibility for bilateral US–UK work to do with a couple of regions of the world. One summer Saturday afternoon I was alone in the embassy working on an urgent problem, when a still more urgent one brought the ambassador, Peter Jay, in from the residence next door. He asked me to accompany him to an immediate appointment he had just secured with the then US secretary of state, Cyrus Vance, to discuss this new and urgent problem and to find a rapid solution. I was to take the note and draft a subsequent reporting telegram to the FCO. Cy Vance was a formal gentleman who always wore a three-piece suit complete with fob watch and chain. Peter Jay was wearing a suit. Most unusually for me and most embarrassingly, I had driven to the chancery dressed in jeans and shirt – no jacket. I borrowed a tie and blazer from the ambassador (who was particularly tall, so the blazer drooped low). Mercifully, for, had they known, my state department colleagues would have never let me live down the sartorial blunder, Peter Jay and I were alone with the US secretary of state. The subject of the discussion with Cy Vance had to do with the then Rhodesia (not, as it happened, directly a chancery responsibility of mine, but that was irrelevant). The meeting was most civilised and constructive professionally, and personally Cy Vance seemed the essence of tolerance and forgiveness. But I never again went to the office, in Washington or anywhere else, wearing other than a suit and tie.

The quality of colleagues in the chancery was probably the highest of my career: too many to mention by name, they included future ambassadors to NATO, the UN and the EU and ambassadors at Tokyo, Warsaw, Kuwait, Tel Aviv, Amman, Vienna, Lisbon, Rome and Paris – and the list is by no means exhaustive.

An unexpected element of my 'JIC rep' duties was concerned with the protection of British classified material which had been shared with the US government over the years and would be shared in future. This was in part the treatment by the US National Archives of historical papers whose release might be detrimental to the British national interest, and in part a matter of our official concerns as the United States devised and developed their Freedom of Information Bill. The protection of historical papers allowed me to work with the responsible senior official at the National Archives, the deeply knowledgeable Alan Thompson. We became good friends, and much enjoyed sailing together in Alan's lovely straight-stemmed, gaff-rigged 'cat boat', *Calico*. Years later, Alan, his splendid wife, Denny, Hilary and I shared two excellent and memorable sailing trips in yachts we chartered in the Caribbean. One such venture was with our younger son Charles, who joined us at short notice – Hilary had accidentally scalded her hands and was pronounced unfit to haul on ropes.

Alan also introduced me to Bob Urbanek, for whom I often crewed in his fine racing yacht, *La Mouette* – from Annapolis in Maryland. We did reasonably well in a memorable offshore race over several days, and had a magical weekend cruise, with Alan Thompson too, in Chesapeake Bay, partly to observe Canada geese resting in thousands during their migration. The geese surrounded *La Mouette* at anchor in the late evening, and settled to sleep. A few awoke at dawn to begin a gentle conversation, which steadily grew in volume and participation until it became a huge cacophony of a debate that recalled question time in the House of Commons. I had many occasions to be grateful for the rigorous nautical training at the British (Army-run) Kiel Yacht Club, while I was serving in the Royal Navy: it proved invaluable in a number of sailing grounds around the world.

On the Freedom of Information front, I learned a good deal in Washington from the Americans, notably when working with the legal staff at the State Department – and in particular an impressive and companionable lawyer there, Jeffrey Smith. Jeffrey and I, with others concerned in London and Washington, worked out a system judged reliable enough to protect, where necessary, classified British information shared with the Americans. I also learned enough to fear, years later, the effect on the national interest of British Freedom of Information legislation: I was unsurprised when (by then former prime minister) Tony Blair, asked what he regretted from his period in office, put that same legislation first in his answer.

Necessary embassy contacts made with the State Department, the Pentagon, the Central Intelligence Agency (CIA), many other official arms of the US government, the White House, Congress, the media, the academic world and, importantly too, with people and organisations beyond the confines of the hotbed of politics that was – and is – Washington 'inside the beltway', all required an able and sufficient staff. The embassy was large, the consular system of posts around the United States was quite extensive: all were worked hard. Subsequent cuts in the number of people on the ground have been made at a real cost to the British official coverage of and influence in the United States, though that cost will have been limited by the quality of the staff deployed, UK-based and locally engaged. In Washington, my own access was privileged, ready and relatively easy. In those days, the US State Department concluded that the British embassy and consulates were the most effective of all. I only hope that remains true.

It was a bonus to serve in Washington during two different US administrations, one Democrat and the other Republican. The personalities of the presidents differed too. Jimmy Carter I found very pleasant and easy to talk to. He was kind, hospitable, serious but smiling. An engineer, he had an engineer's detailed analytical approach to problems, with a human approach to frailty in those who worked for him, and a desire to do good he still demonstrates. Ronald Reagan I thought jovial, and relaxed in Californian style. He could even joke with his wife Nancy and with doctors before surgery on the day he was shot, just down the road from us. He was, as a former actor, the fine communicator his reputation declares. He did have a particular compatibility and a friendship with Prime Minister Margaret Thatcher, who found him more of a soul mate than she had Jimmy Carter. Her relationship with Reagan proved of critical value to the United Kingdom on a number of occasions. Conducting relations with the Carter administration in the British interest was a different task, and, I thought, probably just a little more difficult, despite the mutual recognition of many common national interests.

It was during President Carter's term of office that the US–Iran hostage crisis occurred. Some 50 Americans were taken hostage in Tehran in November 1979, and held for 444 days – until a few hours after Jimmy Carter left office. The April 1980 failed rescue attempt was, of course, a disaster. Much has been written to explain why. In my view, some of the mistakes were to do with inter-Service and inter-Agency rivalry in Washington. For example, as a result of compromise decisions made to ensure all the rival military interests played a part in the operation, helicopters were flown by service personnel insufficiently familiar with them because they belonged to other services. There was also some inadequate practical preparation: despite rehearsals in the deserts of the United States, neither anti-sand shields nor filters were fitted to helicopters flying low under the Iranian radar. Crashes resulted from these errors. The command structure also seemed to me at fault: too many detailed decisions during the operation had to be referred to the highest levels in Washington rather than being left to operational commanders on the ground. The endeavour was a sad affair indeed. Some Iranians claimed that the US failure was due to divine intervention on behalf of Iran; and the Iranians dispersed the hostages to make another attempted rescue impracticable.

During the hostage crisis, there was cooperation between the Americans on the ground and the British embassy in Tehran. It became public knowledge that the Canadians sheltered some US diplomats who otherwise would also have become hostages. It was not then public knowledge that British diplomats in Tehran were similarly sheltering and secreting American diplomatic colleagues, in some numbers. Had that became known, it would have put the Americans concerned, and their British hosts, in immediate and real danger. And such as our ability to influence events for good in Iran by then was, it would have been severely curtailed, probably nullified. Fortunately, sufficient time elapsed before the facts became known. Sadly, our influence in Iran later further declined, mostly for other reasons, though while the United States was the 'great Satan', the United Kingdom was the 'little Satan'. But such is a worthwhile price of our vital transatlantic alliance.

The 1979 British general election brought to power a new British government led by Margaret Thatcher; and brought to an end the political appointment of Peter Jay as ambassador to Washington. I was standing with Peter in the rotunda of the British embassy in Massachusetts Avenue just after we had each given interviews for the American media about the elections, he on television and I on radio. We were following the results as they came in by radio and telephone as part of the 'election watch' event we had organised for the many interested people in Washington. We both pricked up our ears to hear a key result, which would be a strong indicator of the overall result. Labour lost that seat. Peter commented to me that that single result also marked the end of his only diplomatic mission. He had a half-share in an ocean-going yacht, and added that he planned to sail back across the Atlantic in a race. He knew I was a keen sailor, and asked me to join him, as navigator. I said I should love to, but was not adept at astral navigation (essential in those days for transoceanic sailing before electronic means and GPS). He said he would teach me. It was typical that astral navigation was one of his many skills. In the event, this enormously attractive sail was not to come my way, for duty reasons. I have always regretted that.

Our new ambassador was Sir Nicholas Henderson, who had retired from the Diplomatic Service in April 1979 as ambassador to France. Reappointment after the mandatory (but young) retirement age of 60 was almost unknown and allowed the Service to complain, largely in jest, that we had exchanged one political appointee for another. Nicko Henderson, a most successful professional diplomat, was also a character and a little eccentric – which, by the 1980s, was sadly something of a rarity in the Service. He must surely have had a distinctly able tailor as well as a particular dress sense to appear so consistently and stylishly dishevelled.

Nicko had his share of tough times as ambassador, including explaining and defending British policy in Northern Ireland to ill-informed and prejudiced television journalists, whose style was often at the rougher end of an often rough business. (I suffered myself, later, as consul-general in Chicago.) But Nicko came into his own, and much more, over the Falkland Islands conflict.

The days and weeks that began before Christmas 1981 with unauthorised Argentine-backed landings on South Georgia were increasingly tense in the South Atlantic, in London and, as Secretary of State Al Haig attempted to mediate between the military junta in Buenos Aires and the British government, also in Washington. The real intent of the Argentinians was at that stage uncertain, and Haig's efforts, bravely and well meant, were worth pursuing. We did not then know for sure that they were doomed to fail. There was much effort and action in London and Washington. There was also frank disagreement. On 29 March 1982 (when the JIC in London thought imminent invasion likely), the Americans privately but officially called for restraint from both us and the Argentinians, the implications of which 'equal' treatment our ambassador roundly rebuffed.

I was involved at my own level with a number of American arms of government, notably the State Department, the White House and the analytical and intelligence assessment side of the CIA; and with the Foreign Office and the Cabinet Office in London. Two days later, on 31 March 1982, as JIC London's representative in Washington, I presented to Nicko the crucial JIC assessment I had just received from London that the Argentines were indeed going to invade the Falklands – on 2 April. Nicko's reaction was instantaneous: that we must inform the Americans, now. I managed to swallow my own instant reaction to that: that I must first clear that action with London. Nicko had seen the historic imperative, the historic nature of the moment and the need for great speed. We needed to demonstrate that we were right; that we were the key, utterly reliable interlocutor for the United States; and that we should be believed and the correct conclusions drawn. The moral advantage and goodwill that swift ambassadorial action would give us was to pay very important dividends later. I said I would prepare a short classified piece of paper which the ambassador could hand straightaway to the secretary of state. I did so, very quickly, and without consulting London. An immediate appointment was made with Haig. Nicko told him of the British conclusion that the Argentinians would invade. Al Haig did not believe it. He checked by telephone with US intelligence. Admiral Stansfield Turner, the then director of the CIA, took a different view: that the Argentinians were only exercising. Nicko persuaded Haig, however, to take us seriously, very seriously. (I knew Stan Turner and later spoke separately to him and his analysis staff.)

We had already asked Haig to bring pressure on the Galtieri government in Buenos Aires. A message from Prime Minister Margaret Thatcher now followed to President Reagan asking him to press Galtieri to refrain from invasion. President Reagan readily agreed, and did so that day, 1 April – sadly to no avail. That day, the Falklands Islands governor, Rex Hunt, warned the islanders of the coming invasion: that night, he declared a state of emergency.

The Argentinians, of course, invaded as we had expected on 2 April 1982. Nicko Henderson had already begun to make himself the master of Falklands Islands history, geography and politics. He led the embassy in a massive effort to bring the Americans to support Great Britain in detail, in depth, logistically, diplomatically and popularly. In successfully pursuing this huge task, Nicko became widely and well respected in the United States, and something of a television star.

On the Falklands issue, the US government was divided, from the White House and Congress to the Pentagon, via the State Department and most of the others. A few government agencies were almost entirely with us. Some were not. Many were themselves split. As our fleet (which had assembled, as the chief of the naval staff had promised the prime minister it would, in 48 hours) set sail from Portsmouth on 5 April, the US press and broadcast media coverage was in large part scathing in its assessments. I remember American headlines evoking Gilbert and Sullivan as they poured scorn on our effort to recapture the islands 8,000 miles away.

Like it or not, American support was vital to British success. Extra intelligence cooperation was one key example. Logistic support – petrol, oil and lubricants – from Norfolk, Virginia across the Atlantic to Ascension Island for Royal Fleet Auxiliary support to our warships was another. The Pentagon's support for this supply (this sale) was essential. That support was hard won. By no means all the senior US officers favoured the United Kingdom and our action: some had western hemispheric careers and sympathies. Our defence attaché, Major-General Tony Boam, did a splendid job of persuasion and delivery of the British interest. 'Cap' Weinberger, US secretary of defense, was a true ally of Britain who recognised the moral imperative and believed in and supported the British cause.

It was, in truth, more than the narrow British national interest that we had to persuade the Americans to support. The highest of Western, international and moral issues and principles were involved. In crude terms, this was a first-world matter, of the defence of sovereignty, of the democratic will of a people, and of the defeat of aggression. If we had not recaptured the Falkland Islands in those tricky and dangerous Cold War days, it is not fanciful in my view to suppose that one effect might have been to encourage the Soviet Union's leaders in aggressive acts in areas of the free world they wished to influence or subjugate, and in further aggression within the Soviet sphere of influence. Nor is it difficult to believe that a number of other territories (some of strategic importance) around the world that others than the rightful occupants claimed might have been put at risk of invasion.

There were many moments of importance in the frequent exchanges between Nicko Henderson and Al Haig that illustrated the tussle between national interests and the perceptions of those interests. During his early 'shuttle diplomacy' between Buenos Aires and London, we also saw a lot of Al Haig (who, with a fine disregard for British history in India, called me 'Raj'). He and Nicko often played competitive Sunday tennis on the residence court, and had diplomatic battles as well. On one occasion, Haig had just landed in Washington after a difficult session with Galtieri, and called Nicko to his office. There he told the ambassador that unless the British prime minister agreed to pursue a certain course of action, the Galtieri government could easily fall. Nicko's reply was instant and demonstrated his professional judgment of the right way to impress and influence Haig. The ambassador said, in effect, that we were not in the business of keeping the Galtieri government in power, and allowed himself just a little emphasis on the word 'Galtieri'. I suspect that as the message sank in, this was one of the moments in the campaign when Al Haig saw the conflict in wider terms and as an imperative for the first world.

Sterling work was done throughout the campaign in New York by the British ambassador to the United Nations, Sir Anthony (Tony) Parsons, a fine man and diplomat. He worked some diplomatic magic at the United Nations, by dint of very hard work and the application of great skill. His American opposite number at the United Nations, Jeane Kirkpatrick, seemed firmly to favour Argentina. She had written her first book on Argentina, and reputedly was the guest of honour at the Argentinian UN ambassador's table on 2 April 1982, even as the Argentinians were invading the Falklands. She was not an easy colleague for Tony Parsons, who did a magnificent job, often in close consultation with Nicko Henderson.

In the event, and sometimes in the nick of time, our bilateral cooperation with the Americans in Washington worked very well, and was invaluable. In the chancery and in the military attaché's office, those most directly concerned worked all hours. In many ways we diplomats felt we were part of the effort – if at a great distance, though a little less than that from London; and Washington DC is in the same time zone as the Falklands. My office wall opposite the desk was covered with a large-scale map of the Islands. Another wall had a map of the region, from Argentina and Chile to South Georgia and the South Sandwich Islands. The maps were to prove invaluable throughout the campaign.

My job as JIC representative involved particularly close liaison with the Bureau of Intelligence and Research (INR) at the State Department and the non-operational, intelligence assessment side of the CIA at Langley. I spent many long hours at Langley discussing analyses by the JIC and the CIA, quite frequently also with representatives of other close intelligence allies. Occasionally I needed to try to resolve differences of views or analysis across the Atlantic – differences which, during the Cold War, could have key policy implications. I worked closely with three successive fine heads of the section of the

CIA responsible for this liaison work: Charley Allen (from whom I learned a great deal about intelligence assessment), Gary Foster (later inspector-general of the CIA) and Bob Gates (much later US secretary of defense). Frank Carlucci (who followed Cap Weinberger as US secretary of defense) and Evan Hineman were among the able and impressive CIA deputy directors on the analysis side of whom I saw a good deal. We made particular and good friends with Evan and his wife, Barbara, who is a talented organist. Dick Kerr was another bright star; and I remember with admiration, fondness and much sadness Bob Ames, a top Middle East CIA senior analyst with whom I worked and who died so tragically (with 62 other souls) in the appalling terrorist suicide bombing of the US embassy in Beirut of April 1983.

Liaison work with the CIA during both the Iran hostage crisis and the Falklands campaign was especially valuable and rewarding professionally. Discussing assessments with INR at the State Department was also intellectually stimulating and helpful. The head of INR, Bill Bowdler, was a fine professional. Working with him was Bill McAfee, well into his seventies, and as pleasant and wise a colleague as one could wish for: a good example of why we in the British Diplomatic Service were wrong to retire everyone by the age of 60. The brain power in INR was impressive indeed. Hilary and I made good and enduring friends with a senior and very able academic who served in INR for a time: Dr (later Professor) Carol Baumann (a former Marshall scholar – see Chapter 8) and her husband Richard. We cemented the friendship later in Chicago, and have since exchanged memorable family visits around the world.

INR had a 24-hour operation. Soon after the Argentine invasion of the Falklands, I had a late-night session with the duty officer in charge, an admiral on secondment to the State Department. The meeting was memorable for the age it took me to persuade the admiral that INR should help the Brits with important classified information. Finally, he was convinced, and agreed to help, that night and any time thereafter, as a matter of urgency, whenever we needed. It was a wonderful moment at about 2am when he smiled his eventual agreement, a moment marred only by his immediate assault on the English tongue, declaring, with all seriousness: 'Gee, Roj, I guess we're now in an on-going prioritisation situation'.

It was a serious loss to the United Kingdom when on 5 April, three days after the invasion, Lord Carrington resigned as foreign and commonwealth secretary. Parliament was baying for blood; there had been a failure of diplomacy when our negotiations in New York with the Argentinians stalled; and Lord Carrington's honourable resignation united the party in power. I was working with Nicko in his office in the embassy when Peter Carrington telephoned to say he was going to resign. Nicko tried heroically and eloquently but in vain to dissuade him, as, I learned later, others had too. Ministers of state at the FCO Richard (later Lord) Luce and Lord Privy Seal Humphrey Atkins (later Lord Colnbrook) also resigned from the government, in the wake of Lord Carrington.

Far too many times as the campaign proceeded, I heard in my office, terrible night after dreadful day, trenchant and tragic messages of disaster for our sailors and soldiers. There were pithy accounts too, of course, of successes and advances – often made, we knew, against the odds and due to inspired and courageous military tactics and derring-do, and to some slices of well-earned luck. Finally, on 14 June, in that same office we heard, in very close to real time, that the Argentinians were surrendering and the British, having won the battles on the heights above Stanley, were marching into the capital. That was a moment of lasting joy and enormous relief.

Margaret Thatcher had appointed Francis Pym in Lord Carrington's place. During the campaign itself, on 2 May, Francis Pym was visiting Washington for the second time. The British team was working with him in the library of the ambassador's residence, when I was called from the meeting to take a classified telephone call. It was from the permanent under-secretary of state at the FCO, Sir Antony Acland who, together with his immediate and recent predecessor, Sir Michael Palliser, sat at the Falklands cabinet meetings. Antony told me that the cabinet had just met to consider amending the rules of engagement under which the Royal Navy was operating in the South Atlantic. The situation was complex, and I was glad to have the map in my mind. This was, of course, the question of an attack against the Argentine cruiser, the *General Belgrano*, by the British submarine shadowing her. The cabinet were in favour of the proposed amendment, but the prime minister thought it right to have the foreign secretary's view and vote. Time was of the essence. Would I please consult the foreign secretary while Sir Antony waited, and report back? I did as bidden and explained the problem to the foreign secretary, who responded firmly that the rules of engagement should indeed be changed as proposed. I reported back. Time was certainly of the essence: the instruction would have to be transmitted to the submarine within the very limited period when she could receive a signal. It was not long after that that Argentina's light cruiser *General Belgrano* was sunk.

A few Falklands footnotes: to put it mildly, the militarily important (some even say the most decisive) action of the campaign, the sinking of the *Belgrano*, was controversial, both in London and around the world. A few months after the Falklands campaign, while I was doing my subsequent (and very different) job in London, I was asked to give a detailed account of that exchange of views and instructions for the official Franks Inquiry. Weeks later I was relieved to be told by an official of the inquiry that my remembered account tallied exactly with that of the foreign secretary. Years later, Francis Pym and I exchanged reminiscences when seated together at a feast at Magdalene College, Cambridge, where I had been invited by an old school friend and now distinguished and much published historian (who later drew my attention to a different but also confrontational episode in British diplomatic history – see Chapter 9).

The second footnote is that an Argentinian admiral asked, a few months after the Falklands were recaptured, for his view on the *Belgrano* sinking, said that he would have done exactly the same in our circumstances. Another is that two Falkland-related events occurred over a decade later while I was ambassador in, of all apparently unrelated countries, Indonesia. One was a visit to Jakarta by former governor Rex Hunt; the other event involved Margaret Thatcher (see Chapter 9). And the last footnote is that Hilary and I visited the Falkland Islands and South Georgia in 2007, visits that furthered my understanding of the battles and our admiration for the British forces and their exploits in defence of freedom.

Professionally, my four-year tour in Washington was rather like two separate postings. When President Carter was succeeded by President Reagan, well over 2,000 people in Washington left their jobs and, it seemed, rather more than 2,000 arrived to replace them; the real estate rental market leapt. Hilary and I had to move house; and the embassy had to deal with many new senior officials and a different set of US politicians, often with different approaches to world affairs, international problems and bilateral issues.

The British embassy was also atypical of posts abroad in that members of the Diplomatic Service were in a distinct minority. The embassy was a mini-Whitehall – and no doubt still is, especially given the further reductions in FCO resources over the years. Home civil servants were in the majority, and were well rewarded. There was a real need for those officials' wives (I can recall no dependent husbands in those days) to have help with the business of settling into a new environment and living abroad, even in the United States. So there was a British Embassy Wives Association (BEWA), which Hilary chaired for two years. The association organised support for newly arrived wives, with advice and information on housing, schools, doctors, dentists, shopping, driving tests and licences, and much more on social, welfare and charity undertakings. In some ways, BEWA mirrored the then Diplomatic Service Wives Association (DSWA), which was headquartered in London and had a branch in every post abroad with UK-based Diplomatic Service staff. (Nowadays, politically correctly and accurately, DSWA is known as the Diplomatic Service Families Association.) BEWA of course played no part in DSWA lobbying of the FCO for improvements to conditions of service.

Every other year, BEWA organised and ran a massive Christmas charity bazaar, to benefit perhaps the Save the Children Fund or the International Red Cross – always a major international charity. This event needed a great deal of work to attract the great and good of the Washington scene, American and international, and to raise a great deal of money. The bazaar was also a significant Washington social event in the run-up to Christmas – part of its success as a fund-raiser. Charity work is traditionally ancillary to diplomacy, usually run mainly by wives. In the third world, such efforts can do much direct good in themselves and for the reputation of the United Kingdom. In a first-world country such as the United States, it is advisable to benefit international charities rather than to meddle in local welfare matters.

It was just before Christmas 1979 that Margaret Thatcher got to know President Carter during her first visit to Washington as prime minister, accompanied by Lord Carrington. That visit was necessary and proved useful. In many ways it was memorable, including for a most hospitable Christmas party in the White House, when the US secretary of state along with Kirk Douglas and other assorted luminaries led the singing of 'The Twelve Days of Christmas'. Both the Thatchers and Lord Carrington sensibly declined the president's invitation to sing solos. That brisk December evening there was even, incongruously, a brief reminder of the fun of diplomatic life in Bulgaria when the British defence attaché's official Jaguar swept through the opened front gates of the White House. The car removed its exhaust system with a satisfying bang and subsequent roar as its silencer hit the steel locking mechanism set in the ground between the two gates.

Prime Minister Margaret Thatcher's first visit to President Reagan's Washington, and to New York, was also memorable – for her unremitting hard work (from 5.30am to well past midnight), for the reception she received, for the bonds she made with Ronald Reagan, for the major formal dinner party at the ambassador's residence attended by the Reagans, and for a speech she made in New York. The speech followed Mrs Thatcher's acceptance of the Donovan Award (made for services to freedom) after a splendid dinner in the Waldorf Astoria.

As instructed, I had sent to London a first draft of the speech some weeks earlier; I had heard nothing more of it. That last evening of her visit, Mrs Thatcher was unsurprisingly exhausted, but showed no sign of it, save to a few of us British officials with whom she had a drink before dinner. Mrs Thatcher and her principal hosts were seated at a top table, on the stage, but so far apart from each other, that conversation was difficult. Hilary and I were at one of many tables below, in the front stalls, as it were. There must have been a thousand or more at dinner. During the meal, the prime minister took the speech and a fountain pen from her handbag and, turning the pages, wrote at some length. I wondered (and worried, so tired had she shown herself in private) what was happening to the speech.

When she stood to deliver it, there was not a trace of that tiredness. In a strong voice she spoke at length on East–West relations and on how and why to deal with the Soviet Union: a speech transformed by the addition (that evening, in her own hand) of a string of well-judged Winston Churchill references or quotations to illustrate the points and arguments. She received a thunderous standing ovation and her speech was well and widely reported throughout the United States. Such is the force of politically generated adrenalin.

It was at the residence dinner that I much enjoyed conversation with Denis Thatcher. Later, I could not decide whether *Private Eye* caricatured him, or the reverse. At one point I asked if he would like a refill for his glass: his immediate and twinkling reply warmly welcomed the idea of a 'swift sharpener'.

After four years, we were sad indeed to leave Washington. We had made good and enduring friends. We had had an immense variety of fun and experiences. Out of the office, these included flying down into the Grand Canyon; traversing Bryce Canyon on horseback; driving around the United States with our boys one summer holiday; sailing and racing from Annapolis (even, once, in a 45-knot wind); watching a guest, departing from a mulled-wine Christmas party in our own house on an icy and snowy day, walk down the garden path steaming like a plum pudding from his bald pate; eating ice-cream with Jack and Gloria Rivers, the embassy chaplain and his wife, perched atop the roof of the rectory the better to watch the Independence Day fireworks; and enjoying a dance given at the residence by the Jays, at which US National Security Advisor Zbigniew Brzezinski danced an almost impossibly athletic twist. Our younger son Charles went to the Carters' Christmas party at the White House, where he was dazzled by the veteran newscaster Walter Cronkite. There were equally memorable experiences, but much less fun, such as one Sunday having ourselves to clear our first rented house's basement flooded with backed-up sewerage from along the road. Later, our elder son,

John, learned to drive in Washington, passed his test at 16, and then had to wait a clearly most frustrating year back in England before he could qualify there. (Charles passed his test, also at 16, in Chicago, and suffered similar frustration. So that was fair.)

I had a superb job in the embassy, a job once described by Tom Brimelow, who did it many years earlier, as one of the best in the Diplomatic Service – and that when he was about to retire as head of the Service. The job also carried with it a privileged involvement in the international high politics that is the stuff of Washington's official life. As an embassy during those four years, I believe we defended and advanced British interests across a wide front, from the Cold War via bilateral problems and Rhodesia to the Falklands.

So Washington was another fortunate, professionally demanding, stimulating and immensely worthwhile four-year posting. It was the only one from which I had almost to drag a reluctant, weeping Hilary to the aeroplane when we left for London in the summer of 1982. Neither of us dreamt that some three years later, after a most unusual job in London (see Chapter 9), we would return to the United States.

CHAPTER 8

CONSUL-GENERAL, CHICAGO

Hilary and I were indeed surprised as well as thrilled to return to the United States for our next posting, in 1985. The job was British consul general in Chicago, covering ten states of the Midwest. In Royal Navy terms, this was to be my first command. We had driven around and across the United States a few times, but had by-passed Chicago itself. It was a delight to discover this exciting, brilliant if self-conscious city, which is a secret also to many Americans. The politics were often raw, rough – and racist. Irish too. Chicago has a rough, tough trading and political history. It was, for example, the motor force of agriculture, industry and trade, and the cradle of the 'America First' movement. Chicago was Al Capone's stamping ground, and we found Chicagoans who were rather proud of that. Crime and social problems were still rife and serious. The weather is less than attractive for much of the year. Winter is characterised by distinctly sub-zero temperatures, worsened by high winds. Lake Michigan freezes, including its waves, and warnings are broadcast against walking the dog, for paws would stick and freeze to the ground.

However, Chicago is a most civilised city too, with some of the world's most exciting architecture, which, unlike that of less spacious New York, can easily be seen and admired from street level. Chicago is the home of several world class universities, welcoming ones, and of academic breakthroughs and Nobel prizes. The city boasts one of the world's best symphony orchestras – and how glad we were to be present often when Sir Georg Solti conducted. It also has the Chicago Civic Opera, which shares productions with New York's Met and London's Covent Garden, and which we also attended delightedly.

The Art Institution is another international star we followed. Sculpture of the best kind adorns the streets. There are the blues and jazz, theatre, festivals and literary luminaries. Chicago is a vibrant, strong, sporting, passionate city and, so big is Lake Michigan, has a distinctive maritime feel.

Chicago can be a touch neurotic. It tells itself it has a 'Second City Syndrome' – second, by implication, to New York. The financial services industry of Chicago was in our time only just second to, and much appreciated and admired by City of London experts. I once wrote a despatch to London entitled 'Chicago in Psychosis'. That, however, was a piece of colour: a faithful description of a few weeks when the Chicago Bears (American football team) for the first time reached the Superbowl, the grandest of all cup finals, held on 26 January 1986 in New Orleans. The city really went mad. On the day of the Bowl itself, the Chicago Symphony Orchestra's matinée was started an hour or two early, so that all present could go home afterwards and watch the match on television. At the end of the concert, the Chicago Symphony Choir joined the orchestra on stage, with Lady Solti and Hilary leading in the sopranos, and under the baton of Sir Georg Solti wearing a bear's head, performed with the orchestra the only really musical rendering ever heard of the Chicago Bears' fighting song: 'Go, Bears, Go!' The audience, on their feet throughout and joining in, demanded seven encores. I shall never forget as a once-only walk-on bass, the feeling of willpower and musical control emanating from Sir Georg Solti and his baton.

The Bears won the Superbowl. Their triumphant return to Chicago involved an appearance before many thousands, gathered excitedly, adoringly, in the main square, Daley Plaza. The team was so mobbed on the way from the airport that they arrived hours late. The then mayor of Chicago, Harold Washington, was also host that day to Archbishop Tutu, whom he introduced to the vast crowd in Daley Plaza. We watched from my office on the thirteenth floor of our building. Some ten years later aboard the Blue Train between Cape Town and Victoria Falls, it was a delight to meet Archbishop Tutu and to remind him of how brilliantly and effectively he took advantage of the chance to address at length such a huge, captive congregation.

Later that same year, the Chicago Bears, who featured boldly in the Illinois and national sporting scenes, were due to play a pre-season exhibition game at Wembley Stadium against the Dallas Cowboys. Their famously successful coach, Mike Ditka, telephoned me one day to ask if I would come and talk to the team. He explained that they were reluctant to travel to London at all because they feared for their security there. This was in the immediate aftermath of the US bombing of Gaddafi's Libya in April 1986 (which followed the bombing of a Berlin nightclub by Libyan agents and Libyan support for the Irish Republican Army (IRA) and other terrorist organisations. The US raids were from aircraft carriers and, crucially, from two RAF stations in England. Hilary and I both visited the Bears at their pre-season training camp; and then I alone was invited into the 'locker room' – a huge hangar of a building, divided into two, for 'Offense' and 'Defense', by a two-storey high folding door, shoved open with tremendous strength and speed by a defensive lineman, William Perry. He was known for his size and stature, in a reference to American double-door refrigerators, as The Fridge. An inhibiting start to my 'team talk'! I began to speak about the reality of life in London, the welcome the team would receive, the absence of threat and the lack of any need for extra security, but it soon became clear to me that I was not on the right wave-length: I was not putting my message across at all effectively. I sensed that the Midwestern fear of the foreign was only a small part of the problem. Misrepresentation in the US information media about the effect of the US Air Force bombers flying from the British bases was another part; but I felt that there was something more. I tried to reassure, to engage members of the team in conversation, and to understand their irrational fears and what else was worrying them. I found the running back, Walter Payton, particularly helpful. He was a fine, thoughtful man who commanded the respect of the others. Known as 'Sweetness' in American football circles, he was bright and caring. Subtly, intelligently, during the conversation with the whole squad, he alone led me to conclude that there was indeed an underlying issue: the players' union was pressing the team members to refuse to go to England for the planned pre-season game without considerably better terms, for wives' travel and pay. I was a bit cross that Mike Ditka had not briefed me on this key background matter, though I understood why. I shifted my ground and joked with the players, including about how disappointed their wives and girlfriends would be not to visit and to shop in London. I contrasted the Bears' reluctance with the evident keenness of the Dallas Cowboys to take them on at Wembley, and I even suggested that there might be accusations that the Bears feared losing to the Cowboys. Finally I felt I was gaining some ground. We parted on friendly and positive terms. I remonstrated later, fairly gently, with Mike Ditka, and suggested he should further develop some of my themes in discussions with the union. The game at Wembley did take place. So sadly, Walter Payton died at 45, from a rare cancer.

For spectators, American football is more of a family game than we expected. Whole families happily attend and enjoy weekend matches, complete sometimes with picnics – and sit on hard benches, even when they are covered in ice as they were for us, once, at the Bears' home stadium, Soldier Field. Violence and bad temper seem unknown in the crowds, largely because violence is experienced vicariously and in a remarkably organised and predictable way on the field of play. No wonder the players wear such ample armour.

Harold Washington was, of course, a loyal fan of the Chicago Bears and a successful politician with a robust sense of humour. It was that same mayor who heard Hilary deliver a speech in my stead one evening when I had been double-booked and spoke elsewhere in Chicago. The following morning Harold Washington telephoned to say that he had chosen the better of the two events to attend: could Hilary please give more of my speeches?

It was a sad and politically important moment when, in late November 1987, Harold Washington died of a heart attack. A lying-in-state was arranged, and we were invited to pay our respects, by way of a separate entry for VIPs. The logistic arrangements had been made hastily and were less than perfect, which meant that we were ushered to pass by and pause at Harold Washington's body three times instead of the expected once. Harold would have enjoyed the joke of triple respect paid. The error was probably in part because of the enormous press of mostly black people from Chicago's South Side,

Harold's political stronghold. There Harold Washington was loved and revered, and the emotion at his lying-in-state was visible, audible, palpable and impressive. Thousands came. It was a memorable time.

Irish politicians took charge and installed an interim mayor for just eight days, while the City Council elected Eugene Sawyer to complete Harold Washington's term. Later, at a dinner we gave for our ambassador, visiting from Washington – by now the most accomplished and amusing Antony Acland (now KG GCMG GCVO), former permanent-under Secretary at the FCO where I had worked for him – Antony asked Hilary who would be mayor of Chicago following the next elections. Unhesitatingly, Hilary answered, 'Richard Daly'. After dinner, I explained how the politics were rather more complicated than that implied and that it was not certain that Rich Daly would win. I should have stayed silent: Hilary was proved resoundingly right. Rich Daly was a courageous and dynamic mayor, whose father had been mayor during the visit aboard the royal yacht in 1959 by the young Queen and the Duke of Edinburgh. Chicago folklore insists that as Daley senior waved off HMY *Britannia*, he yelled across the widening gap of Lake Michigan waters, 'Next time, bring the kids'; thus no doubt ensuring even more political support in Chicago. Rich Daley Junior proved to be the longest serving mayor in Chicago's history.

The job in Chicago was manifold and fascinating. My initial superior as ambassador in Washington was the witty, wise and friendly Sir Oliver Wright, who kindly and supportively also let me get on with the job. It was, in important part, a job of commercial diplomacy: several of the first-class staff were devoted full-time to that work – and were good at it. The Confederation of British Industry (CBI) had told me when I went to see them shortly before I took up the post that, to them, the Midwest of the United States was a black hole. Staff in the consulate-general took that as a challenge. We wrote an article for the CBI's journal to illuminate that black hole and to offer advice on how best to exploit it: subsequently, the trade figures rose further, most satisfactorily. The Midwest market place for British goods was a tough one, but a rich one, too, and rewarding when intelligently and assiduously approached.

The promotion of inward investment from the Midwest to the United Kingdom was a high priority task, for me and for some more expert full-time investment promotion staff. However, there were unnecessary and seriously inhibiting rivalries and divisions at home among the United Kingdom's Regional Development Agencies (RDAs), several of whom had sent representatives to be based in Chicago. They were competing among each other for investment by Midwest American companies. Negotiations could take months: the American companies quickly spotted that the (varying) RDA offers of tax breaks and rent deals on factory and other space could each be improved by a little pressure and references to rival offers. This process swiftly and sometimes even sharply depleted the value of potential American investment to the UK economy as the deals became sweeter at every stage of negotiation. The Americans naturally pressed home and even occasionally, at the last moment, let in our commercial rivals in Europe, such as the French, to win the business.

We argued with London and did something in the field to reduce this waste of opportunity and effort: those measures may have helped. Certainly, both US investments in the UK economy and UK investments in the US economy, running into hundreds of billions of pounds sterling, have increased significantly since my time in Chicago.

I was particularly keen to promote Northern Ireland as a destination for Midwest investment in Europe, and we had some real advantages in this work. There were the especially favourable tax and other arrangements the British government had put in place. There was an excellent man from Belfast on my staff, James Gray. However, try as I might, I could not, in my three years in the post, persuade that massive external investor from Chicago, McDonald's, to open a franchise in Belfast. Their senior decision-makers seemed transfixed both by press accounts of the bombings and troubles in Northern Ireland and by their own experience with a fairly recent bomb in a McDonald's restaurant in California. I argued the case, and might eventually have overcome at any rate the first of these inhibitions; but it was not to be until some years after I left Chicago that McDonald's hamburgers appeared in Belfast.

The Irishness, so often really pseudo-Irishness, of the Midwest was a key to the most testing and difficult of the constant problems the consulate-general faced. The same difficulty, with variations, applied in Boston, New York and to the embassy in Washington. The Chicago river was dyed bright emerald green on St Patrick's Day every year; the pubs sold bright green beer; and a massive parade marched several miles through the centre of Chicago. 'Noraid' collections were taken up along the way, the money going to the IRA. These were bad times in the Province; and the Chicago view was based very largely on prejudice and on history embroidered, sadly distorted and thus transmitted down the generations as gospel truth since the Irish first emigrated to the United States as a result of the potato famine.

Chicago is a television town, and Hilary and I were very glad to have attended a first-class course the BBC ran in the 1980s for the FCO on the art of being interviewed by TV journalists ranging from the gentle, via the rough and tough to the really hard Chicagoans. When the problems in Northern Ireland seemed to reach new lows nearly every week for a long time, I would often be interviewed on television to argue the UK case. I remembered the lessons learned at the BBC, and survived – all except once. I had always followed the wise BBC advice to avoid any but live interviews. On this occasion there was good reason to state the facts and to argue the British government position on the latest developments, but I had an unbreakable engagement many miles away from Chicago. I declined the request, made that morning, to be interviewed, as usual, live on the evening news of one of the several Midwest channels, and I explained why. Later that morning the presenter himself asked me if I would record an interview the channel would then play on the news. I declined again, politely. He pressed. He was a well-known television personality, something of a Jeremy Paxman of the Midwest, and I thought there was a good chance he would not wish his reputation to suffer by being associated with editing that might be partial or unfair. There was that good reason for not letting the UK case go by default; and the TV station would not accept my deputy since he was not in formal charge. Eventually I agreed to record 30 seconds, on the clear understanding that the 30 seconds would be shown, uncut and in one piece. We shook hands to seal the agreement.

I wrote, memorised and rehearsed the 30 second script. The TV team arrived, and I said my piece to camera. I half suspected something might be amiss when the cameraman and the junior producer with him were so evidently surprised that I had stuck to my side of the bargain, recording exactly 30 seconds. So I reminded them of the terms of the agreement, which I said firmly I expected to be honoured. I ensured that we, too, shook hands. That evening, as I recall the video I saw the next day, my 30 seconds had been cut into seven or eight pretty inchoate snippets, which were interspersed with longer, passionate pieces from the sobbing mother of a girl terrorist the British police had just arrested. The UK government position and case went completely by the board; and all over again I learned the BBC lesson – the hardest way.

In Springfield, the capital of Illinois, I spoke to both houses of the legislature together, principally about Northern Ireland. It went well enough that I thought I should try to repeat the exercise in another, even more 'Irish' state, Minnesota. I told my Republic of Ireland consular colleague what I was planning. He was professional and supportive: the Republic government too had an interest in objective facts overcoming poetic and passionate misreadings and beliefs.

It proved more difficult to negotiate with the Minnesota legislature in St Paul, but we reached an agreement. I was to speak for 15 minutes to both houses gathered together. As I rose after the speaker's introduction, an army of emerald-green blazers stood up all around the semi-circular balcony, and unfurled anti-British banners. I said my piece, to only occasional heckling. Either the speaker was reasonably satisfied or he had undertaken to the IRA sympathisers that they could have another go at me, because, in accordance with our agreement, he announced that his chambers behind the chair were now available for further discussion with the consul-general.

In the chambers, discussion was free and uninhibited. A good few green blazers joined us, and I fielded a good number of questions. I was thinking that survival was possible, then likely, when the sergeant at arms arrived, complete with mace. He came smartly to attention before me and announced that I was behaving contrary to the provisions of the Foreign Agents Act, and that he would now escort me from the legislature.

I had only once glanced at the US act to which he referred, and certainly never expected to have to know its provisions in detail, still less to be challenged under it. This was a friendly country with which the United Kingdom had thoroughly good, frank and warm relations, for heaven's sake. I said none of this, deciding simply and hopefully to call his bluff. I said as lightly as I could something like 'Nonsense, sir', and resumed answering the question I had been addressing. The Minnesota sergeant at arms said no more, subsided and withdrew to the back of the room. After another five or ten minutes, I brought proceedings to a close and made thankfully for the exit and the official Jaguar outside. I may say that the supportive presence of Hilary and of Caroline Cracraft, the information officer at the consulate-general, helped, as ever, enormously, at such events.

A footnote to this and similar episodes was that each time we regained the Jaguar and its flag, a large Irish wolfhound, with demonstrators as escorts, was being led a repeated circular walk around and close to the car. This seemed to be designed to inhibit us and our stalwart Derbyshire driver, David Beakey, and perhaps to provide a photo-opportunity. The dog and his handlers were persistent, following us to several of the ten states of the consular district. However, neither photo-opportunity nor inhibition occurred: we made good and familiar friends with the wolfhound.

The Northern Ireland issues and the importance of putting our case across in the United States also explained why, when he was secretary of state for Northern Ireland, Tom King (later Lord King) accepted an invitation from the well-respected Chicago Council on Foreign Relations to speak to an influential audience there. It was quite a difficult evening, and I recall Tom King working hard to ensure that during his thoughtful speech, the inevitable television camera in the centre of the hall, complete with long lens, could record a sound-bite of use to the UK cause and illuminating the truth, rather than the imaginative nonsense so often portrayed in the Midwest.

In an effort to keep up to date and to improve my credentials and credibility when speaking on Northern Ireland issues around the Midwest, I visited the Province several times, and Hilary and I spent a working week there. We were extremely well looked after, including by the police, and during an intensive programme saw much of Northern Ireland, met the leading politicians, and became fully and deeply informed on issues, attitudes and policies. We were much struck, at those difficult of times for the Province, by the sheer weight of numbers of good people doing good work there quietly, carefully and, by increments, effectively. The passions we encountered helped our understanding of the depths of the divides, but the positives we found were even then remarkably many and widespread. We visited Londonderry and there met a thoughtful, hard-working and deeply caring mayor. We also encountered dogs especially and well trained to chase and bark at British Army vehicles. The whole visit was impressive and educational in so many ways, including discussions with politicians of both sides of the divide. Then, one fine afternoon and evening, we were astounded to be lent a lovely yacht by a fine gentleman architect who did not know me from Adam, but said he had been reading about me. The relevant charts were already open on the chart table below. The kind and trusting architect left for home. He did leave a crew member aboard, sitting right astern, shucking fresh oysters. We sailed the length of Strangford Lough into the Irish Sea and back. No wonder we fell for Northern Ireland.

On one visit I made there alone, I called on the then secretary of state for the Province, Douglas Hurd. Half that day was spent at Long Kesh in the H-Blocks at the Maze prison, meeting convicted IRA terrorists. I had a jokey exchange of views with a prisoner I met in the washrooms he was cleaning. Only after the chance encounter did the governor let me know that this was the infamous 'Shankhill butcher'.

Duty visits to Chicago did become frequent among Northern Ireland politicians, Westminster and London luminaries, some senior officials, cabinet ministers and royals. The most delightful of all the cabinet ministerial guests was probably the then foreign secretary, Geoffrey Howe, who performed his official duties with grace, diligence and effectiveness, and for whom we made time for a little rare relaxation at the weekend, to practise his also rare skill with a camera. His pictures of Chicago architecture seen from the river should be a prize collection.

Among royal visitors, HRH The Prince of Wales did particularly well as a commercial ambassador for Britain. He opened a British week that the consulate-general and the up-market Marshall Field's had organised together, and worked hard at a wider brief too. He also did well on the demanding polo field, despite once, at speed, being thrown off his mount, who then also fell – on top of the prince. Both were badly winded. In the stand, I was just a little concerned for some minutes, until the prince, who had been surrounded by team mates and hidden from view, climbed to his feet and later mounted another polo pony. My concern was increased by the thought that I might have to use the rather heavy and cumbersome radio telephone I had with me. Incredible as it would be today, it was then the only means of instant communication from the polo ground, which was a long way outside Chicago. Part of my brief was to telephone the Princess of Wales if Prince Charles was at all seriously hurt, so that Her Royal Highness immediately had the facts, rather than a press story that might be inaccurate. The twist in the tale was that when the double fall occurred on the polo field, the rather numerous British press at the polo ground promptly offered me (vainly, I hasten to add) considerable sums for the use of the radio telephone!

Towards the end of his clearly successful visit to Chicago it seemed to me that the Prince of Wales was in thoughtful, even doubting mood, questioning whether the job he was doing for the United Kingdom was effective. In answer to his question I said that I was sure his visit would indeed help the cause of UK trade and inward investment promotion. He came back down the steps of his aircraft just before it took off from Chicago to challenge me to prove what I had said in a quantified report say six months later. And could the same please be done for Boston, where he had been just before Chicago? The trade part of the question was easy to prove and quantify. The inward investment part was more complex, but we had constructed our various guest lists with some care to include potential investors we were pursuing, and Prince Charles had read and used his brief well.

We followed up with those guests, and in the report could and did make a causal connection of some validity.

My predecessor as consul-general, Gordon Jewkes (thereafter post-conflict governor of the Falkland Islands in succession to Rex Hunt), had a good deal to do with the initiation of a major cultural three-month British festival of Minnesota in late 1985. Supported by the British Council and by Honeywell, the festival was led and organised in large part by the chairman of the organising committee, an imaginative, generous-minded and splendidly effective vice-president of Honeywell, Dick Weber. The Minnesota Symphony Orchestra was among the leading attractions, conducted by the then just knighted Sir Neville Marriner. The wonderful Sir David Willcocks conducted the King's Singers (whose then counter-tenor, Nigel Perrin, is now a top-rank choral conductor in his own right). There was children's theatre, new opera from Glasgow, the Guthrie Theater and much more. There were festival publications galore, including magazines and a cookery book. David Hockney designed a carrier bag. The streets of St Paul and Minneapolis were decorated with expertly and attractively designed banners.

Especially welcome and delightful Royal visitors who came to support the Festival were HRH Princess Alexandra and her husband, Angus Ogilvie. They spent six days in Minnesota, and impressed many Americans mightily with their professionalism and genuine enjoyment of the experience. They charmed Hilary and me when they sought 'time off' on the Saturday for a private picnic lunch. We arranged for their Illinois state police driver to take them to a little known beauty spot, where he left them discreetly alone. Only later did they explain what I suppose I should have known: that this was their wedding anniversary. Oh, for those days less pressured by today's inescapable demands of close security.

The good done for Britain, the goodwill created and the evident rise in our national standing and cultural influence lasted a long while and helped in trade and even in political endeavour. Without that festival it is possible that we would have had no hearing at all on Northern Ireland in that part of the United States. It is sad indeed, and a national loss, that the British Council no longer has the resources to include such major international events in the fine work it does and supports around the world.

The Duchess of Gloucester stayed with us in Chicago during a charity visit, and was among the many house guests whose company we much enjoyed. Perhaps there was a little fellow feeling: she was once a member of the Danish embassy in London. HRH The Princess Margaret came to Chicago on a private visit as the guest of the Louises. John Louis had been American ambassador in London. An excellent dinner *chez* Louis was followed by Princess Margaret playing the grand piano. There was even some impressive singing.

Having ten states of the Midwest in the Chicago consular district meant travel around them for various official purposes. In Kansas City and St Louis within the consular district there were honorary British consuls who helped a good deal in securing British national interests, mainly with consular and representational work. This was a good arrangement, repeated, with appropriate variations, in many countries around the world. Put baldly, the honorary consul had a formal unpaid appointment and an official plaque bearing the UK coat of arms for his office, which helped with his standing and reputation – and implicitly with his own business. In return the consul carried out representational duties, provided invaluable advice (including commercial and investment advice on occasion), and was the first port of call for consular work such as help with British citizens in serious difficulties. The honorary consuls had to be well chosen: my experience throughout my career was always of excellent ones.

In St Louis, Missouri, the honorary British consul was Frank Cornwell and later R.A.K. Smith. The consulate-general cooperated with both regularly. Hilary and I did some useful work with them spreading the UK message and working in support of British industry. Also in Missouri is Westminster College, a liberal arts college at Fulton, which has the only Sir Christopher Wren church in the United States. This is a wonderful story, which began in the Second World War after the Luftwaffe reduced the City of London church of St Mary Aldermanbury to rubble. The post-war rationalisation of the many churches in the City resulted, after negotiations, in a piece of inspired thinking by the then president of Westminster College. Fund-raising followed, as did much devoted work in labelling the pieces of stone, shattered wood and rubble; transporting it all across the Atlantic and on to Fulton; and rebuilding it there, with the vital aid of Christopher Wren's 1667 drawings. A most successful architectural decision was to rebuild the church omitting the frills and furbelows added by the Victorians: the church is a pure and lovely example of Wren's work. A fine organ was commissioned from a London organ-builder. Under the church, an extensive undercroft was first constructed, to house what later became a thriving centre for the academic study of Churchill, his life and his times.

Westminster College and its Christopher Wren church also became the centre for an annual speech by a world leader, a tradition started when the president of the college invited Winston Churchill to speak there in 1946 after he lost the general election that followed the Second World War. The college president had the good sense to pass the invitation through the White House, whose incumbent was 'I'm from Missouri' Harry Truman. Truman wrote on the bottom of the letter of invitation words to the effect that if Churchill accepted, Truman would accompany him from the US east coast to Missouri, by train. This duly happened. The train journey would have taken two days, and the two leaders evidently talked extensively, played a lot of cards and consumed quantities of brandy. The speech Churchill made at Fulton, Missouri was entitled 'Sinews of Peace', but is widely known as 'The Iron Curtain Speech': it was the first time Churchill used the phrase in public, 'From Stettin in the Baltic to Trieste in the Adriatic, an Iron Curtain has descended across the Continent'.

Winston Churchill has been followed at the Fulton rostrum by US presidents, by Margaret Thatcher and by other world leaders. Westminster College has a tradition of appointing academic worthies, benefactors and even British consuls-general in Chicago as honorary Churchill fellows. After we had left Chicago, Gorbachev in the Soviet Union introduced *perestroika* and *glasnost*. I wrote to the college from Indonesia, suggesting that they invite President Gorbachev. They did so in 1992. He accepted. His speech had to be given in the open air, because thousands flocked to hear it and no building there could accommodate them. I heard from someone present that while Gorbachev's speech is known in the United States as a declaration of the end of the Cold War, it also contained far less than complimentary references to Churchill. It even implicitly accused him of responsibility for the Second World War! Such, perhaps, was a strand in Soviet revisionist history, even in Gorbachev's day – or perhaps Gorbachev may have needed some political counterweight to his more open policies. The speech was not, I gathered, well received. The episode certainly illuminates the circumspection with which advice from Churchill fellows should be viewed.

The honorary British consul in Kansas City was the President of Hallmark International, Stanley Hamilton OBE. Stanley's advice was always of the soundest, he was a great support in many and varied ways, and he did much work for the United Kingdom. Stanley was our host on many useful visits to Kansas, including one with Mary Soames, when she was presented with a particularly fine set of reproductions of her father's paintings: ones she did not herself possess.

Travel around the consular district included, inter alia, a poignant one to Ames, Iowa in the deep winter of December 1985. We made the 360 miles-long snowy journey there in the official Jaguar to honour four British students who had just been killed in a tragic air accident. They had been studying at Iowa State University, and played in the ladies' hockey team there. The team had been flying back to the university from a match in two small university aircraft – that being the normal means of transport in the Midwest where distances are so great. Both aircraft had crashed. The hockey team was a source of much collegiate pride. A stage erected in the centre of the large university stadium was the setting for a memorial service to all those killed in the dreadful crash. The stadium was crowded. After the moving service, those who wished were invited to meet the clergy and the British consul-general and his wife. Hundreds of young students came to express their evidently abundant grief. It seemed both Midwestern and compelling that male students formed a long queue to speak to me about these so popular girls, while an even longer line of young ladies came to weep on Hilary's increasingly dampened shoulder. All told how wonderful the British girls had been and how shattering was their loss to this (huge) university. All this helped when I wrote to parents at home in the United Kingdom, and when the team coach flew there to call on them, to explain, to offer condolences and to pay tribute.

A particularly rewarding task for the consul-general was membership of the regional Marshall scholarships committee. Its chairman, Bill Gaines, himself a former Fulbright scholar, conducted a rigorous and disciplined sifting system, and chaired lengthy and searching interviews of splendidly bright young post-graduate Americans who were seeking one of up to 40 of these prestigious scholarships to the best British universities. The 'Marshalls', known to the cognoscenti as the academic version of the Rhodes scholarships, are funded by the British taxpayer, and were founded by Parliament as a tribute to US Secretary of State General George Marshall and the Marshall Plan, which was so important to post-war reconstruction in the United Kingdom and Western Europe. The Midwest Marshalls Committee made recommendations to the national committee in Washington DC and thence to that in London. It was a source of much intellectual stimulation, fun and satisfaction to meet and debate with some of the brightest and best young people in the United States, to present our selected cases against the competition from around the United States, and to know that the winners would become familiar with Great Britain at its brightest and best. Many winners became serious Anglophiles and later held positions in US business, government and academia of influence and importance. Win, win.

In place of the old, outdated and costly consul-general's residence on the fashionable but arguably a little faded North Side of Chicago (in Astor Street, just up from where Al Capone once lived), and with excellent expert help from the FCO, we selected a new apartment; a duplex on the 61st and 62nd floors of a new, exciting 63-storey building in a fine downtown location. This new residence was a superb tool of diplomacy, widely admired.

Hilary provided a major input into the design of the new apartment. She worked well with the architect. After careful thought he accepted her suggestion that instead of visitors arriving on the 61st floor and looking up and out through the huge triple-glazed windows to the view, they should rather enter the apartment on the

62nd floor, where the door led to a small hall and thence to a landing at the inner corner of that floor. Visitors would then descend a wide spiral staircase of oak and bronze, stepping, as it were, down into the stunning, indeed breathtaking view of the city and its lake to reach the reception room. We lived in that apartment for only a few weeks. Oliver Wright's successor as ambassador in Washington came to stay there. This was the Sir Antony Acland of the sharp question about mayoral succession in Chicago. Hilary and I have a longstanding and great regard for Antony. His enthusiastic and effective wife Jenny (a magistrate in the United Kingdom) also came to Chicago with Antony. Unknown to us then, the good Jenny suffers from vertigo, but bravely negotiated the double-width spiral staircase from the upper floor down into the drawing room, despite the inescapable feeling that one was walking into that splendid view and almost into the vast Lake Michigan. While Antony and I helped Jenny down the stairs, Hilary dashed into the principal guest bedroom to close the blinds on the floor-to ceiling window and banish its view over Lake Michigan.

It was in that new apartment that we made some of our regretful farewells to Chicago. In 1986, a brand new, financially strapped but impressive and promising little Shakespeare repertory theatre company, performing in the upper back room of a pub, had asked me to help in a first benefit performance to try to raise some money. They performed a collection of Shakespearean extracts in a warehouse space on the North Side of Chicago. After some strong persuasion, I played a part for them in one of the extracts. Hilary and I supported their successful efforts to grow their repertoire and, importantly, their audience. Barbara Gaines, a serious devotee and original scholar of Shakespeare, was their inspirational director. She directed superb and thrilling performances and attracted first-rate actors. Just before we left Chicago in 1988 we invited Barbara, members of her company, some of their supporters and others to one of our farewell parties in the new residence. The company returned the compliment that evening in great style, with some marvellous Shakespearean acting. They used the spiral staircase and the landing and balcony above it to wonderful effect. (I had pleaded with them to eschew sword-fighting on the new staircase!) The Chicago Shakespeare Theater company grew to international stature and recognition and in 1999 moved to a huge, purpose-built theatre complex on Navy Pier in about the best location Chicago could ever provide. In my view their theatre space and supporting facilities outdo those of the rebuilt Stratford-upon-Avon theatre by an almost sickening margin. The Chicago company contributed two of the history plays to the Royal Shakespeare Company's production of all Shakespeare's plays in the summer of 2006; and exceptionally fine performances they were. On Navy Pier, the Chicago Shakespeare Theater produces world-renowned performances of Shakespeare and more, runs a festival and an outstanding educational programme, and wins the highest awards. That's the Chicago spirit, in Barbara Gaines's inspired and excellent exegesis. Since then, and to enormous acclaim, Barbara Gaines has directed Verdi's *Macbeth* at the Chicago Lyric Opera.

The Chicago spirit was also well and sparklingly to the fore for a naval visit, only the second in history, following the royal visit in 1959. In May 1987, two Royal Navy ships arrived in fine fettle out of the Lake Michigan mist: HMS *Juno* and the larger, then midshipmen training ship, HMS *Fife*. As only those of the Royal Navy can, the ships performed an array of ceremonial, formal, informal, charitable and sporting duties and events during their visit. They did the United Kingdom and the RN proud. From the skyscraper of the new residence, we hung the largest White Ensign ever constructed: it had covered the deck of an RN aircraft carrier on a visit to Australia, and was flown from the United Kingdom to Chicago on an RAF aircraft regular flight, rolled up along the floor of the passenger cabin. HMSs *Juno* and *Fife* must have been pleased to see it through the Lake Michigan morning mist as they approached their moorings at Navy Pier. Most of Chicago could not fail to see the Ensign during the visit.

I had some concerns about the naval visit, which I had worked hard to secure at a time when RN ships in the western hemisphere were heavily committed to the Falklands Islands' defence and to anti-drug running and other operations in the Caribbean and elsewhere. The initial answer to my proposal had been 'No: a diversion via the St Lawrence Seaway would take far too long'. But eventually the visit

A pause in the ascent: the main E1 road across Europe in 1962.

Morris Minor, Hilary and worldly goods high in the Balkan Mountains.

Hilary, by Elizaveta Gruncharova, Sofia 1964.

Paris événements, May 1968.

Lieutenant Sam Falle RN, later Sir
Sam Falle KCMG KCVO DSC.

John and Charles Carrick,
Singapore 1972.

Nearly complete British High Commission building, Singapore 1973.

Far East Fleet Steampast of some 20 ships off Singapore, 1971.

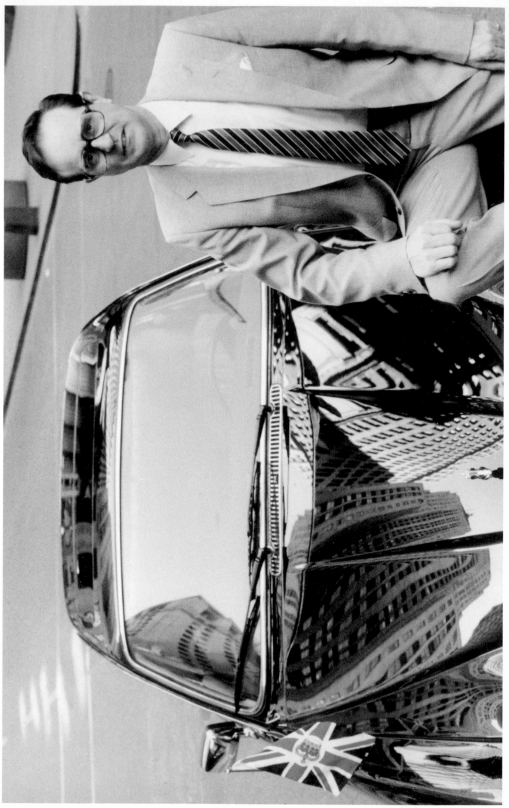

HRM Consul-General 1985–88; official Jaguar and Chicago Board of Trade

Mayor of Chicago Harold Washington and the British Consul-General.

President Richard Nixon in political rehabilitation and in conversation with British Consul-General.

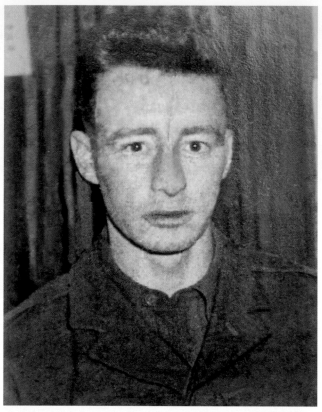

Corporal Tommy Collins, Royal Marines, 1963.

Indonesian forces honour Corporal Collins, Royal Marines, 1991.

18 September 1963: rioters storm and burn the
British embassy in Jakarta ...

... despite the earlier efforts of bagpiper Assistant
Military Attaché Rory Walker to divert the mob.

Commonwealth War Graves Commission Australian First World War graves, St John's churchyard, Sutton Veny, Wiltshire

Australian Prime Minister John Howard and the High Commissioner

British High Commissioner outside refurbished office building, Canberra

was arranged. One problem was that while the young midshipmen could drink some alcohol aboard RN ships, not only was the US Navy strictly 'dry', but the equally strictly enforced legal drinking age in Chicago was 21. Yet the midshipmen would be expecting, along with their duties on land, a 'good run ashore', essential to which was the consumption of alcohol. I went to see the necessarily very tough chief of police in Chicago. His attitude gave new meaning to that badly over-worked phrase the 'special relationship'. After a cheerful discussion, we reached easy agreement. When the ships arrived, Chicago police cars queued like taxis on the quayside to ferry all the many under-age midshipmen from *Fife* to two carefully selected, hospitable and friendly bars. Later, the police cars queued outside the two bars and returned all the young midshipmen safely home to their ship.

Among the wealth of happy memories from the naval visit is that of a senior RN engineer officer, wearing the top half of his best uniform and Chicago police jodhpurs beneath, riding a police horse on the famously rough South Side of Chicago and handing parking tickets down from the saddle.

While on a nautical theme, I should record being much favoured by an early invitation from the owner, Chris Bodine, to help sail a Beneteau yacht on Lake Michigan at some weekends in the season. It was a joy to do so frequently during our time in Chicago, including in a 350-plus miles race from Chicago to Mackinac Island. Chris also readily allowed me to bring on board some occasional sailing visitors from the United Kingdom for a weekend day sail. The visitors were usually nonplussed at and disbelieving of the opposite 'hand' way in which red and green navigation buoys were laid in American waters. Later, after careful preparation, including for the saltier, international waters, Chris sailed that same yacht around the world, with a variety of crew members. One was an English girl whom he married.

The Chicago Council on Foreign Relations, run during my time in Chicago by the former Hubert Humphrey aide, John Rielly, attracted a good number of world leaders. One was Helmut Kohl, from hearing whom I learned a good deal about the German (then West German) approach to Europe and the European project: that insight was to be useful in my next job in the FCO in London. One evening at the council I also heard the deeply impressive Henry Kissinger answering a lady's question about the source of his attraction for women with his legendary response, 'Power'. Mention of Kissinger recalls former President Richard Nixon, whom I met at another Chicago venue and event at which he was speaking. By then President Gerald Ford had (if controversially) pardoned Nixon after his fall from grace and office after Watergate. Indeed Nixon's rehabilitation was well under way towards his status as elder statesman. I well recall Nixon much enjoying a careful re-entry into the international scene. In conversation, he was eager both to exchange political pleasantries and to seek the latest gossip about foreign affairs and personalities.

Edward Heath was another former leader who used to visit Chicago most years, as a member of the advisory body to Arthur Andersen LLP, then one of the 'big five' international accounting and consulting firms and based in Illinois. I used to send the former prime minister a note of welcome and to have a conversation (never gossip) with him, which he said he found agreeable – a characteristic response from a real political patriot if, by then, also a rather sad figure for a man of such huge achievements, and a man I will always admire.

It was something of a contrast when Jeffrey Archer, then vice-chairman of the British Conservative Party, visited. He and I were invited to be guests on an important, hour-long radio 'chat show', moderated by the leading commentator, Sondra Gair. That was a stimulating hour, in which I found myself too often at odds with Mr Archer over such subjects as Northern Ireland. I had wrongly assumed that since the Tories were then in government, their party vice-chairman would follow the government line – and indeed the facts. Not so, and I fancied that Sondra Gair was enjoying the differences she (or I) exposed between the two Brits during the discussion. However, there was no rancour: after the broadcast Mr Archer proposed lunch à deux, and evidently enjoyed a long gossipy exchange of views.

The British consul-general in Chicago is also an unofficial ambassador to an important part of American academia: it was a particular delight to attend seminars and the occasional lecture, and to know faculty members at several fine universities (my sabbatical at

Berkeley helped, of course). The Anglo-American academic exchange scene was of importance, I thought, for Britain's reputation and even sometimes for our invisible exports. On the latter front, Chicago, home of market trading in futures and derivatives, had much admiration for the City of London: frequently animated discussions among experts from both sides of the Atlantic were valued by both, and were productive. A leading light in this aspect of Chicago life was the bright, friendly and welcoming Bill Brodsky who headed the Chicago Mercantile Exchange. He was most helpful in explaining and demonstrating his complex, even arcane part of the financial services industry to visiting British minister, Christopher Patten. I wonder if Lord Patten recalls his own gesture in conversation on a trading floor: a gesture that I thought moved the market! I had first met Christopher when he was a young MP visiting the United States and I was the duty officer in the embassy in Washington. Christopher came to dinner and Hilary and I have been firm admirers ever since. Admiration and the excitement of the futures trading floor apart, the intellectually interesting financial products and devices did seem, even then, rather worrying. Only the good and very able people controlling the market really understood it, I thought, so there could be some potential for manipulation by insiders, and government regulation posed such complexities that might defeat its object.

Sitting at my desk in Chicago one day in the early summer of 1988, I was shocked to receive a telephone call from Sir Mark Russell, an FCO deputy under-secretary of state, known also, archaically but attractively, as the 'chief clerk'. The shock was in his message: could I please leave Chicago earlier than expected and return to the FCO very soon to be assistant under-secretary of state (economics). A compliment, but I cavilled just a little, seeking time to do more from and in Chicago which, by now, was 'our kind of town'.

There followed the required round of farewell calls on captains of industry, senior politicians and officials around as much of the consular district as time allowed: a busy, even rushed time of some purely representational but also as much substantive work as possible. The job, as ever, was to seize opportunities, to capitalise on goodwill for the United Kingdom, and to advance British interests.

It was a real wrench to leave Chicago in August 1988, and to leave the enduring friends we had made there among Americans and the staff of the consulate-general, to whom particular tribute should be paid: they were first-class, effective and fine people. But the FCO had spoken, and once again we returned to London.

CHAPTER 9

LONDON APPOINTMENTS:
DESK OFFICER TO UNDER-SECRETARY

O ur return to the Foreign Office in 1965 was unexpected – as is much Diplomatic Service life, we learned. We had gathered that another foreign posting was likely, and we relished the thought. However, I had (at the second attempt) succeeded in an internal FO limited competition for advancement to what later became known as the fast track, and it became sensible and good career planning for me now to become a desk officer in a political department in London. This meant a radical change of work content. I was posted to eastern department, whose name dated from early FO days when there was a department for each four cardinal points of the compass, and only a few more, such as the Levant department – still existing in 1965. In eastern department, my new job was dealing with Britain's relations with Jordan and some other minor Middle East subjects. In a department of some 14 diplomats when I arrived, there were perhaps five non-Arabists: two of these spoke Farsi and another Mandarin. I shared an office with the fourth, whose desk was Israel. (I, of course, was the fifth.) My further education in eastern department was intensive and valuable, though I never learned Arabic – to Hilary's satisfaction, since she did not relish the prospect of the privations of living in some of the Arab countries where, for example, as a woman she would not have been allowed to drive, even as a diplomatic wife.

On the domestic front, Hilary was now pregnant with our first son, so housing and hospital were high priorities. We had to buy a house while there was a mortgage famine, and when my salary was still that of a distinctly junior diplomat. The problem was eventually solved with the help of the Civil Service Housing Association (a broker) and of the unexpected combination of success in the limited competition and a promotion. We had to pay above the going interest rate for the mortgage, and to live 69 miles by commuter train from London. However, our small house quickly became what my father called a happy home, and our son John fared well there, as did his reliable escort and guardian from Bulgaria, mongrel Fergus.

The translation of Fergus from Bulgarian to British citizen-dog was a near epic tale in its own right. We flew home on the inaugural flight to London of TABSO, the then Bulgarian airline. I recall being invited to stand (*sic*) in the flight deck and film the take-off. Fergus followed alone on the third flight, if I recall aright. The communist government had decided to use that flight to insert, or to replace, a number of their spies in London, all at once. The British authorities were alive to this arguably less than wise move and the flight was made to wait, stationary on a taxiway some miles from the then terminal, while the offending personnel were interviewed and arrested or however the authorities processed them.

The quarantine rules for dogs were strict and only the kennel owner from Folkestone was licensed to collect Fergus, once he had been delivered from the aeroplane to the RSPCA holding kennels. This gentleman had driven from outside Folkestone in his specially equipped Mini Estate car to await, collect and drive Fergus to his new home. He had left his wife at home, allowing plenty of time to drive to and from London airport. Even though she was heavily pregnant, his wife was not anxious, because the dog collection operation was, to them, routine and predictable.

However, the British authorities were letting no one off the aeroplane while they conducted all their interviews. Our kennel owner was properly concerned for Fergus's well-being, and after a long wait persuaded the RSPCA to take up his case. Eventually, a tired and thirsty Fergus was allowed to be the first to leave the TABSO aircraft (only in Britain!). By then, well before the days of mobile telephones, the kennel owner was also concerned about his wife, who had planned to give birth at home. He collected Fergus, completed the necessary complex formalities, put him in the metal box kennel in the back of the Mini Estate car and drove home. It was now hours late, and dark. Well before the construction of the M25, his route was through London. From sheer familiarity, our man knew all the short cuts and every inch of the roads. He drove through west London and out through the south-east. That night, in that area, there had been a robbery – of a whole safe. The police knew that the getaway car was probably a Mini Estate. Well through south-east London, a police car pulled swiftly out of the side road in which it had been waiting and fell in behind our hero's speeding Mini Estate. Our man, now thoroughly fearful for his wife, had been breaking the speed limit for miles, and thought he might as well be hung for a sheep as a lamb: he led the police car a merry chase through Kent and on, fast, towards the darkened kennels half a mile down a long hill.

Such was our man's local knowledge and driving skills that the police car was well behind him, when, to avoid waking a small army of dogs, he switched off his engine and coasted the last 500 yards down the hill and into the kennel yard. He offered a quick word of reassurance to Fergus and rushed into the house. The police followed, found Fergus and his travelling kennel instead of the expected stolen safe, and were soon giving valuable assistance at the birth of a child of Kent.

We visited Fergus every other weekend. He made full use of his generous but, by regulation, all-concrete run and charmed the kennel maids. He forgave us his imprisonment, which the kennel staff all made as pleasant as possible, and joined us happily at the end of his six-month sentence to become an extra baby-sitter for our new baby son.

The work at the FO Jordan desk involved that complex of Middle East and Arab-Israel problems at a time when Great Britain was still, it felt, a weighty player in the region. There were, too, minor and mundane oddities such as authorising the monthly pension payments to King Hussein of Jordan's then father-in-law, a former British Army officer who had supervised the administration of the water supply in Jordan – and whose daughter was later to marry King Hussein. Coincidentally, Princess Muna had been at school with Hilary in Kuala Lumpur. There was the then classic task of drafting the formal

FO despatch to the British ambassador, setting out and arguing future British policy towards Jordan. Swallowing a sheep's eyeball as a guest in a diplomatic flat in Dolphin Square in London was among the more testing aspects of the otherwise pleasant duty of working with the Jordanian embassy in London. The embassy was good enough to offer me an official visit to Jordan, but I was instructed that FO policy of the day was to refuse such visits – I supposed to avoid any chance of them resulting in less than complete objectivity in judging how best to pursue British interests in the country concerned, even one with which we had such good and friendly relations.

There was policy cooperation with the Overseas Development Administration over the then fairly substantial British aid to Jordan. The ODA was then part of the Foreign Office and our cooperation was close and effective. Relations between these two arms of government since the 1960s have often been less good: the British interest has, in consequence, not always been well served. As assistant under-secretary of state (economic) many years later, I and others sought to improve cooperation in this sometimes tense area of government and of the furtherance of the broad British interest abroad. As I write, I am conscious that the separate ministry, now named the Department for International Development (DFID), is strong and calls the tune widely – a function of its very much increased (and protected) budget, about whose enduring value and accountability to the British taxpayer I wonder. Can such large sums be spent well, defensibly and always without the fear of misuse by some recipients? I will return to this subject in the concluding Chapter 12.

A highlight of my two years in eastern department was the stimulus of working with an impressive array of colleagues. All were top class. The intellectually brilliant Percy Cradock later became head of the cabinet office assessments staff, HM ambassador to China and the prime minister's foreign policy adviser. Willie Morris, the marvellous head of department, was later ambassador to Saudi Arabia and Egypt. His early death was a tragic and irreplaceable loss to his wife Ghislaine, his family, all who knew him, his Service and his country. Alan Goodison, another of the array of fine Arabists, was a delight, a colourful colleague and later also a successful ambassador in Dublin.

David Hannay, Farsi speaker, was a tigerish worker whose fine brain took him to Brussels for over a decade to work in several positions of signal importance for the United Kingdom and the EEC, including later as permanent representative to the European Communities, to the UN as ambassador, and to the House of Lords.

The Israel desk officer and I shared not only an office but also an open fire, lit each morning in winter with half of a shilling bundle of firewood. The fire was tended during the day with a coal shovel whose handle was wrapped in FO blue draft paper for cleanliness. The coal was delivered in a scuttle by a frock-coated messenger. The Israel desk officer was Colin McLean, a most welcome and unusual scientist in the Service. A zoologist by first degree, micro-palaeontologist by doctorate, he had been a district officer and vice-principal of the Institute of Administration in Kenya, and was full of common sense and wisdom. All in the department were fine people. Willie Morris's PA, the vivacious and first-class Pat Essex, left the department for the private office of the then foreign secretary, Michael Stewart, the sadly barely remembered but honest, conscientious and patient politician who worked so hard, notably trying to solve the Vietnam conundrum. But Pat did not altogether leave eastern department, for she later married another of its denizens, Robert Alston. Robert is another Farsi speaker, accomplished Middle Eastern diplomat, later HM ambassador to Muscat and high commissioner in New Zealand while Hilary and I were across the Tasman Sea in Australia. The Alstons succeeded us in our posting to Paris. Eastern department friendships endured, notably with the Alstons, but with others too, including the Montgomerys. David, who among much else after leaving eastern department became a Thai speaker and did excellent commercial diplomatic work in Bangkok, is an able Scot with an acerbic wit. Later still, when deputy high commissioner in Barbados, he was influential and effective at the highest levels and did especially fine (and once rather dangerous) work on Grenada at a time of crisis, some of which has been mentioned in histories and biographies. David should, and would, have had another senior posting had he not chosen premature retirement – to the real regret of many of us.

Among many highlights of that FO posting was a state visit to Great Britain by HM King Hussein of Jordan in 1966. At my junior desk, I was asked to draft a couple of the king's speeches, and to include jokes in one in particular. This was an interesting task: I recall sitting through the speech at a grand dinner in the Guildhall in the City of London and waiting a little nervously for the jokes. King Hussein had been to Harrow School and had perfect, if delightfully accented, English, but the telling of jokes in a second language can be a difficult art. He brought it off – just. The Guildhall dinner, for which the dress was white tie and decorations, was indeed a grand affair. Guests were announced before they walked the length of Guildhall between serried ranks of robed liverymen and great men of the City before being presented by the lord mayor to King Hussein and Princess Muna. The guests announced ahead of us in the line were the Earl and Countess Attlee. Given his then advanced age, they walked very slowly towards the royal dais to well-merited and loud applause on either side, sustained for every inch of the way. When Hilary and I were announced, by name and 'from the Foreign Office', the little applause there was quickly petered out as we rather hurried forward: unsurprising and just more amusing than embarrassing. King Hussein was something of a hero to many British people, and warmly liked in our own royal family. The state visit was a great success, in part due to Princess Muna whose modest charm was widely appreciated. Rather unusually for a state visit, and to much acclaim, the king and the princess went to Scotland. The king also attended the Wembley semi-final of the football World Cup in which England defeated Portugal (partly because of an unforgettable goal by Bobby Charlton): another an unusual event for a state visit, but one much appreciated and much enjoyed.

Towards the end of the state visit, an elegantly robed member of King Hussein's household appeared in my office to thank me and say that His Majesty proposed to invest me with a Jordanian order. I explained that while this thought and honour were deeply appreciated, I could not accept it. Our rules effectively then forbade acceptance of foreign honours or awards. I did offer that members of the FO protocol department, some of whom had been involved in the state visit, had a dispensation. My interlocutor was not satisfied, and my refusal needed another rather insistent visit before it was apparently accepted. My Jordanian colleague, however, appeared a third time, in splendid robes; bowed; said, 'By the king's command'; placed two royally wrapped boxes on my desk; and swept out. Oh dear. One of the boxes was labelled for the head of eastern department, the other for me. I consulted Willie Morris, who sighed understandingly and advised that I write a minute (memo) of explanation to him. I did so, telling the tale, arguing that to return the gold watches the boxes contained would be an insult, and seeking instructions. There were no hard rules about such gifts in those days, as there are today. It now seems quite unbelievable, but the minute was not only added to in endorsement by Willie, but submitted upwards, via assistant under-secretary of state, deputy under-secretary of state and permanent under-secretary of state to the secretary of state. Each of these added a comment; the secretary of state's being to mark the minute across King Charles Street to HM Treasury with a request for advice. The rest of the story, as I recall it, also seems incredible today: the chancellor of the exchequer marked the minute down the Treasury hierarchy for comment. After it reached a level at which a desk officer opined, the minute travelled upwards again, via each hierarchical step until the chancellor endorsed the advice and sent the papers back across the street to the foreign secretary's office whence, with suitable endorsement, it journeyed down again to eastern department, finally for action. As I recall it, the import of the minutes was that the watches could be kept – but only if certain set conditions were adhered to. One condition, a not unreasonable one, was that the watches should be insured at the officers' expense. Another was that they should in no circumstances ever be sold or given away – I wondered if the Treasury official had contemplated the eventual deaths of the two officers and, if so, decided that that was too difficult a matter to resolve. Nowadays, strict and sensible rules provide for surrendering any such gifts, their valuation and the opportunity offered to the recipients to purchase the gifts for the sum assessed. Otherwise the gifts are, I think, eventually sold for charity.

I was saddened, professionally, to have left eastern department before the 1967 Middle East war, a war which the department expected. I had been sent earlier on an intensive 22-week course in economics and statistics at the Treasury Centre for Administrative Studies (later the Civil Service College) in London. The course was quite tough, mainly in its advanced mathematics which, at least initially, was beyond the abilities of many of the 20 or so course members from across the Civil Service, including of some with economics degrees. The book prescribed for reading before the course was also beyond the headmaster of a grammar school near our home who was himself a mathematician. The Treasury Centre teaching was of the highest international standards. I gained experience and knowledge that would stand me in good stead immediately in our next posting to the embassy in Paris and, indeed, for the rest of my career.

I was next to return to London after Singapore (Chapter 5) in late 1973, and to an appointment I found a surprise: assistant head of personnel operations department (POD) with responsibility for overseas and home postings, promotions and career planning in grades up to and including first secretary in the then branch A (the senior branch of the Service). There were two other assistants covering the other branches; a deputy head who dealt primarily with the counsellor grade; and a head of department who looked after the most senior grades. With the deputy head he ran the department as a whole, which was organised geographically with specific units dealing with the two most junior grades, with home appointments and with welfare. The head of department when I joined it was Richard Parsons, subsequently ambassador to Hungary and, later, as Sir Richard, ambassador to Spain. The deputy was Ken Scott, who after distinguished service in Washington and in the FCO heading East European and Soviet department, was appointed ambassador to the then Yugoslavia. Later, as Sir Kenneth, he became deputy private secretary to HM The Queen. Richard and Ken ran an impressive operation, with grace, good humour and effectiveness. Again, a high proportion of the members of POD went on ultimately to become heads of mission in posts of importance: a few examples are Moscow, Cairo, Dublin, Harare and Bogotá.

Previously I had stood rather in awe of POD so I had a lot to learn, and quickly. It is entirely right that members of the Service should serve in its administration. This view was sometimes countered with the opinion that a cadre of people serving only at home should fulfil the Service's administration duties, in which the expertise required is different, that diplomats are trained for diplomacy and should serve abroad, or if at home only in front-line 'political' departments. In my view, the necessary administration expertise is readily acquired and the advantage of diplomats administering diplomats is overwhelming. An understanding of diplomatic practice abroad is vital for proper, defensible and accountable management of the Service, its members and, indeed, its families. Nonetheless, it was a shock to find myself planning colleagues' postings, promotions and even careers. Decisions on such matters were subject to collegiate discussions and then proposals and cases made to boards. Decisions were made with devotion and care, and quite frequently, to meet unpredictable operational demands. There is a separate debate about staffing 'functional' departments in the FCO, such as that dealing with energy. There is another debate about commercial diplomatic policy and action, to which I shall return.

The FO has intermittently experimented with exchanges of people between business and academia on the one hand and its overseas posts on the other, with mixed success. One problem, the disparity of salary levels, could sometimes be mitigated if a company valued the experience their secondee would receive while working for government and so topped up the salary the FCO paid. Another problem could arise with secondments in either direction if the people concerned felt they might suffer from temporary absence from the core of their career streams. There was also the varying quality and adaptability of secondees, again, both ways. While I served in POD, we brought in a small number of academics to work for a year or two on political desks in the FCO: this too produced mixed success. The best among them was an economist from Glasgow University who had worked in Kenya, Dr Vince Cable.

Personnel work in the FCO was, in that overworked word, challenging. When postings and promotions worked well; when sound career planning could be fulfilled and the national interest met; when embassies, high commissions, multilateral missions, consulates and departments at home were performing to the maximum; I found this work immensely rewarding. When things went wrong; when (rarely) staff performed at a level lower than that at which their superiors and POD judged they should and could; or (more frequently) when we could not solve personal problems for colleagues at home or abroad; then the frustration, disappointment and sense of failure were often acute. Understanding human problems and how to help solve them, and understanding the needs of British diplomacy and helping to meet them with personnel management decisions were, of course, vital. The work was obviously different from most diplomatic work; but also demanding. Most Diplomatic Service officers appointed to POD adapted and performed well: just a few able and effective diplomats were proved not to be cut out for personnel work, and returned successfully to the mainstream. The department did have a remarkable and positive collegiate feel and way of working. As in so many walks of life, to have some fun is a distinctly positive contribution to work. This seemed especially true in POD: we were well led; yet also a cohesive, happy group who worked well together.

During the three-day week in early 1974 when the electricity supply was cut, some of us slept on camp beds in the office and worked by candlelight; some stayed with colleagues who lived close to the office. Richard Parsons held a departmental meeting at his hospitable nearby home.

There seemed to me a good deal of troubleshooting work to do in POD. I became concerned at the frequency with which the inevitable strains of life and work in the Service led to divorce. I asked the next door department, who dealt with the terms and conditions of service and allied matters, to establish the rate of divorce in the Diplomatic Service and to compare it with the national average. The work was done and the answer clear. To my surprise, though not to my comfort, the rates were precisely the same. Clearly, I should stop worrying and get on with the job. I began to learn an important lesson: that while divorce is almost always sad, perhaps especially where children are concerned (though they often learn quickly to cope surprisingly well), it is nearly always right.

The troubleshooting work occasionally meant that a 'pastoral' visit to a post or posts abroad by the head of department became necessary. The care with which such work was approached and executed was remarkable, and much good was done. The department worked to an assistant under-secretary (AUS) and a deputy under-secretary (DUS), the latter known as the chief clerk, who probably made rather more pastoral visits than the head of POD, since he was responsible for all the management of the Diplomatic Service. During my four years in the department, there were two splendid chief clerks. Donald Tebbit, a diplomat's diplomat, was much admired throughout the Service. He had been No. 2 in the embassy in Washington. Donald's was the determining voice in the most senior diplomatic appointments, a deeply respected voice on which the permanent under-secretary and the secretary of state relied. When visiting the Office on leave, the most senior diplomats would frequently call on the chief clerk. I recall one, a rare exception indeed, who had committed some peccadillo in a far flung, probably tropical, post. He rather gingerly enquired of Donald whether his peccadillo had been forgiven. Donald's reply demonstrated his humanity, his humour, his judgment and his professionalism: 'Forgiven, yes; forgotten, no.' Partly because of pressure on resources and partly because of his diplomatic and political skills, Donald took on another job while chief clerk: he became deputy to the permanent under-secretary, Sir Michael Palliser. I think this appointment was unprecedented. Even in such a Service, few people could successfully have combined two such demanding and senior jobs. Sir Donald went on to be high commissioner to Australia for his last, well-deserved posting before retirement at the absurdly young age of 60 – on which more in Chapter 12. In Australia, Donald continued to do outstanding work, with characteristically high skill and devotion. He and Lady Tebbit left a deep, enduring and much respected mark. Donald also successfully managed both a unique and occasionally surprisingly awkward bilateral relationship, and the sometimes testy relations between two prime ministers, Malcolm Fraser and Margaret Thatcher.

Donald Tebbit's successor as chief clerk was the steely-eyed Curtis Keeble, who had been ambassador at East Berlin and was later, as Sir

Curtis, to be ambassador in Moscow. Curtis had also been head of the FO's security department. He was a fine tough diplomat with a lust for life and a good sense of humour, hidden when necessary but not deeply so to those who knew him well. For example, while chief clerk he responded to an advertisement seeking leeks for a production then running at the Old Vic: Shakespeare's *Henry V* was playing and the company needed large fresh leeks for each performance. So every day of the play's run, Curtis delivered large fresh leeks from his Thames Ditton garden to the Old Vic stage door on his way to the Foreign Office.

POD needed to find a successor as deputy head of the department to Ken Scott, who had been posted as head of chancery in Washington. The deputy head was a counsellor and the No. 2; the assistant heads were first secretaries and at the next level down. To identify a candidate to succeed Ken, the usual sifting and selecting procedures, for which I was primarily responsible, followed. We proposed a candidate to Curtis as a precursor to putting the name to the appropriate board. Unusually, and because Curtis did not know him, he asked to see the candidate. The interview resulted in Curtis letting us know by telephone just before the candidate came on to see me that he did not think the man was quite right for the job. I had not foreseen that. It also presented a problem of timing, since Ken had to be at his next post abroad quickly for good operational reasons, and the staffing cupboard was bare and likely to remain so for rather longer than we thought the department should sensibly carry a gap. I searched and sifted further, without finding a good solution. Richard Parsons came into my office later with the message that he and Curtis thought that since I had failed to produce a successful candidate, I had better do the job myself. It took a little while for it to sink in that this meant promotion – as well as another two years or so in the department. I hasten to add that the failed candidate, a distinctly pleasant and able man, took it all well. He may just even have been a little relieved, and continued a good diplomatic career.

It was as deputy head of POD that I acted as secretary to the No. 1 FCO board when it debated and recommended the 'political' appointment of Peter Jay to be ambassador to the United States (see

Chapter 7). Altogether, my four years in POD were surprisingly varied. At one end of the spectrum of the departmental experience was that unforgettable board meeting. At the other end was the early morning when a member of the Service came into my office looking bedraggled and soaking wet, having walked the streets of London all night trying to come to terms with the fact that his wife of many years had walked out. There were also good times a-plenty: those that did not mean wakeful nights trying to find solutions for operational personnel problems, but rather moments of real pleasure as the right practical answer was found to the Service's and the national need. Personnel work, perhaps especially for those who spend an intensive few years rather than a whole career in it, can be hard work – or, in the modern term, 'stressful'. The hard work was helped by excellent colleagues and a collegiate atmosphere. It was also relieved for some by coffee. I once asked my splendid and efficient PA, Rita Wisker, to count the number of cups of coffee she so kindly made for me and I consumed in a day. When she told me the answer, 17, I stopped drinking coffee in the office. Thereafter, I probably made rather better decisions.

Two postings later, in Washington in 1982 and with the Falklands conflict about to erupt, Ambassador Nicko Henderson called me into his office and handed me a letter from the then FCO chief clerk, Derek Day, which had arrived in the diplomatic bag as the enclosure to an explanatory letter to the ambassador. Both letters said that for my next posting I had been selected to be the first head of a new and much enlarged overseas estate department (OED) in the FCO. Ministers had decided that responsibility (together with the associated resources, financial and personnel) for the diplomatic estate overseas would be transferred from the property services agency (PSA) of the Department of the Environment (DoE) to the FCO. Shock was my first – and indeed long-lasting – reaction. I had not joined the Diplomatic Service to manage land and buildings, however spread around the world they were. I knew that professional and technical skills of which I had almost no knowledge would be vital. I guessed that there would be unedifying and unpleasant Whitehall battles to be fought. All this was a long way from mainstream diplomacy. Yet neither had anyone else I knew in the Service joined it to run real estate. Derek Day's letter to me hastened 'to explain what may, at first sight, seem a bizarre proposition'. His letter to Nicko said: 'I do not imagine that he will be immediately enchanted at the prospect' and 'he should regard his selection as a compliment and I hope you will encourage him, if necessary, to approach it in a positive frame of mind'. Nicko asked me if he should 'tell them "no"'.

I asked Nicko for 24 hours to think. Thinking did not help much: the new department would be huge for the FCO, approaching 200 people, and based in Croydon. It would be manned by professional estate and other surveyors, architects, engineers, technical and executive staff all from the DoE and transferred to the FCO unwillingly. Many of them would believe themselves gamekeepers forced to become poachers. Relations between the two departments and their predecessors had been unfriendly for generations. This would be a poisoned chalice and a huge job of management with some limited policy work but only a spattering of real diplomacy. I assumed the FCO expected me not to try to refuse: I had joined a service in which one simply did not refuse postings. Nicko might think it fair game to 'tell them "no"' and his was a kind offer. I would not, however, take it up. Yet, as I learned much later to my surprise, the FCO had a 'fall-back' candidate in mind in case I should refuse. That plan was, in my POD experience, unprecedented, and marked the singular nature of the appointment – or exile, as some colleagues regarded it.

The transfer of responsibility (known in Whitehall by the arcane phrase 'vote transfer') for the overseas estate was evidently the culmination of a long turf war between the DoE, with its Property Services Agency (PSA), and the FCO. The secretary of state at the FCO, Lord Carrington, as he later confirmed to me, firmly favoured the change. He had had his own disagreements with the PSA's predecessor when he had served as Britain's youngest high commissioner to Australia (as a political appointee). In accepting the headship of OED, and for the only time in my career, I did attempt to secure a couple of conditions. That I should be allowed to carry forward a chunk of leave not taken while serving in Washington was readily agreed (but, unsurprisingly, never proved possible to implement). I also put down markers about strengthening the staff in the new department, to which I would return when I had taken the measure of the job; about the need I guessed there would be for an office in the FCO proper in London as well as that in Croydon; and that I thought it reasonable to expect a mainstream job abroad after OED. The chief clerk 'took note'. I then put the new posting out of my mind while the Falklands conflict raged.

My chancery and JIC rep work and the post-Falkland matters on my desk included many a thank-you letter to American officials. With the benefit then of a little background reading during an all-too-brief driving holiday with Hilary and our boys, I began work in an unfamiliar role and in, initially at least, a rather antagonistic and charged atmosphere in Croydon. It did not take long to secure the extra office in London: it was to have a good deal of use. I became accustomed to driving legs of the triangular course between our then home near Tunbridge Wells, Croydon and London – sometimes all three in one day. (I found a quiet, quick, mostly country and barely used route for the first of these legs. One night I stopped to enjoy the sight in my headlights of a family of badgers at play. Much more recently I have come to mistrust and even to dislike the badger for the damage he does where we live in retirement in Exmoor.)

It seemed important to take time to assess staffing questions in OED, the management problems I faced and where I should direct most energy and seek most reform in the overseas estate and its management. The staff, it was quickly clear, certainly included a fair number who resented that they were to work for, instead of traditionally and sadly, against, the FCO. Some resisted having a diplomat as head of the new department. I would have much to do to counter and to alter those views. There was a huge amount to learn about the estate itself and about the technical, professional and decision-making processes needed and best suited to manage it. There were decisions to take about how best to identify and secure necessary and probably radical changes in policies and practices. The need became increasingly clear for a deputy head of the same rank as

I. My clear assumption was that this would have to be a Diplomatic Service colleague. But first I should ensure a sensible organisation of OED. The large and unwieldy department, with its 'silo' structure of professional disciplines, needed instead a geographically-based integrated approach to the estate. The next needs were for new integrated policies or strategies for the estates of perhaps half the posts abroad, particularly the larger ones, and to drive tough rationalisation of the estates that needed it most.

In exploring ways forward and in getting to know the professional engineers, architects, building surveyors, estate surveyors, technicians and others, I began to learn how to recognise quality in these people, and to form views about how best to overcome prejudice and suspicions of the FCO and the Diplomatic Service. Among some distinctly able professionals, one in particular stood out. The more I listened to and discussed with the superintending architect Mark Bertram, the more I recognised professional expertise, analytical and intellectual ability, moral integrity, the openness and clarity of a good mind. It was clear he had an objective keenness to make the new arrangements work well and to the advantage of British interests. It was then a careful but not a difficult step to change my mind about having a Diplomatic Service deputy head of department. Mark accepted the job and applied himself to the reciprocal of my task. Mine was to learn about the overseas estate Mark already knew well: his to learn about the FCO and the Diplomatic Service. Mark was a superlative deputy head.

Mark and I had some high-quality help. John Owen was a splendid and wise assistant head of department. Earlier described by the redoubtable Sir Percy Cradock in Peking as the best administration officer in the Service, John ended his career as governor of the Cayman Islands. Some of the technical and professional members of the department were excellent in their complex fields. Clive Newey, structural engineer *par excellence*; Ken Campbell, architect – whose admirable work I knew from Singapore (Chapter 5) and who in OED was to produce a formidable design for new embassy offices in Moscow; and Jeremy Neate, estate surveyor, who made that difficult transition with great care and probity, are just three.

In 1982, the British overseas estate, spread right around the world, consisted of about 4,000 properties – owned, rented, old, a few new, some well and some badly located buildings: offices, residences, houses, apartments, some in good repair, many not. This mixed portfolio had one overriding characteristic: too much of it was distinctly less than fit for present or future purpose. There were several reasons for this. Operational diplomatic requirements change, in some places quite rapidly. Many ambassadors, set down in their residences to do their job for three or four years before being uprooted again, are understandably resistant to the additional distraction of a change of house or office. Overseas countries and governments, for varying reasons, can also resist change. Yet the chief reason for the unsuitability of so much of the estate seemed to me the consequence of a straitjacket imposed by the Treasury. In simple terms, if a building in the estate were a white elephant or for some other reason no longer needed, and were sold, the money went to the Treasury via a reduction in the budget they provided that year to run the estate. Thus there was no gain to invest in the estate – rather the opposite. Proceeds from operationally necessary sales not planned over a year in advance went straight to the Treasury coffers with no question of any gain to the estate. If a new building were needed, then the FCO had to make a case to the Treasury for new money. There was thus no incentive at all to modernise the portfolio in order to create a more efficient and cost-effective estate. Further, and because of these and other antiquated arrangements that added to the need for essential flexibility in the estate holdings, there was too large an incentive to rent rather than to buy or build.

With the help of the finance department of the FCO and, at the last of a series of battles, of the then chief clerk, John Whitehead (later ambassador in Tokyo), OED eventually persuaded the Treasury to agree to an 'asset recycling' scheme. This allowed OED to sell outdated or operationally unsuitable property in one part of the estate and to reinvest the money there or elsewhere in the world. The previous Treasury rules were Whitehall-wide: part of the reason for the many wasted months it took to reach agreement was, I believed, that the Treasury feared contagion. For example, the Ministry of Defence held large UK land holdings and might well see the same advantage in asset recycling that we did. If that was the Treasury position, I thought it unreasonable, short-sighted and, indeed, against the public interest. The FCO agreement with the Treasury was detailed and complex – and took far too long to negotiate. The settlement provided that while OED could, as necessary, carry forward a large amount of receipts each financial year, the Treasury would receive an annual 'slice off the bottom' of those receipts. That slice seemed to me unjustified in principle but inevitable in the bloody battles of Whitehall. The Treasury settled for a surprisingly small amount for their slice, given what we judged the estate could sensibly generate for years to come. OED undertook to reduce rent expenditure – as we were in any case determined to do.

The first deal we did abroad under the new arrangements was in Kuala Lumpur, and involved a crucial telephone call to my home late one Christmas Eve from the then mayor of KL. He needed fully to satisfy himself about sensitive Malaysian political implications. Within a month or so of that telephone call, OED spent much of the multi-million proceeds from our KL changes on apartments in New York and thus greatly reduced a large rent bill that was increasingly becoming indefensible. The asset recycling agreement with the Treasury was for ten years. It lasted its course, and, I understand, became embedded in general practice.

In parallel with the asset recycling negotiations, and as a precursor to using the new system, OED developed strategies for estate rationalisation, which were useful guides and stirred useful action. To my colleagues in overseas posts the strategies were sometimes controversial, but agreement was usually reached amicably, if occasionally with emotion and even a certain rancour. The end results were certainly worth the efforts. Within a decade or less, much of Britain's official property abroad was looking more representational for modern Britain. More importantly, the estate was doing its financial and operational jobs well and better earning its keep in furthering national interests.

To be head of OED was certainly not what I expected, aspired to, nor felt qualified to be. Yet it did seem right that the FCO rather than the DoE or any of its 'Ministry of Works' predecessors should be responsible for the diplomatic estate abroad: the estate is primarily a tool of diplomacy. Like the curate's egg, I enjoyed parts of the job. There was, for example, a fair amount of essential travel to posts abroad with which I was not acquainted. The construction by Taylor Woodrow of new embassy offices, residence and staff housing in Riyadh when the Saudi Arabian government moved there from Jeddah allowed me to order a redesign on the spot. Part of the motor pool was arranged such that an entirely unintended insult to Allah was about to be perpetrated. The redesign and rebuild happened very quickly. That visit also included a memorable evening off in Jeddah. I was sitting on the steps of the residence with the British ambassador. We were speculating about who might become our next head of the service and permanent under-secretary. We enjoyed swapping names of possible candidates and their chances for half an hour before I suggested that he might be a good contender. His surprise seemed utterly genuine and modest, but it was a widely admired and popular move when Sir Patrick (now Lord) Wright became the permanent under-secretary.

On the same journey I settled on a site for a new high commission office building in Dacca. A key criterion was that it should be well above the flood plain but, as I recall, we built it on stilts to try to be sure. The high commissioner was Terry Streeton, who had been the assistant under-secretary supervising (with, mercifully, a light touch) OED when I took it on. Terry was a pilot and used this skill to considerable effect in supervising British aid work throughout Bangladesh. To illustrate a part of the OED job I did not enjoy at all, budgetary constraints as I judged them meant that I had to refuse him a change of carpet in the main reception room in his residence in Dacca – despite that I hated the carpet as much as did he and his wife.

Another visit abroad was to the capital of the then USSR for some negotiations on a possible exchange of sites for new embassy offices in London and Moscow. This was a large, detailed and complicated matter, which we thought best handled by a delegation whose leader could be devoted to just this project. The FCO was fortunate in that a former ambassador to Moscow and chief clerk, Sir Curtis Keeble, by then retired, agreed to take on the job as a consultant to OED. It was a joy to be working with Curtis again. There were many working sessions in OED, and it was good to see how integrated the various professions could be in such a cause. Curtis visited Moscow, and, with a couple of us from OED, potential sites in London several times in the run-up to the main negotiations of a formal agreement. I was Curtis's deputy head of delegation. Mark Bertram brought his essential architectural expertise and wisdom. OED'S splendid legal adviser, Jeremy Hill (who later, unprecedently, I think, joined the Diplomatic Service and became ambassador to Bulgaria), was another essential member of the delegation. Christopher Meyer, then head of chancery in the embassy in Moscow (later ambassador in Washington) joined us too, as was standard practice, to provide local up-to-date advice.

The negotiations proceeded to our plan, toughly but well – until the last day. As hosts, the Soviet delegation proposed on the penultimate day that since we had by then reached agreement in substance, we should follow their normal practice, under which the heads of delegations would have the following day off and their deputies would review and agree the detailed texts of the agreement. The Soviet No. 2 was clearly the KGB man on the Russian team. The next day, he tried to pull all the tricks in the book, and some more. There were to be two texts, Russian and English, both of equal authority in any later question of interpretation. The texts had been 'tidied' and retyped overnight by the hosts – again normal practice. My Russian was very rusty. Christopher's was not. But even I could spot no doubt deliberate new 'translations' in the Russian text. I insisted on crawling through the texts, word by word, and making corrections in both languages. Revised versions were retyped. Some of the corrections had been made. Some other changes, to which we had not agreed, had been added. This process continued as the Soviet deputy head of delegation, knowing that we had a British Airways flight to catch back to the United Kingdom, sought to wear us down and allow changes to the Soviet advantage to slip through. Jeremy and Christopher were letting me know quietly (but unnecessarily) of their concern. I believed that the Soviet government needed the agreement rather more than we did. It was a freezing, snowy day in Moscow. We had taken the precaution of having our transport ready, waiting and warm in the road outside the Russian offices. At what I thought was the right, convincing moment, I stood, announced that I could not recommend the text of the agreement as it now stood to the British government, and said goodbye: we walked out. As we drove into the then British embassy offices (now the residence), Curtis was waiting with his luggage. I wound down the window of the car as we drew level with him. He asked: 'Well, is the deed done?' I answered 'No, sir' and opened the door for him to join me in the car and to set off for Sheremetyevo airport. Curtis's steely gaze had never been steelier as, taking due account of the fact that the car was no doubt bugged, I began to explain. He quickly said I had done the right thing. We spoke regretfully and turned to other things.

We arrived at Sheremetyevo and were directed to the VIP lounge. There waiting for us, unexpectedly, was the head of the Soviet delegation, who carried the rank of ambassador. He was bearing two copies of the disputed text. He calmly said that he understood it had not been possible for the deputies to reach final agreement and asked if Curtis and I would look at the copies he had had retyped: he hoped they would meet our concerns. Time was against us by now, so we said we would consider whether that would be possible, quietly sought a delay in the flight and repaired to a separate room (doubtless, of course, also bugged).

We crawled through the retyped text in both copies and in both languages (Curtis's Russian was well up to the task). I found, and let Curtis know silently, that all the remaining 'mistakes' had been corrected and the text restored to the agreed one. Curtis wisely checked too. However, we now had the moral advantage. We wrote to each other on scraps of paper. In English and Russian, Curtis then wrote in the margins of the typed copies of the agreement two extra clauses to suit the British need over the Soviet. We then took the copies back to the Soviet ambassador. Curtis invited him to read the extra clauses and, if he were content, to join Curtis in initialling them. If he agreed, the documents thus amended would form the agreements to be submitted to the two governments for ratification. The Soviet ambassador read, thought and consented. The deed was now done, to British advantage. Bearing our copy, Curtis and I boarded the aeroplane and walked down the fuselage to our seats without a word. Curtis remained steely-eyed and silent until the captain of the delayed flight, in common BA practice at the time, finally announced that we had left Soviet airspace. Curtis then pulled the switch for the steward, upon whose arrival this fine and tough diplomat gave just one command: 'Champagne'. Our colleagues were thus both updated and relieved.

That Moscow foray was instructive and interesting in many ways. There was the unavoidable evening in the inevitable dacha outside Moscow when our hosts plied us with predictably large quantities of vodka. The roots of the equally inevitable large aspidistra profited from the spirit far more than did I. That evening, I thought that rusty as my Russian certainly was – I had had to suppress it to an extent in order to master the also Slavonic but in important respects quite different Bulgarian – I really should use it. So I spoke to the leader of the USSR delegation in Russian. I soon concluded from his expression and reaction that there could be no more haughty or disdainful interlocutor than an elderly, old-school Muscovite who felt himself and his beautiful language seriously insulted by being addressed in that language not only by a Westerner, but, of all things, in a Bulgarian accent.

By contrast, there was the British ambassador's dinner for both delegations, held in the 1890s residence opposite the Kremlin on the Sofiskaya Naberezhnaya (embankment or quay) of the River Moskva. That extraordinary and extraordinarily effective residence was the subject of Anglo-Soviet disputes from at least the days of Ernest Bevin and Vyacheslav Molotov to those of Margaret Thatcher and Mikhail Gorbachev. The residence dining room was lit by candelabra and had walls bearing life-size portraits in oil of members of the British royal family. I walked in to the room accompanying the head of the USSR delegation. Opposite the door was a portrait of King George V. My Soviet companion stopped in his tracks, breathed the Russian words for 'My God: it's the Tsar', and even more surprisingly crossed himself. That was a wonderful moment that no one else saw or heard, and that I have cherished ever since. This senior Soviet official had reverted entirely to type when he later visited London for some consequential work. During a break in his schedule I took him to the gallery of the House of Lords to witness a debate. As we looked down we saw a member of their Lordships' House lying down on a back bench fast asleep. The Soviet visitor could not be shaken from his conclusion that we had arranged that spectacle especially for him. I could only speculate quite how he imagined we were seeking to impress him with this demonstration of democracy in action.

So, to my surprise, there were parts of OED's endeavours that required classical diplomacy – but they were few: most of the work was, as predicted, management and firm decision-making. Some had to do with persuading British heads of diplomatic missions that change in 'their' local estate was necessary and would be achieved in their time. I recall one ambassador coining the acronym NIMTOD, for 'not in my tour of duty': an understandable attitude given the distraction of radical estate change from the front-line tasks of a mission. However, that attitude had to be overcome in the interests of essential reform and rationalisation – if at the risk of my Diplomatic Service colleagues erroneously concluding that I had defected to the enemy.

There was also important work to be done in briefing the permanent under-secretary and supporting him at a hearing – or perhaps grilling – by the Public Accounts Committee (PAC) of the House of Commons. A few members of this committee displayed a strong prejudice against the FCO. At times their questioning resembled the worst of the inquisition. They seemed to me to take rather little account of the National Audit Office's generally objective if also cautious report to them. Sir Antony Acland was politeness itself in handling this questioning, of course. We had prepared a defence against the PAC's likely line of attack; Sir Antony deployed it to good effect and the results were satisfactory from the taxpayers' and OED's point of view. Sir Antony's gentlemanly handling of the hearing and his brief, together with his convincing demonstration to the PAC of his and the FCO's determination to manage the overseas estate in the taxpayers' best interests, efficiently and effectively, made the right impression, too, on our heads of mission around the world. The exercise, I thought, also helped to bind the disparate OED together and contributed something towards a more cohesive department working for the national interest.

An unusual illustration of the need for diplomacy in managing the overseas estate is also a cautionary diplomatic tale. OED were responsible for the construction of new offices in an African country whose economy was then rather depressed. Our new building, a modest one, was nonetheless the only construction project of any size in the capital of that country, and provided jobs not only for the British building company but importantly for the country concerned. At the end of one week's work on the site, it was closed by the local police. The head of mission and I had an exchange of telegrams and a telephone conversation. He professed to being baffled by why this unfriendly and apparently absurd act had occurred. In answer to my questions, the head of mission, a good operator and diplomat, said he had secured all the necessary permissions and that all the culturally required precautions, including the prescribed sacrifice at each corner of the planned building, had been taken. We asked him to call on the ministers concerned and make firm representations. This he did, and I am sure spoke well; but the site remained closed. I wrote a submission to the then minister of state in the FCO covering Africa, Malcolm Rifkind, and attached a firm draft personal (yet also official) message from him to the head of government, whom he knew. Malcolm Rifkind (later, inter alia, secretary of state for defence and foreign secretary) summoned me to discuss the problem. He told me that he accepted the arguments in the submission, but wanted to be significantly tougher in the personal message. I rewrote the draft and persuaded the head of the FCO African department concerned not to object to it. The toughened message, which now included a clear implication that the United Kingdom might have to consider the value of continuing diplomatic relations with the country concerned, did the trick: the site was reopened and work resumed, with next to no extra cost to Britain. It was another three months or so before the head of mission established the underlying – and astonishing – truth: the minister concerned had a mother-in-law who was in living in the United Kingdom. She had overstayed her visa and, just as our construction work had begun, was deported back home – where the minister evidently did not want her to be at all. Left and right hands in Whitehall (Home Office and FCO) were not in effective communication at all.

The history of the British diplomatic estate is a fascinating and often surprising one, with much political content and some intrigue, even conspiracy. I left OED in mid-1985 convinced that three years of effort had led at any rate to some useful modernising reforms and to some increased efficiency in the estate of the day. I concluded that the decision to move the responsibility and budget from a home department to the FCO had been the correct one; that the estate professions made essential contributions to good decisions and continuing good management of the diplomatic estate; that the department needed to be run with sensitivity and with professional diplomatic skills; and that there was still, and would continue to be, a great deal to do, both in estate management and in policy work. Crucially, I also believed that despite (and, by now, also because of) the vital need for understanding of and familiarity with the business of diplomacy, architect Mark Bertram, rather than another diplomat, should succeed me.

I was delighted that the FCO accepted my proposal to this effect. In a development unprecedented in the FCO, Mark succeeded me when I moved on after some three years. With a later promotion to under-secretary grade, he headed OED with great success and distinction for the next 12 years. (Later, there was still further reorganisation; unsurprisingly, given the modern Whitehall penchant for change, often seemingly just for the sake of change.) As a savant and researcher, too, Mark was thus uniquely qualified to write an authoritative and seminal history of the British diplomatic estate. He has done so in *Room for Diplomacy*. All our heads of diplomatic missions and a good number of our politicians would profit much from reading it.

Assistant under-secretary (economic) in the FCO in 1988 was a job for which I did feel I had some qualifications and aptitude. AUS is the third rank in the FCO among officials (below both deputy under-secretary and permanent under-secretary), and classically supervises departments, in the AUS (economic) case only two in my time: the commercial management and exports department (COMED) and the economic relations department (ERD). There was also some joint work with the overseas development administration (ODA). The deputy under-secretary to whom I worked at first was the excellent and immensely likeable Roderick Braithwaite – but soon he left to become ambassador to Russia. Roderick was succeeded by the academically very able and distinguished Nicholas Bayne, who had served as head of ERD and more recently as ambassador and permanent representative to the Organisation for Economic Cooperation and Development (OECD) based in Paris. In practice, subjects were mostly divided between us, Nicholas taking, for example, such heavyweight economic work as G7 'summitry'. He was the most pleasant of colleagues and a formidably effective and always gentlemanly operator. After a successful posting as high commissioner in Canada, Sir Nicholas became a distinguished and published academic at the London School of Economics and a fellow of its international relations department. He recently wrote a most readable memoir, *Economic Diplomat*.

With Nicholas's and his wife Diana's permission, I should record a uniquely tragic example of the worst of life in the Diplomatic Service. In 1984, while he was serving as ambassador to Zaire (and accredited also to the Congo, Rwanda and Burundi), their second son, Charles, visited his parents after completing his schooling. While on an expedition and a thousand miles from his parents' then home in Kinshasa he had a most dreadful accident. He dived from a boat into the Zaire (formerly Congo) river where it was unexpectedly shallow, hit his head on the river bed, broke his neck and nearly drowned. He was paralysed from the neck down. Thirty-six hours and 3,000 miles of travel by dug-out, boat, Land Rover, light aeroplane, ambulances and a scheduled flight took Charlie to hospital in Pretoria (South Africa), where he had an operation on his neck and metal braces applied. Months later, this very brave young man was in Stoke Mandeville Hospital. He learned how to cope with the extreme disabilities and dependencies of being a tetraplegic. Eventually he was able to operate an electric wheelchair of special design and a mouth-stick with which to write by electric typewriter and later computer. Ten months after his horrendous accident, Charlie was discharged from Stoke Mandeville.

Before Charlie had his accident, he had won a place at Trinity College, Cambridge. He went there in 1985. A generous and most thoughtful college and wonderful full-time community service volunteers made life and work possible for him. During vacations, he travelled to Paris, whither Nicholas had been posted, in a specially adapted van and with loyal, supportive companions. Charlie studied hard at Cambridge, first at Anglo-Saxon and then social anthropology. He wrote much, if inevitably laboriously, including long exams working by mouth-stick. He did very well in his Part I exams the summer his parents moved back to England from Paris. Charlie went travelling by van again in 1988, ambitiously and successfully, in Scandinavia. In the following summer of 1989, despite all the privations and some additional illness, Charlie secured a 2.1 in his finals at Cambridge. He followed this by travelling again, with two companions by car – in the USSR, in Soviet bloc Eastern Europe, and in the USA. In January 1990, Charlie began work full-time at the Department of the Environment, on noise control and domestic waste recycling. The department provided special equipment to enable him to work: he did so, to excellent effect. Charlie died unexpectedly in the summer of 1990, at home.

I was much privileged to meet Charlie once at his home with Nicholas and Diana. I was also much stirred. I am greatly impressed by how his parents and his brothers worked for him with love, devotion, imagination and understanding. The FCO was most sympathetic and helpful throughout. The Office arranged for Charlie to go to Stoke Mandeville; for Nicholas and Diana to travel frequently between Kinshasa, Pretoria and London; for Nicholas's posting to Zaire to be cut short; and for him to be posted to the civil service selection board in London for six months so that the family could be together. The FCO then appointed Nicholas to the OECD ambassadorship in Paris (in which position he did so well), because it was readily accessible to the United Kingdom. It also authorised works on the house in Paris to make it accessible for Charlie. I had my own by far less serious reasons (from Sofia) to know that when the welfare need is there, the FCO responds as an excellent employer.

It is intensely moving to read Charlie's book *A Travelling Man*, which his brother Dick edited from Charlie's writings. This is a book of prose and poetry, of travelogue, of deep thought, of equally deep frustration, of love for family, of rationalisation, of explanation, not quite of reconciliation, but implicitly of enormous and inspiring courage.

That AUS(E) job was indeed varied. It included some necessary coordination work with the ODA, on aid policy, principally as a member of the Aid Policy Board. The ODA was then part of the FCO, with a separate minister of state for overseas development reporting to the foreign secretary. I attended that minister's weekly morning meetings of junior ministerial and senior official staff. Initially, the minister was Chris (now Lord) Patten, whom I had first met years before in Washington. His intellectual and human grasp of the sometimes complex issues was most impressive, and he conducted thoughtful, valuable and often searching meetings. It was no surprise when he was later promoted to the cabinet (though how much he relished the Department of the Environment's chalice loaded then with the community charge – poll tax – was perhaps another question). He was later, and famously, the last governor of Hong Kong. I was among regional heads of mission who attended a memorable conference there and who Chris and Lavender kindly entertained to dinner. Chris's successor at the ODA was Lynda (later Baroness) Chalker, whose warmth and humanity endeared her to so many, including officials and, it seemed, all of Africa – not only aid recipients. Lynda had a fear of flying, perhaps especially in small aeroplanes. Yet she flew a lot, including in bad weather, in the course of her distinguished and effective service as minister of state for overseas development. Lynda's parliamentary private secretary was the intellectually able and pleasant David Nicholson, MP for Taunton, whose knowledge, sense of political history and humour I came much to admire and enjoy after I had retired, and whose friendship I value highly.

There were some problems between the FCO and the ODA. But they were few, mostly concerned policy matters and mostly were resolved well. I recall only one tricky one that needed Nicholas Bayne's help to settle amicably and usefully. I thought that the then arrangement that the ODA was part of the FCO but with its own minister worked well in the national interest. There was a joint ODA/FCO department–aid policy department, with whose under-secretary, Barrie Ireton, I worked happily. I recall the overseas aid target of 0.7% of national income being then discussed as a long-term aspiration, but not one that could be achieved at the time, or in the then foreseeable future. The cost and the concerns we had even then about the defensibility of such a high expenditure and the risk of corruption in some countries and governments militated against such an aim. Budgetary aid can be disbursed with speed, but not always with assurance of value for money for the British taxpayer. Project aid can carry risks too, but when well managed can both provide long term much needed gain for recipient communities, and help preserve jobs in the United Kingdom.

Other AUS policy work in the FCO proper included the negotiation of mutual legal aid treaties (MLATs). With drug agreements, these were the work of a desk in economic relations department. ERD conducted international negotiations to secure these agreements bilaterally with individual overseas governments and multilaterally with several. When successful, these agreements led to cooperative international systems and work to counter, for example, drug money laundering. I had come across the then new Whitehall fashion for employing British consultants as head of OED in the 1980s, where it mostly worked well. It was still new to the rest of the FCO in the 1990s and as AUS(E) it was rather against my instinct to employ consultants to write reports on the scope for new effective agreements in these very different, more classically diplomatic, international legal fields. We did employ consultants, under a contract that I thought generous to the company, to write such a report on the Caribbean within six weeks, and to a brief drafted in ERD. Despite my attempts to guide and chase the company, and despite their visits to the region and their assurances of endeavour, the eventual report was weeks late in delivery. In my view it was also lightweight and of poor quality.

I asked a first secretary member of ERD, Nicola Brewer, to start from scratch and write a report at her desk in ten days. Nicola did a job of sheer excellence, which led directly to productive international agreements. Lesson learned, I hoped. (To the surprise of none who know her Nicola's career has further blossomed. Dame Nicola is now British high commissioner to South Africa – and due to regrettable FCO cuts, also accredited to Swaziland and Lesotho.)

ERD worked on some subjects, such as economic summitry, directly to Nicholas Bayne. Others, such as vexed questions in extraterritoriality and international debt, came to me. Only fairly occasionally did we need to combine forces, or I work directly to Nicholas. The two first-class heads of the department with whom I served, notably different in styles, were Tom Richardson (later ambassador in Rome where he was knighted) and Roger Bone (later ambassador to Sweden and then to Brazil, where he became Sir Roger).

COMED involved much policy work. I regret that there had been frequent bad blood between the FCO and the then Department of Trade and Industry (DTI) over commercial diplomatic (export and inward investment promotion) policy and practice in overseas markets. That bad blood was but a few drops compared to that shed in the turf wars I had witnessed among arms of the US administration in Washington. However, it was a serious waste of British taxpayers' money and often counter-productive in what should have been the joint pursuit of commercial and investment opportunities and market share abroad for British companies. I do hope that latter aim has by now been achieved.

With the splendidly calm and sensible Roy Reeve as head of COMED, we pursued genuine joint trade promotion work across Whitehall. Nicholas Bayne, Roy Reeve and I negotiated at DUS level with the DTI, with COMED doing much underlying work, towards a joint FCO/DTI directorate. Joint exports promotion department was established with staff from both departments. This was the first time the FTO and DTI joined forces, under joint ministerial direction, to settle and pursue policy and practice in exports and inward investment promotion. Nowadays, after much enlargement and several name changes, there is a large joint trade and inward investment promotion organisation called United Kingdom Trade and Industry (UKTI) that covers work in Whitehall and in posts abroad and works to ministers in both departments. I hope UKTI is not too cumbersome to work well for industry. The fact that it fairly recently took on defence sales promotion work from the Ministry of Defence did concern me, but the defence industry evidently wanted the work to stay there when the government changed in May 2010. Certainly yet further change for its own sake alone would have be costly and, at least for a while, detrimental.

The good Roy Reeve had started in the FCO as a Russian specialist. A well-begun career suffered in 1988 when he had to leave Moscow in a reciprocal expulsion of diplomats. Roy became both a political and a commercial operator in the Service. After very sound leadership of and work in COMED, he was appointed consul-general in Sydney, where I was delighted to find him four years after I came to the end of my time as an AUS.

I was particularly encouraged by William Hague's strong emphasis on commercial diplomatic work soon after he became foreign secretary. This development was first affirmed in an important speech that he made in September 2011 on his view of the future of the FCO and the Diplomatic Service. William Hague noted what he called the 'staggering decision by Ministers in 2007 to remove the FCO's protection against exchange rate movements' (the Treasury at work again in arguing for the abandonment of the Overseas Price Mechanism that compensated for unforeseen movements against sterling). He analysed and criticised shrewdly and wisely much that was amiss, and described what had been done and would be done to correct faults where corrective action was practicable. One such action was in the economic and commercial field, action which he had heralded in an earlier speech. The new declared intention was to equip our diplomats with sharper economic skills and specialist knowledge to enable them better to spot commercial opportunities and to build relationships to develop greater trade and inward investment. Following a discussion and exchange of letters I had with Lord Strathclyde, Leader of the House of Lords, the FCO kindly invited me to a meeting to discuss some of the implementation of William Hague's policy plans. I do hope sufficient resources will be allocated to that work, and that the foreign and commonwealth secretary's initiative to bring commercial work to the fore (again) in diplomacy works well. It ought to, to the benefit of the UK economy.

COMED also covered CoCom policy work, which I had pursued as UK delegate to the coordinating committee in Paris, and on which I had written in Berkeley. At AUS level there was an occasional need to visit Paris for 'high level' CoCom meetings and, once, for a call on the then French finance minister. I found a good way to reach Paris quickly in the late 1980s was to travel along the River Thames by fast catamaran, to board a bus for a short ride to City airport, and thence to fly at interestingly low level to Paris. I could pick out our boys' school as we flew over Tonbridge.

The desk officer for CoCom work in COMED was Donald, the MacLaren of MacLaren, a fine Diplomatic Service brain and character who had served in Berlin and Moscow. Later, in the FCO planning staff, Donald wrote the only paper of which I am aware that accurately predicted the fall of the Berlin Wall and made policy suggestions about how we should react. Donald later served in Cuba, Venezuela and Ukraine, and became ambassador to Georgia before retiring early to my and others' regret.

One of the less than enjoyable tasks I had as an AUS was to be the FCO member of a review of exports credits guarantee department (ECGD) – a task, however, greatly relieved by the sheer pleasure of working with its widely experienced and wise chief executive, Malcolm Stephens. The review was initiated by the Treasury, who seemed to want what they described as 'the zero option' – i.e. the British government would in effect abnegate all responsibility for insuring British companies against foreign risk: ECGD would be privatised. I had nothing against privatisation in principle, but some of ECGD's work involved sovereign debt, and I could not see how private insurance could possibly manage that, nor commercially complex political risk, long-term large international debts, nor international guarantees of bank loans. The battle, which involved DUS Nicholas Bayne as well, was long. At times it seemed both bitter and sadly divorced from the real world of overseas governments, finance, politics and markets. The end result was that HM Government sold the short term credit guarantee business of ECGD to, interestingly, a Dutch bidder (though work and jobs went to Wales). I am glad to note that ECGD guaranteed almost £3 billion in British exports in 2010–11, an increase of one-third; and was the first major export credit agency to resume cover for Libya after the upheavals of 2011.

There was some interesting work, too, on arms sales policy. A tussle seemed inevitable between the need to make sales abroad for the good of the economy and the creation or preservation of jobs in the United Kingdom on the one hand, and the risk of how the defence equipment might be used (that is, the human rights concerns) on the other. CoCom constraints and enforcement were designed to deal in those late Cold War times with military risk to us and our allies. Human rights concerns were usually met by strict, monitored 'end-use' controls. Yet the debates and difficulties were sometimes rightly tough and tense. A particular problem in this field will be discussed in the next chapter.

Such broad policy matters apart, it was interesting as an AUS, and usually useful in the British interest, to receive calls by ambassadors and high commissioners accredited in London, to lobby or to discuss both bilateral and multilateral matters. We debated topics ranging from aid coordination policy, via CoCom subjects to exploration of how the British arranged their work, and settled upon policies in economic and commercial fields. It was always a pleasure and helpful to work with the FCO economic advisers – a very small band of professional economists, then led by Simon Broadbent. One afternoon, Simon, David Ratford – a fellow AUS (for Eastern Europe) – and I had a long and captivating, even thrilling conversation with George Soros, mainly about his native Hungary, its finances and what HM Government ought to do, if anything, about them. We also ranged across most of Eastern Europe with this superb financial and economic mind. Once or twice I felt I might flounder in a farrago of financial hypothesising, but Simon was a match for Soros and held the government's line to good effect.

Another fascinating session in which Simon was involved was when we met economists from the then West German government to discuss new economic consequences and policies should West and East Germany reunify after the fall of the Berlin Wall. This meeting began with economic analyses exchanged across the table, and broadly agreed. The West Germans asked us to consider and let them have our view of the possibility that the Ostmark and the Deutschmark would be merged – at par; and what economic and commercial consequences we foresaw. This proposition, never breathed before, was a shock. The two currencies were so evidently and grossly unequal. We adjourned until the following day. Simon and I worked far into the night with statistics and calculators. Next morning, we told our West German colleagues that we thought the cost of such a move would be huge for the West German economy. Our interlocutors asked if we had an estimate of that cost. Carefully, we gave them a figure, with some caveats. The burden of our message was the Sir Humphreyesque one – that we thought such a policy 'brave'. The West German representatives' reply was, in crudely summarised form: 'We agree both with your figure and your comment – and we shall do it anyway'. This was a fine example of the fact that (and whatever one thinks of President Clinton's electorally related remark 'it's the economy, stupid') politics so often rules economics. And today, reunited Germany is once again the economic powerhouse of Europe, though only after great trials and tribulations both for the Germans and our fellow Europeans, and with still more difficulties in prospect.

Also a source of much enjoyment and professional satisfaction were meetings with British ministers – once with three secretaries of state: our own Geoffrey Howe (who mastered his every brief with the skill of a leading lawyer) was host to Lord Young from Trade and Industry and George Younger, then at Defence. One official adviser from each department of state completed the cast around a tense but very well-behaved table. After exchanges and debate, a disputatious, difficult and important matter of export policy was settled by the gentle and effective chairmanship of Geoffrey Howe.

There was a good deal of work with other ministers, too, in the FCO and elsewhere in Whitehall. Outside the FCO, I was particularly impressed with Michael Portillo, whom I first met when, as minister of state for transport, he spoke to the export group for the construction industries. I was also impressed with Tim Eggar, minister for energy. I thought later that both were serious losses to HM Government.

Several of these ministers paid official visits to us abroad. To have known and worked to them in Whitehall as an AUS was a bonus in designing their visits to best effect. Also in Whitehall, work with HM Treasury included subjects such as ECGD; the French-proposed European Bank for Reconstruction and Development, whose base we secured for London, with a first head from France; international debt/equity swaps; and difficult country cases, such as Zambia.

Attendance at some meetings of the court of the Bank of England was another privilege, flowing in part from work with the then British Invisibles Export Council, so well chaired by the late, admirable Lord Limerick, who had served as minister for trade in Ted Heath's government. (Pat Limerick became a good friend and colleague after I retired. He died young and is much missed by many.) In the chair at the bank court was the governor, the distinguished and accomplished Robin Leigh-Pemberton, later Baron Kingsdown (and a fellow trustee of the Chevening Estate years later).

The AUS job took me behind the Iron Curtain in support of British companies. Hungary was then doing better than most of the Comecon states, which is not to say a lot. Romania I found a sad economic as well as political story. Bulgaria allowed me mixed success and some nostalgia (see Chapter 3). I visited Moscow a couple of times. It was good to see our commercial diplomatic work in these countries on the ground being carried out so much more effectively in the late 1980s than in the 1960s, despite all the Soviet bloc constraints that still raged. How much greater the commercial opportunities for UK plc must be now that three of those countries are members of our biggest market abroad, the rest of the European Union – despite the failure of the EU yet to complete the Single Market.

In the context of commercial work, it was a very good move for the then permanent under-secretary, Patrick Wright, to give regular working (sandwich) lunches for senior British businessmen in the FCO. COMED organised these and proposed agendas and guest lists. We co-opted a few other guests from Whitehall. We listened to business people's beefs and suggestions; and some good policy adjustments, as well as action by the FCO and posts abroad on specific cases needing help, emanated from the discussions. Certainly there was no shortage of people from the City and industry keen to attend. Among the general policy subjects discussed was the plan, on which ministers were unsurprisingly keen, to charge British companies for commercial diplomatic work done on their behalf by our posts abroad. I could see some advantages, such as filtering out some unnecessary effort in which companies did not themselves believe. Even there, however, my experience suggested that such filtering could well be done at posts without much waste of time, and sometimes with advantage in moving effort to more productive work on industry's behalf. Overall, I was personally opposed to the new policy, believing it would raise no great sums, since charges were to be set at rates a good deal lower than any realistic estimate of our costs. Some companies would be deterred from seeking new markets overseas. And charging would create largely nugatory extra work. However, charging was government policy, which of course I therefore had to advance, explain and defend – in short, sell – to British industry. Charging was introduced and eventually accepted by most British industrialists, who recognised remarkably good value for their money. I recall that, after a year or so, I invited trade ministers to increase the charges for the sake of achieving a little more credibility and even respect for our commercial service abroad – to no avail.

For an AUS, there was some representational work, as the Diplomatic Service refers to the many forms of being on parade for Britain – activity more common in posts abroad where its most frequent manifestation is the much disliked but often useful cocktail party. The highest form by far in London for the under-secretaries was attendance at the Queen's diplomatic reception at Buckingham Palace. The principal guests were senior members of foreign high commissions and embassies, and luminaries such as the Commonwealth secretary-general. Dress for the evening was 'white tie' or national dress, complete with decorations. The arrangements for this extensive and generous reception were detailed and, for under-secretaries, involved advance briefing at the palace. The main floor of the palace would be filled by guests. The royal family would begin a progress among all present at one end of the picture gallery. The under-secretaries were 'allocated' a member of the Royal Family other than the Queen and the Duke of

Edinburgh to accompany and escort throughout the floor, ending in the ballroom. As we progressed we presented the diplomatic guests to the royals. It was, of course, a glittering and elegant occasion. The royal family all worked hard and impressively and a great deal of good was done –and no doubt still is every year. The extra joy was that wives of under-secretaries were also invited. After a couple of hours of my royal duty, Hilary and I met and danced in the ballroom where a wonderful military orchestra played all evening.

At a different level, Nicholas Bayne and I held an annual 'economic' summer reception for our official contacts in the London diplomatic world and beyond, and for staff. In 1989 we used the Durbar Court Conference Room in the FCO where, in 1965, I had taken the note at Anglo-German talks on the Middle East, on the Monday our son, John, was born. In those days one would not have dreamed of seeking time away from the Office, although I had been with Hilary in the hospital for most of the previous weekend during a tense and prolonged labour. So I contrived breaks in the talks to rush across the corridor to a room with a telephone to borrow (and eventually to hear John's first cries).

In the summer of 1990, my last as an AUS, we thought of using the beautifully restored and rather splendid Locarno rooms for a rather larger party, following Nicholas's latest (and difficult) summit meeting at Houston. A defensive FCO official thought that the secretary of state, Douglas Hurd, would want to give the first reception in the restored historic rooms and that we should go elsewhere. The official might have been more defensive still had he known that when an FO official, Douglas himself had worked in economic relations department in the Locarno rooms. The rooms were then partitioned into small offices with plywood walls under a lowered protective ceiling and had been, I believe, since the Second World War. Douglas Hurd, however, was delighted that we should go ahead. I recall him telling me that the Locarno Treaties of 1925, after which the rooms were named, were negotiated in Switzerland but signed in London – and earned Austen Chamberlain a Nobel Peace Prize. The 'spirit of Locarno' was however rather short-lived: Adolf Hitler tore up the treaties, most importantly their Rhineland Pact, in 1936, when he sent the German Army to occupy the Rhineland. Nonetheless the FCO and the United Kingdom are fortunate to have the Locarno rooms in the wonderful building between Downing and King Charles Streets.

On that summer evening in July 1990, I left my office in good time to take up my place at the entrance to the Locarno rooms alongside Nicholas. Guests arrived in a stream. Among them, I recall with particular pleasure, was Sam Wanamaker. But there was no sign of Nicholas. It was well into the party before I received a message that he had been admitted to hospital for an emergency operation. Nicholas recovered well over time: other colleagues and I guessed that the root cause of his initially serious illness was probably stress (though he showed no overt sign in the Office) from various personal and work causes, including the dietary and other disadvantages of excessive international travel and work.

Other 'representational' duties in London included attending De La Rue's annual diplomatic dinner: a fine evening for the heads of mission of the Diplomatic Corps accredited to the Court of St James. The dinner was a much admired promotional exercise for this famous and fine British company with extensive commercial interests worldwide, notably with overseas governments; a fixture in London's calendar, and an occasion for major speeches. At the first I attended, the speaker was the Princess Royal.

For the same foreign and commonwealth diplomats in London there was also the secretary of state's diplomatic banquet. I recall one held in the British Museum when I sat not far from the Elgin Marbles and next to the Burmese ambassador, with whom I had less than an enjoyable evening of debate. Another in that same summer of 1990 was held in the FCO's marvellous Durbar Court which, with its marble and other glories, also suitably protected and hidden, had once housed the FCO's communications department. The profusion of so much marble made the Durbar Court acoustics dreadful for years after its restoration, and meant that red wine could not be served lest any spilled and stained the floor.

The De La Rue dinner continues. I imagine the secretary of state's banquet has been at the least severely scaled down.

It was a joy to participate in a 'British Invisibles' promotional event aboard HMY *Britannia* in the pool of London – and indeed to be aboard *Britannia* once again after the triumph of the 1972 state visit to Singapore (see Chapter 5). Beyond her royal functions, in themselves of serious economic importance to the United Kingdom, the royal yacht performed valuable service for the British economy right around the world. I well understood the financial constraints of replacing an ageing ship and of manning and maintaining a successor, but I am among many who deeply regret her demise.

Service in the FCO in Whitehall during a diplomatic career is said to enhance the career, and there is some truth in that. It is also to endure a rather grey commuting existence, as for so many others in Whitehall and elsewhere. As I hope this chapter illustrates, London postings also offer much varied and worthwhile work in the national interest and a generally rewarding if sometimes frustrating experience. Yet the FCO's involvement with Parliament is a good deal less than for many home civil service departments for whom legislation and its progress or otherwise is the stuff of life. FCO officials are from time to time summoned to appear before appropriate select committees in Parliament (as at the PAC described earlier) but direct involvement with the whole House of Commons is rarer. I was therefore grateful to be in support of the ODA when some aid legislation was debated and progressed there – one of very few official ventures I made into the House. Another had to do with East–West Export Policy and CoCom.

I spent some time in the summer of 1990 preparing for my next posting, as ambassador to Indonesia. I learned some of the language, Bahasa Indonesia, in the evenings. A few colleagues and I went to Hereford for two days to be inducted – just in case – by the Special Air Service into various methods and consequences of being taken hostage abroad. The SAS majored on attempted rescue, sometimes in darkness, with multiple skirmishing, much shouting, great noise of gunshots and most impressive military professionalism. Those two days were quite a change from international economics and politics; but not a huge change, save in weaponry, from equally memorable Whitehall turf battles I had also survived.

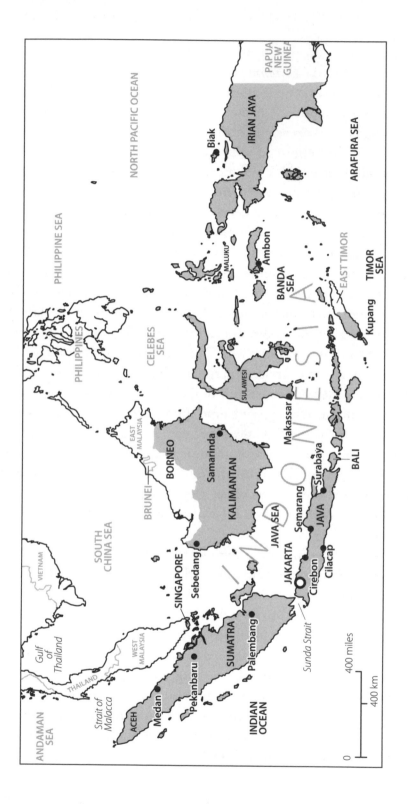

CHAPTER 10

AMBASSADOR TO INDONESIA, LAND OF COMPLEX DIPLOMACY

Before leaving the United Kingdom in mid-1990 Hilary and I were granted an audience with HM The Queen whom, of course, and whose government we were to represent in Indonesia. Her Majesty's ambassadors pay such calls as a matter of normal practice whenever possible. Such a call is, of course, a highlight among all the also necessary Whitehall, City and business briefing calls. It is a truism to say that the Queen is immensely experienced and knowledgeable. Hilary and I hugely enjoyed the private audience, which also included a good story or two and laughs.

After an absorbing and busy time in London as an assistant under-secretary, I was keen to serve abroad again. The job of ambassador to Indonesia was in some senses a natural, I having become familiar with aid policy and practice, and Indonesia having a large British aid programme. There was much scope for commercial diplomacy. I had served nearby, in Singapore. The prospect of Indonesia was both enticing and daunting, with its stratified and complex culture and politics; its broad and rich potential allied sadly with corruption, but more sadly also with subsistence-level poverty; its geographical spread; and its sheer size. Yet I was to learn that there is so much more than all this in the pursuit of British interests in beautiful and intriguing Indonesia.

The Indonesian protocol of the day meant that until I had presented my letters of credence to President Soeharto in person, I could have official dealings only with the foreign minister, Ali Alatas – and with no other minister or ministry. Ali Alatas kindly welcomed me for a courtesy call that included much substance on our first morning in Indonesia. The standard wait for a credentials ceremony was a month. Hilary and I decided to spend half of that month in Jogjakarta. We stayed with an hospitable and welcoming Indonesian family and attended language classes at Realia, a well-staffed and professionally impressive school for foreigners. This was an immersion course and we spoke nothing but Indonesian all the working day and with the family morning and evening. We failed to follow just one of the school rules – that we should also speak only Indonesian when alone, including in our bedroom. The course certainly helped professionally: I was able eventually to undertake short television and radio interviews in Bahasa Indonesia and to make parts of speeches in the language.

I could not have done the latter, however, without the professional skills of the United Kingdom-based member of the embassy staff of whom I thought, in a rather old-fashioned way, as the Oriental Secretary. That title originated in the Middle East, of course, but applied exactly to the functions of the third later second secretary (political) in the embassy in Jakarta, Jon Benjamin. Jon, who has fine political sense, had spent a year in Jogjakarta learning Bahasa Indonesia in great depth before joining the embassy, and was well established in Jakarta when we arrived. His Indonesian was in the true sense fluent: he even spoke some of the Jakartan patois. He had the Indonesian staff literally rolling on the floor with laughter at the embassy Christmas pantomime. Jon has outstanding linguistic ability. I recall my German ambassadorial colleague telling me that at one of his morning meetings he asked his staff who was the young German expatriate he had seen and heard the evening before: it was Jon. This gifted young man became British ambassador to Chile in 2009. My counsellor and head of chancery, Peter Collecott, was also especially able and effective. He and his wife were beneficiaries of an enlightened FCO personnel policy of cooperation with the Australian Department of Foreign Affairs and Trade. Both organisations tried hard to send Australian-British married couples to the same or nearby posts. Peter and Judith had met while both were serving in Khartoum. Married, they worked for their respective services in Canberra,

London, Jakarta, Bonn/Stockholm, and London again, before the Australians finally lost Judith when she accompanied Peter to his final post as ambassador to Brazil. All our embassy staff, senior and junior, were skilled and of great help in inducting a new ambassador into the complexities of Indonesian culture, politics, trade practices and much more, and indeed into the consular pitfalls the British faced in the almost countless islands of Indonesia.

A few facts and a brief look at Indonesia's history might help to set this scene that was new to us, despite our earlier service across the Strait of Malacca in Singapore. At some 238 million people, Indonesia is the fourth most populous country in the world. It has the world's largest Muslim population – more Muslims than in all the Middle East. The country is some 742,000 square miles (nearly 2 million square kilometres) in area and has some 17,500 islands, stretching over 3,300 miles (5,310kms) from east to west and 1,100 miles (1,770kms) north to south. The volcanic archipelago is a major part of the Pacific 'Ring of Fire'. It demonstrates the fact with frequent eruptions. Traders from India brought Hinduism and Buddhism to Indonesia from the first century AD. In the fifteenth century, Arab traders brought the Muslim religion, which largely but not completely, superseded these faiths. Christianity, Animism and mixtures of religions and beliefs are also scattered among the islands today. There are some 300 local languages.

The Portuguese began spice trading in the sixteenth century. So did the British and the Dutch. The Dutch East India Company achieved partial authority over the Indonesian archipelago, and the Netherlands East Indies government consolidated control during the nineteenth century. The British were in charge for five years during the Napoleonic wars, but otherwise the Dutch were in power until the Japanese occupation during the Second World War. In 1945, Indonesian Nationalists proclaimed the Republic of Indonesia. Negotiations with the Dutch, and some recurring hostilities, lasted until 1950, when the republic was admitted to the United Nations.

Thomas Stamford Raffles, who later founded the British settlement of Singapore, was lieutenant-governor of Java and its dependencies from 1811 to 1816. He wrote a scholarly and seminal two-volume

History of Java, published in 1817. In it he described the Javanese as 'a highly polished people, considerably advanced in science, highly imaginative and full of penetration'.

Raffles also wrote, penetratingly:

> Where not corrupted by indulgence on the one hand, or stupefied by oppression on the other, the Javans appear to be a generous and warm-hearted people. In their domestic relations they are kind, affectionate, gentle and contented; in their public, they are obedient, honest and faithful. In their intercourse with society, they display, in a high degree, the virtues of honesty, plain dealing and candour ... No people possess a quicker apprehension of what is stated, or obtain a more rapid proficiency in what they have a desire to learn ... Their religious enthusiasm is no sooner excited than they become at once adventurous, esteeming no labour too arduous, no result impossible, and no privation painful.

One last brief Rafflesian observation about the Javanese: 'The further they are removed from European influence, the better are their morals and the happier are the people.'

Indonesians have many other traits too, of course, of which just one is the ability to think, act, and above all discourse, at a plurality of levels. After a serious talk with an Indonesian official, from then President Soeharto down, I found it necessary to sit and think carefully before establishing usually at least three levels of meaning, senses or interpretations of what I had been told.

Raffles's five-year-long British administration of Java from 1811 to 1816 resulted from an Anglo-Dutch deal done when the Netherlands saw a need to concentrate their efforts at home against Napoleon. The Dutch and we had also agreed on swaps of land around the region and the world. For example, we British gave the Dutch a beautiful and productive little coral spice island in the Banda Sea called Rhun. We British had occupied Rhun informally from 1603 and formally from 1616: some scholars argue it was thus the first British colony. A fort was built there to protect our trading interests.

In direct exchange for Rhun with its high importance in the spice trade in nutmeg and mace, and by virtue of land exchanges agreed as part of the 1667 Treaty of Breda at the end of the second Anglo-Dutch war, we acquired the business end of an island in the western North Atlantic, just off the coast of one of our then colonies: a territory the Dutch had named Nieu Amsterdam. When Hilary and I and my marvellous PA, Ann Douthwaite, visited Rhun and walked along its sandy main street among its houses made of coral, we met the delightful islanders on our way to the ruins of the former English fort and came to the one crossroads on the island. Here we were to enjoy the humour of the islanders, and to be reminded of the modern name of Nieu Amsterdam. Slung above the golden sandy crossroads between two great coconut palms was a banner reading 'Welcome to Manhattan'.

In Surabaya, East Java around the end of the Second World War in 1945, a British Indian Army brigadier, A.W.S. Mallaby CIE OBE, was the senior British officer in Eastern Java. With then President Sukarno and his senior officers, Mallaby negotiated a truce and the ceasefire arrangements for the establishment of the Republic after the British action to secure Indonesia following the Japanese surrender. The day the truce was agreed in principle and when details were being worked out, Mallaby was cruelly and pointlessly shot dead at close range in the Lincoln car the Indonesians had allocated to him. British officers with him threw a grenade (the only weapon they had) at the Indonesian assailant – probably unauthorised and possibly crazed. (In the temper of the time, the British retaliated by bombing Surabaya, killing thousands.) Brigadier Mallaby's body was buried in Surabaya. His remains were later reburied in the British Commonwealth section of a Dutch war cemetery and later still in the British cemetery in Jakarta.

Margaret Thatcher visited Jakarta for five days in December 1992 – when President Soeharto invested her as the first foreign honorary member of the Indonesian Institute of Engineers. I took Mrs Thatcher (as Lady Thatcher then was) to the British cemetery. She and I both know, and much like, Mallaby's son, Christopher, who was nine years old when his father was killed – and who, many years later, became British ambassador to France. As we walked alone in the cemetery, we talked of Brigadier Mallaby, of his widow and their son. We talked of the soldiers, sailors and airmen lost in the world wars – sacrificed in the defence of freedom. Soberly and sadly, Mrs Thatcher spoke of the men whom she had sent 'with great reluctance' to their similar deaths in the Falklands. She 'knew some of them would die'. Mrs Thatcher then laid a tribute at Brigadier Mallaby's grave. We stood, silently; then walked very slowly the 25 yards or so back to the cross of remembrance where the embassy chaplain awaited us. Throughout that walk, tears ran profusely down Margaret Thatcher's face.

After the British secured Indonesia in 1945, reassertion of Dutch colonial control there was problematic. For five years or so, Indonesia struggled determinedly and increasingly effectively towards independence. Cold war economic and strategic competition was rife in South-East Asia. With Soviet urging, communist insurrections broke out in Indonesia and around the region. The Dutch attacked Jogjakarta, captured President Sukarno, and initially rejected international pressure to withdraw from their colony. The United Nations eventually admitted the Republic of Indonesia to membership in 1950. Irian Jaya as I knew it, West Irian as the Dutch knew it, (West) Papua, or Papua (Barat) as it is now called, became part of the republic a good deal later, in 1963.

In that same year, 1963, Sukarno began his campaign against, to use one of Sukarno's neologisms, 'Nekolim' (neo-colonialism, colonialism, imperialism). That campaign heralded 'Konfrontasi' (Confrontation) against, initially, the eastern states of Malaysia – Sarawak and Sabah, which border Indonesian Borneo, or Kalimantan. Soviet-armed Indonesian troops staged raids into Malaysia. Sukarno, of course, eventually lost that conflict, in part, perhaps, because his plan for, or expectation of, support from the Chinese communities within east Malaysia came to naught. But in my view he failed principally because of the active and effective military support for Malaysia provided by British, Australian and New Zealand forces.

I should like to record two true stories of Confrontation. The first took place in September 1963, the day rioting students and others sacked and burned the British embassy building in Jakarta. The building had been opened in August 1962. The ambassador, Sir Andrew Gilchrist, was a fine Scot and diplomat – who, by happenstance, was also a predecessor of mine as consul-general in Chicago, where he introduced the sport of curling to the United States. On 16 September 1963, Andrew was working in his Jakarta office while also observing an anti-British demonstration outside. Major Rory Walker, another Scot and Andrew's assistant military attaché, arrived in uniform to request permission from the ambassador to go down and play the bagpipes to calm or divert the demonstrators. Andrew agreed. But he also kept a closer eye on developments below his window, and soon saw that the bagpipe playing was arousing, even antagonising the demonstrators. (Sassenachs in the Embassy might have expected that reaction.) Sir Andrew ran down the stairs and ushered his fellow Scot back into the embassy. My own military attaché, Colonel Ker, tells me that he has seen a photograph, taken a little later, of the determined if arguably ill-advised Rory, piping from the embassy roof.

Two days later, on 18 September, ambassadorial Union flag pulled down, Indonesian flag brandished; the demonstration became a riot, a fire and a rout. Contingency plans for destroying classified papers and evacuating the embassy were implemented. The staff retreated calmly, leaving the mob to their mayhem. Cars were overturned; some were set on fire. The embassy itself was largely burnt out. (Thirty years later in the roof space I found a few beams that had not been replaced at the subsequent reconstruction: they were still blackened from the flames of September 1963.) That evening in his residence, then just down Jalan Teuku Umar, the ambassador completed his reporting telegram for dispatch to London by the stand-by secure communications system. One brief paragraph of the ambassadorial telegram referred to his official car, the Flag car, a fine Austin Princess limousine of which he was inordinately fond, and which had its own privileged parking space at the roadside in front of the embassy. The paragraph read, 'The charred corpse of my beloved Princess is even now causing an elegant traffic jam outside the Embassy.'

The ambassador's telegram was distributed that evening in Whitehall. A copy was put in the prime minister's box. In an illustration of the wit and prescience of both men, Harold Macmillan wrote in the margin: 'It is to be hoped that one day an historian does not misunderstand this paragraph.'

Thirty years later, it was a school friend of mine, now a distinguished and much published historian at Cambridge, Dr Ronald Hyam, who, when the Public Records Office released this document, discovered it and wrote to tell me of it while I was serving in Indonesia. I read his letter while sitting in the office Andrew Gilchrist had once used.

The second story of that period of Confrontation that I believe firmly merits recording is of a lance corporal in 42 Commando, Royal Marines. Corporal Tommy Collins played a key part in a secret cross-border raid into Kalimantan (Indonesian Borneo) to attack and destroy a base from which the Indonesians had been mortaring the Royal Marines for some time. The raid, called Operation Lively Cricket, was part of the wider cross-border Operation Claret. Lively Cricket was not a success, but Corporal Collins did very well indeed, firing his machine gun alone, wounded and under heavy fire. He kept the Indonesians at bay to cover his companions' retreat until he exhausted his ammunition. We now know that he was captured and died later that day in obscure circumstances: a very gallant young man.

Tommy Collins's young wife, Irene (then living in a married quarter in Singapore), his sister and their mother, Margaret, in Liverpool, were told simply (and truthfully) that he was missing in action, presumed dead: no geographic, nor any other detail, was supplied.

For many years on each anniversary of Collins's death, his mother mounted a 24-hour vigil outside the Ministry of Defence in London in the hope of persuading the authorities to tell her more. She hoped against hope to be able to see her son decently buried. Mrs Collins also wrote over the years to everyone of whom she could think: senior officers, ministers, prime ministers, senior Indonesians – to try to establish the truth of his death. She found the official account she was given by the authorities, even from the highest level, unconvincing to say the least. Such is the security surrounding Claret operations that even 28 years after the event, Tommy Collins's mother still knew no more; and there was no official intent that the true details should ever be released.

My splendid military attaché in Indonesia, Colonel Ian Ker of the Black Watch, had other ideas. He obtained the Commando log, which had the military details of the operation, including the map coordinates. We knew that Collins had been wearing a dog-tag and a wedding ring. We then knew nothing reliable about the manner of his death. Ian proposed to me that he should investigate further. We decided it was worth a try. Colonel Ker went off alone on multiple trips into deepest Kalimantan. He tramped and cut his way through the jungle until he found the location of the Commando operation – near a village called Sadjingen. There was no trace of anything useful to identify: the jungle had reclaimed its own. After much persevering and painstaking effort in both nearby and increasingly distant jungle villages, Colonel Ker established that shortly after Collins was killed, some Indonesians had carried a white man's body away along jungle tracks and (mostly) by dug-out canoe some 50 kilometres to another village called Sebedang, outside which it was buried.

Ian Ker found Sebedang. In the village he also found an elderly Catholic priest, who had forgotten nearly all his native Dutch and spoke only the local language and Indonesian. Ian questioned him slowly in Bahasa Indonesia, never leading, always asking open questions, and never mentioning any names. The priest, whom Ian came to know as Pastor Mo (for Modestus), remembered burying a white soldier whose body had been brought through the jungle to Sebedang. Indeed, the Indonesian military had paid much respect at the burial, providing both escort and bugler. On another of Ian Ker's visits he learned that a Chinese Indonesian villager, another Catholic, Ah Choi, had, at the age of 16, dug the grave in question. Ah Choi thought he knew where in the cemetery it was: he remembered digging it near a prominent tree. Ian went to see the gravesite and posed more careful enquiries to both. Neither Pastor Mo nor Ah Choi had any memory of the name of the white man. Ian and the priest talked of other things: of Confrontation, of the Dutch administration, of Sukarno.

On the next visit, the priest greeted Ian saying that he had thought long and hard since their last meeting. It was their conversation about Sukarno that had led the priest to what he now thought was the name of the dead man. Pastor Mo said that he had sat recalling Sukarno making speeches denouncing colonialism. He remembered how Sukarno had not been able to pronounce 'colonialism' correctly. He had used 'Nekolim' but had also said 'Collinism': that recollection of Sukarno's muddle had further triggered the priest's memory. The name of the man he had buried in the Chinese cemetery, said the priest, was Collins.

A wonderful moment: it was enough for Ian Ker to come back to the embassy in Jakarta and to agree with me the next step we should take. Deliberately with only half an eye over our shoulder towards the British Ministry of Defence, we approached the Indonesian military authorities. We both saw the chief of the naval staff, Admiral Soedibyo, and the chief of the defence staff, General Faisal Tanjung. I also raised the subject during a call to discuss other matters on President Soeharto, who was commander-in-chief. They all cooperated readily and efficiently. Soon after, Colonel Ker set off once again for West Kalimantan and Sebedang, this time in Indonesian military transport and accompanied by senior Indonesian officers, a pathologist, a dentist, PR staff and police. Indonesian logistic support abounded. Ian Ker also made the now necessary calls on the West Kalimantan governor and military chiefs.

Two curiosities are relevant at this point in the history. The first is that today's Christian cemetery at Sebedang was begun with an enemy grave – that of Tommy Collins. The second is that soon after Tommy was buried, President Sukarno visited Kalimantan and was told about Collins and the cross-border raid: in response, Sukarno joked that 'Collinism' was as dead as Colonialism. Sukarno did indeed find it difficult to pronounce the latter word – and a muddled pun is a much appreciated form of humour in Indonesia.

In Sebedang the remains from the fairly shallow Chinese Christian grave that Ah Choi had indicated and Colonel Ker had noted were exhumed. Sadly, not much remained beyond part of the skull and bones – decomposing fast during more than a quarter of a century in warm, wet volcanic soil. There was a piece of rotting wood at the uphill end of the grave that might well have been part of a cross. There was neither dog-tag nor wedding ring. Pastor Mo remembered the ring and was embarrassed that it was absent. Ian Ker wondered if it might have been taken as payment for carriage of the body – if the remains really were those of Corporal Collins. There were no boots; it is hardly unsurprising that such valuable items would also have been removed before burial. But there was some green woven material, identified by

Ah Choi as that in which the body had been wrapped when buried. It could once have been part of a military rubberised groundsheet. There were five small rubberised buttons which may have been attached to an Aertex, jungle-green military shirt. Tiny scraps of dingy green material adhered to two buckles of the sort Royal Marines used to secure the cross-over waist straps of olive green military trousers. A small screw-top glass bottle, the top secured with tape, cotton wool in the neck, still containing white powder and 20 or more tablets also rested in the grave. These, Ian Ker and I thought as we later studied the bottle, might be standard issue anti-malarial Paludrine or a water purifying compound. And there was, and this I also held in my hand, a recognisable dual-purpose compass of the sort then issued to the Commandos. The glass was intact. But water had penetrated the instrument. The compass card was damp dust. The just identifiable compass needle was brown rust. But on the back of the base was high quality chromium plate, for use both as a shaving mirror and as a heliograph to signal in Morse using flashes of sunlight. The chromium still shone as brightly as the day it left the factory in Sheffield: it was stamped 'Made in England'. Colonel Ian Ker photographed the key items from the grave.

A procession with hearse and other cars formed and was about to move off. Very bravely, particularly given his lowly status and the presence of powerful senior Indonesian officers from Jakarta, Ah Choi hammered on the senior officer's car and demanded that the Christian grave should not be emptied and the contents removed from Sebedang, where it had been kept safe for over 25 years, without the villagers' and God's blessing. After a pause, the senior officer politely agreed. Ah Choi, greatly relieved and overjoyed, rushed to the hearse, opened the back door, sank to his knees, clasped his hands and rested them on the flag-covered coffin. He stayed there for five minutes, evidently in silent prayer.

Corporal Collins's remains were thereafter driven respectfully to a waiting aeroplane; flown to Jakarta and laid out in a simple coffin in the Jakarta military headquarters chapel. The Indonesian military mounted a vigil.

At dawn next day, Colonel Ker and I attended a military parade with all the Indonesian services, their marines to the fore. The parade did solemn honour to, and marched past Corporal Collins. There was serious ceremony. Admiral Soedibyo was present. The Indonesian chief of armed services personnel, Air Marshal Suakadirul, and I signed and exchanged the necessary papers. The coffin was formally and ceremonially handed over to me as ambassador. Tribute was paid in speeches. The coffin was saluted, carried to and placed in the Indonesian military's best hearse. (I thought it might even be President Soeharto's hearse, which I had inadvertently seen in the Istana garages during an official call on the President.) The coffin was driven slowly away, the immaculately polished hearse shining in tropic dawn as brightly as that compass base. Ah Choi and Pastor Mo, present to see Lance Corporal Collins leave Indonesia for home, were thanked formally. Pastor Mo was clearly a very good soul. Of Ah Choi, Colonel Ker has said: 'There are occasions when you meet someone whose position in life and behaviour in adverse circumstances cement that person in your mind for always. Ah Choi was one of these.'

The remains were flown to the United Kingdom. A few days later in Liverpool, Corporal Collins was given a British funeral, with Royal Marine pall bearers and official representatives of the Royal Marines present. His mother Margaret was present; sad, grieving still, but at last at peace, and proud. Ian Ker later went to see her in St Helens, Merseyside, whence Tommy had come. Ian told her the true story, though rightly not all the truth: that might have been too much for her to bear.

With Indonesian military help, Colonel Ker also tracked down and interviewed the commanding officer of the infantry battalion that Tommy Collins and his Royal Marine colleagues attacked in 1963 near Sadjingen, one Major Sanyussi. It was he who had ordered the trek through the jungle and ensured proper respect at Collins's burial service conducted by Pastor Mo in Sebedang.

As I construe it, that piece of history is about heroism and sacrifice. It is also about a mother's love and military officers' devotion to the men. It has much to do with recognition of, and persistence in pursuit of, a good, even noble cause. It concerns the genuine respect that soldiers can have for their enemies. Ultimately, it relates directly to and illustrates the real stuff of international relations: cooperation and friendship.

The embassy in Jakarta had constant dealings with the Indonesian military, who played a key, even determining part in the running of the country. Royal Navy visits were rare, but there were a few valuable ones, including by the task force Orient 92 and one by HMS *Opossum*, a diesel-powered submarine. The naval attaché (NA) and I were invited to join her at sea off Surabaya, taking two Indonesian admirals with us, for a submerged exercise; a computer-driven simulated attack. One admiral carefully followed every underwater manoeuvre. The other preferred watching an adventure video in the wardroom. I had suggested to the NA that Hilary might come too. The NA was horrified at the thought that a lady might go to sea in a submarine and said the Admiralty would never countenance such a thing. At the crammed but hospitable drinks party in the submarine, alongside in Surabaya that evening, the young captain made it clear that Hilary would have been more than welcome. Royal Navy generation gap, I concluded. Hilary did join another RN vessel hove to in the Java Sea, climbing a rope ladder high up the side of HMS *Boxer*, a Type 22 frigate, from a small boat, and doing better than the NA, who, in tropical rig, cut his knees on the steel plates and bloodied his white trousers.

The naval attaché was importantly instrumental in organising a visit by a band of 'pilgrims' to a Commonwealth war graves cemetery on the site of a Japanese prisoner of war camp on the lovely island of Ambon in the Moluccas. The pilgrims, nearly 90 of them, were survivors and widows of survivors of the camp. I was concerned that 40 years after the experience of imprisonment, the survivors and the widows might find the tropical heat and the emotion of the service we planned a little hard to bear. The British Army kindly sent a small medical team from Hong Kong to help. A resident elderly but sprightly Dutch priest conducted the remembrance service in English at the cross of remembrance at the cemetery. The cemetery has some 3,000 Second World War graves, about half Australian, many Dutch and some 800 British, mostly RN and RAF, and is in a memorably beautiful setting on a slight rise from the turquoise sea. Many flame trees bloomed that day among the many graves. Each pilgrim laid a wreath after the Last Post and Reveille, while a well-rehearsed choir from the musically gifted Ambonese sang English and Indonesian hymns and songs of tribute and peace. Hilary, at the far edge of the proceedings, made a video recording. As the assembly of wreaths began to grow in impressive numbers, a tropical breeze arose from the sea, warmly ascended the gentle slope and caused hundreds of poppy-red flame tree flowers to float slowly down over the service and its participants. That was the only time the video quivered.

In defence sales, we worked hard to help secure the acquisition of the BAe Hawk aircraft by the Indonesian Air Force. The Hawk is an astonishingly developable and versatile aircraft. It is the aeroplane of the RAF Red Arrows display team, and arguably the finest jet trainer in the world. The campaign to sell the Hawk to Indonesia was long and careful. British Aerospace needed to design and supply the right specification and, with the embassy's help, to convince the Indonesians on price and quality and to defeat the competition from other European countries. The Indonesian military, political, cultural and financing intricacies involved had to be learned, understood and managed. A primary aim of mine in this campaign was at least to preserve over 100 jobs in England, if not to create more. Crucially, too, it was essential to ensure that the aircraft would never be used in a way which would violate British policies and views on human rights.

I had many discussions on human rights matters with the Indonesian foreign minister, Ali Alatas. This was at a time when he could deploy the argument that while Indonesia had signed the Universal Declaration of Human Rights, his country had a different set of human rights priorities from those of Western countries, and, if in argument I were to exceed what he judged were the bounds of diplomacy, he could accuse me of interfering in the sovereign rights of Indonesia. We came close, but never quite reached that point, though the debates between us were free and frank. When, as foreign secretary, Douglas Hurd came to Indonesia and also debated with Ali Alatas, he found, as had I, that the able Ali was most professional. (Like Douglas Hurd, Ali Alatas had been a diplomat himself.)

The essential assurances on the 'end use' of the Hawk aircraft were secured, including at an extended official call I made, accompanied by Colonel Ker, on the chief of the Indonesian defence staff, General Faisal Tanjung. I am confident that the Hawks were not used against the civilian population in East Timor or anywhere else – notwithstanding the assertions by journalist Mr John Pilger and his cleverly edited and in my view prejudiced film.

I also discussed Hawks in calls on the defence minister, General Leonardus Benjamin (Benny) Moerdani, a physically tough and politically courageous ex-soldier who, as a major, had fought the Brits, including at close quarters, during Confrontation. He had a soldier's respect for the British, particularly our special forces, whom he claimed in conversation, not at all boastingly and indeed accurately, to have frustrated tactically in one incident in Borneo. Benny's father was a central Javanese Muslim railway worker, his mother a half-German Indo-Eurasian. Like his mother, Benny was a Roman Catholic. He had begun his military career as a student, fighting against the Dutch in the struggle for Indonesian independence. He also fought against separatists in several Indonesian islands, and was ever afterwards concerned to promote national unity. Paratrooper, special forces instructor, military attaché in Peking, diplomat in post-Confrontation Malaysia and in South Korea, intelligence officer, planner of the invasion of East Timor, leader of a successful operation to storm and retake a hijacked Indonesian aeroplane and its passengers in Bangkok, and radical reorganiser as commander-in-chief of the Indonesian Armed Forces; his was an erratic and extraordinary military career. There was even a tale that President Soeharto had wanted Benny to marry one of his daughters, and that Benny had refused.

It was important for me to understand Benny. His wife was well-educated, well-travelled, cultivated and pleasant. Devoted patriot Benny once told me that they spoke Dutch at home because Bahasa Indonesia was often not subtle or rich enough a language for them. (I imagine that literary and court classical Javanese might have served well, but the Moerdanis had both been educated at Dutch colonial schools.) Quite quickly, I found Benny good to deal with, in part because, unusually for a Javanese, he meant exactly what he said. He rarely spoke ambiguously or at multiple levels, and when he did it was with unusual clarity. He criticised President Soeharto implicitly for corruption, and if Benny had further political ambition, as I thought likely, it was thwarted: after five years as defence minister, he was not reappointed to the cabinet. I found him interesting and likeable. We shall return to him.

There was much necessary and useful official travel in Indonesia. Hilary came with me on many such trips, so they were especially enjoyable as well as productive. One among so many was to Tanah Toraja, a highland region of Sulawesi where we were 'honoured guests' on the last of the three days of a funeral, for which temporary three-storey 'houses' had been built of bamboo. Men and women separated, both were invited to partake of popular local drugs by smoking or chewing. Hilary and I just managed to avoid causing offence as we practised drug avoidance without actually saying 'no'. The Tanah Toraja religion of choice is a mixture of Animist and Christian, with a touch of mysticism. The funeral neared its climax with the coffin borne by strong, young men processing around the temporary village. A bible was held high as they repeatedly tossed the coffin, spinning into the air amid applause and cheers to ward off evil spirits and ensure safe passage for the deceased. As the coffin neared our 'house', a fine water buffalo, evidently recently shampooed for the occasion, appeared before us and was ritually and gushingly slaughtered. Rather later and more calmly, the coffin was hoisted high up nearby cliffs and manoeuvred into a cave, its final resting place.

I did not accompany Hilary on her trips for charities. Nor was I included in her ten-day-long exploration up long rivers in the interior of Kalimantan by dug-out canoe. With a small group of similarly intrepid ladies, she stayed overnight with a succession of Dayaks in their longhouses. Hilary did much international charity work with Oxfam, including helping traditional midwives learn and accept modern, much healthier techniques. The expatriate British (and other) companies were glad to channel their charitable giving in Indonesia through Hilary and her committees because they knew that the money would all be used, accountably and directly, to help the needy – rather than being diluted, as most such charity was, by siphoning off to other, often corrupt purposes. I borrowed Hilary's direct approach when earthquake and tsunami caused great loss and urgent need in the large island of Flores. The Indonesian government of the day announced that foreign emergency aid would be welcomed and should all be channelled through a government office. I ignored that instruction. The ODA authorised a sum of money, which was used quickly, efficiently and to good effect. For example, a member of our embassy staff, Second Secretary Peter Wilson, despite flight and ferry cancellations and the inaccessibility of many of the affected areas, swiftly reached Flores with his invaluable rucksack and much needed, effective medical supplies.

In far more generous days, the British ambassadors to Thailand and Indonesia used to share the use of an aeroplane piloted by their air attachés. The seasons were such that, broadly, the aeroplane was based for six months of the year in Bangkok and for the other six months in Jakarta. So extensive is the Indonesian archipelago and so much the need to visit much of it officially, that that provision would have been amply justified, until the development of Indonesia's own airlines.

Of Indonesia's 27 provinces, I visited 20 officially. My intelligent and accomplished Australian colleague, Philip Flood (with whom I was also to work in two later incarnations), reached all 27. We cooperated closely with the Australians in several ways. While they had the benefit of the services of a British nurse, for example in Beijing, they provided a doctor in Jakarta who also cared for our UK-based staff medical needs. Dr Bruce Arthur, a former British GP in Norfolk, had become disillusioned with the National Health Service and emigrated to Australia, only later to find himself in Jakarta applying NHS norms for members of the British Embassy. An excellent doctor, he spotted that Hilary had contracted the notoriously difficult to diagnose tropical Hashimoto's disease – a form of hypothyroidism that can be managed chemically, though not cured. Bruce also did me notable service when I was threatened with partial paralysis. My problem was cured by an operation named Cloward's procedure, performed in London by Mr Michael Powell, an excellent neuro-surgeon, champion skier and 1989 *Observer* cook of the year!

Sadly, illness was quite frequent among the embassy staff. We were all scrupulous about hygiene and cleanliness in our own homes, but there was almost always someone suffering from giardiasis, which was acquired usually from infected water or food, and rife among expatriates in our day. Particularly unfortunate was the experience of a second secretary who flew home for his wedding and collapsed during the ceremony – from malaria.

Try as we and the house staff did, bold rats as well as malarial mosquitoes abounded in and around the residence, and throughout Jakarta. Perhaps the boldest, however, was the rat the air attaché's wife found in her hair as she stepped into the shower and donned the shower cap in which the rat had been resting – or was it nesting? Our rats were beyond the house cat, and Chico the well-behaved residence ridgeback seemed uninterested. Modern commercial methods were of little avail in keeping the rodents at bay. The splendid house staff used a Javanese method known as a glue board to catch them seven and eight at a time. We had a civet cat in the roof space for far too long. At night, it sounded like the Charge of the Light Brigade as it galloped above our heads. I rather think it spent such a long time with us because the security staff were slow to hone their skills with bow and arrow – the preferred weapon because it did little or no damage to the eventual meal they enjoyed.

During a brief visit to Singapore on our way to or from London, Hilary and I had a drink in the second of the two houses we had lived in there, with Giles Paxman, then head of chancery in Singapore (and later ambassador to Mexico and to Spain). It was interesting far beyond nostalgia how different the same job was twenty years later, though politically there were also similarities. We much liked the gentle and quietly most impressive Giles, so different in style from the image I have from television of his brother Jeremy.

Given the sheer spread and archipelagic nature of the country, Indonesia's diversity of geography, geology, ethnicity, local languages, religions, cultures, textiles, agricultural and other practices should not surprise; yet it does – and charms too. The cultural differences explain in part the relative unsuccess, as I saw it, of the policy named 'transmigrasi' (transmigration), under which populations were compulsorily moved from crowded islands to those the government thought would benefit from and grow economically with an increased population. Transmigrasi had begun under the Dutch colonial government, though in their latter years the Dutch sensibly scaled back the policy. Revived under Soeharto, transmigrasi was even funded at times by the World

Bank, by the Asian Development Bank and by aid donors. The 1979 energy crisis was the occasion (and perhaps the excuse) for widespread and considerable cutbacks, and transmigrasi was not flourishing in our time. The transmigrants to whom I spoke in the outer islands commonly complained that despite the subsidised infrastructure built for them, they had been moved from productive to poor quality land.

I avoided the most obvious tourist destinations as a rule, though we did spend a long weekend in Hindu, relatively rich Bali – just across the Bali Strait from Muslim, relatively poor Lombok whose geography, geology and economy we found such a contrast to its neighbour. That visit was as hosts to a gathering of British volunteers normally scattered and working alone among the far-flung and poorer islands. The British Council brought them to geographically central Bali for a work conference and some relaxation – which some of them badly needed. We also met some far beyond Bali in their places of voluntary work. They were the best of not always young British volunteers abroad, working in, and sharing seriously deprived and often unhealthy environments; and achieving valuable, practical and lasting results for the Indonesians they were helping.

In September 1993 I went again to Bali. I had been asked to speak on 'Indonesia 2000' for 25 minutes at the Pacific Rim Forum – a gathering of nearly a thousand people, including delegates from all around the Pacific Rim. The Indonesian minister of finance, Mar'ie Muhammad, was on the platform, so I had one friend. The declared language of the meeting was English, so that was a help too. But of those present, some 800 were Indonesian, so I thought I might try a joke in Bahasa Indonesia. Early in the speech, by way of setting 'Indonesia 2000' in a broad historical context, I introduced myself as a successor to the first British ambassador to the country who, in 1602, had travelled to Aceh by elephant, and explained that I had travelled there by the national Indonesian airline, Garuda Indonesia. The joke had to do with a pun: Gajah (elephant) and Garuda (a mythical bird in the official seal of Indonesia). It produced a full throated and sustained roar of laughter and applause from the 800, and wonderful consternation among dignitaries from China, Australia and elsewhere seated on the stage and madly seeking translation that would not help them at all: the joke neither translates nor works at all in English. I learned later that several of them were worried that I might have said something uncomplimentary about their countries. Mar'ie Muhammad was convulsed with laughter. Later that day we were talking together about British history in the Far East, and he told me that at the 1963 sacking of the British embassy in Jakarta, he, then a student, had argued within the crowd against the attack. At a time of endemic and deep corruption at almost all levels of the Indonesian government, Mar'ie, an East Javanese of strong character, was known as Mr Clean. It is no surprise that he now chairs the Indonesian Red Cross Humanitarian Committee and Transparency Society.

The British expatriate businessmen in Indonesia were a tough breed. Mostly commercial operators, many of them came together in the Indonesia-Britain Association (IBA), a close ally of the embassy and rather more than a chamber of commerce. Among its leading lights was a splendid and scholarly Indonesian called Hadjiwibowo who had served in the Dutch Merchant Navy during the Second World War, and spent time in the same Japanese prisoner of war camp as Sam Falle (Chapter 5). It was a joy to bring the two together unexpectedly and so happily at dinner when Sam visited Jakarta. 'Hadji' and I corresponded until he died. He too was an accomplished linguist: in his eighties he learned the Thai language for fun.

The IBA membership was mostly of those tenacious British expats. There is something about hard-lying places in the torrid tropics that brings out the best in such people and their wives (never the other way round in our time, though many wives did valuable voluntary work and one, Joanna Brierley, wrote a good book on the spice trade). Norman Campbell OBE ran a British Ropes factory and was a notably successful chieftain of the Java St Andrew's Society, which ran the largest annual Highland Gathering in the southern hemisphere. Three days long, the event attracted competitors in sports, dancing, drumming and piping from across the world. I recall 13 pipe bands at one Gathering. The 1992 event was opened by the governor of Jakarta and the British ambassador riding abreast around the stadium on motor bicycles, I on First Secretary Jim Malcolm's vintage Matchless, and the governor on his new Harley Davidson. Our wives rode close behind in a yellow bajai (or tuktuk, a motorised rickshaw) decorated with a tartan kilt and driven by the embassy's assistant administration officer. The standard of competition in all the disciplines was always high. In 1993, the Black Watch entered teams who flew down from their then base in Hong Kong. They were hard pressed to win, though they did so in the senior section of the pipes and drums competition. Traditionally, the winner played at a post-Gathering barbecue party at the ambassador's residence, on the steps down to the garden. I had a yen to play a side drum with the Black Watch. Just before their rehearsal in a room in our house, I asked, respectfully. They responded politely, frostily. I persisted, gently. They allowed me to audition, after which they agreed I could play, provided that I was invisible to the audience. I was more than happy with their condition, rehearsed rather feverishly and later found myself on the steps with Black Watch drummers all around me, yet evidently appearing to be in formation. That was a good twenty minutes.

Before I left Whitehall for Jakarta I had pursued a particular problem – to no avail. Indonesia was then concentrating effort and resources on the acquisition of modern technology. The Indonesian minister of technology, later described to me by Margaret Thatcher as a genius, was Bachruddin J. Habibie. Born in 1936 in Sulawesi, B.J. Habibie was a very successful, even visionary aviation engineer who had worked for MBB in Germany and had become vice president for technology there. He told me that at the head of a band of Indonesian engineers he had returned to Indonesia at President Soeharto's request. He was a protégé of Soeharto and seemed to have a free hand as a minister. Habibie had technology advisers from a few countries who were leading exporters to or investors in Indonesia. The advisers were paid by their own countries and were strongly placed to help companies from their countries to secure valuable deals with Indonesia. There was no adviser from the United Kingdom despite our being a prominent supplier of technology globally. The reason seemed to be mostly a combination of lack of imagination in Whitehall and a malaise not unknown among British industry, certainly at that time: complacency. In my briefing tour in London, I had found no willingness at all in any government department to emulate – or to try to catch – our international competitors. I banged my head against several metaphorical brick walls in Whitehall then and more still when I tried from Jakarta, with more knowledge and arguments to deploy.

However, an early call at the embassy by the then chief executive of BAe, Dick (later Sir Richard) Evans, provided another possible avenue. I explained the problem to Dick and why I thought his company was among an important few who could stand to gain a great deal from the appointment of a British adviser to Habibie. Could not British industry supply both the adviser and the salary? Dick responded robustly, saying that I had thrown the ball to him: he would take it home and try to run with it. He did, to excellent effect. He talked to colleague captains of industry, including Rolls-Royce plc chief executive Sir Ralph Robins, whose company later collected financial contributions from some 30 companies. I was unavoidably elsewhere when the first candidate for the position flew to Jakarta. He was not keen to live in Indonesia and did not pursue the appointment. The second candidate, John Coplin CBE, who knew Habibie from visits to Germany in the 1960s and was full of enthusiasm, ideas and drive, came to visit with his wife Jean – a sound move. A visiting professor at Oxford, widely known in government and academic aerospace circles, John was, among much else, the chief designer of the famous Rolls-Royce RB211 jet engine. To add to his impeccable credentials, John quickly mastered the formidable matter of managing the brilliant, loquacious, charming but difficult to pin down Habibie, and delivered much, quietly and effectively, for British industry. Moreover, Jean and he threw themselves into life in Indonesia happily and most successfully. They were wonderful expatriate colleagues and lasting friends. John was later appointed a CBE. We shall also return to B.J. Habibie.

A different challenge was to help persuade British Airways to reinstate their flights to Jakarta. In June 1982, a BA Boeing 747 aeroplane on its way to New Zealand flew through the ash cloud of a volcanic eruption in West Java. The volcano was the active Mount Galunggung (some 80kms south-east of Bandung), whose eruption caused many deaths and a huge and extensive cloud of volcanic ash and gases. The aeroplane, carrying 248 passengers and 15 crew, entered the ash cloud at night some 150kms downwind from the volcano at 37,000 feet: and sequentially lost all power from all four engines. Following the 'flame outs', the aircraft lost height of course, but at around 13,000 feet the crew restarted enough damaged engines to enable a safe landing at Jakarta, notwithstanding the no doubt great harm to engine components, landing and other systems from the ingested ash and gases – and the limited visibility through the damaged windscreen. John Coplin explained to me how restarting would have been possible, even inevitable, provided that normal procedures were followed. Whatever the reason for the mistaken entry into an apparently known ash cloud, it is unsurprising that BA were unwilling to resume flights to Jakarta.

Nine years later, the popular belief in Jakarta was that the offending active volcano was Mount Merapi, much closer to Jakarta and the best known and most active of all volcanoes in Indonesia. I argued for a resumption of flights, which would do so much good for commercial, political and people-to-people relations. BA decided to go ahead. The necessary clearances and 'slots' were secured. David Jones of BA arrived as local manager and quickly learned the relevant Jakartan and Indonesian ropes. David organised the inaugural flight, which arrived with the precision of the Queen's Flight, and in similar fashion too, taxied to the terminal with British and Indonesian flags flying atop the cockpit. The then BA chairman, Lord King, brought guests from aviation, politics and journalism and, wonderfully, the BA band. We held a celebratory dinner in the residence garden. The Indonesians were most welcoming and much good was done. David Jones became an influential member of the British expatriate community in Jakarta and an invaluable ally to the embassy, including in complicated and sensitive handling of VIP visitors who, for example, needed to avoid the attentions of the press.

The active volcanic nature of the Indonesian archipelago and the starring role the country plays in the 'Ring of Fire' has much cultural and economic effect and causes recurrent personal tragedy. Many deaths followed the 1982 eruption of Mount Galunggung. There were plenty other eruptions in our time in Indonesia. Warnings have become rather timelier and more accurate over the years, at least in some cases. Krakatau, in the Sunda Strait between Java and Sumatra, exploded famously in 1883 with effects right around the world. Over 30,000 deaths were recorded officially by the Dutch colonial authorities, and there were probably many tens of thousands more. In lay terms, Krakatau blew itself to bits in 1883, but also spawned a new volcanic island first seen in 1927. Anak (child of) Krakatau has been growing and exploding ever since. One of the eruptions in our time was fiercer and more dramatic than most. Enterprising West Javan fishermen plied an alternative trade, ferrying the curious across the Sunda Strait close to the island, and even landing passengers there. I issued an instruction to embassy and British Council staff to stay well away from the area and the fishermen, and encouraged British expatriates and companies to do the same.

Such was the thrill anticipated from proximity to an active volcano that a small group from the British Council ignored the instruction. A locally engaged US national employee of the Council, who did fine work in English language teaching, was among that group – of very amateur vulcanologists. Some of the group landed on Anak Krakatau and began to clamber upwards. The volcano shot out hot ash and rocks, one of which, described to me as the size of a large refrigerator, struck this so very unfortunate lady. Her companions carried her, semi-conscious, down to the boat, which put off back towards the West Java mainland. The poor young lady died before they reached the shore. Her parents flew from the United States for her funeral in Jakarta, at which I spoke. The kindly mother and father took some genuine comfort from the fact that their daughter had died doing what she loved to do. Hilary and I knew it was a horrid and tragic waste of a young life. As ever, the British community rallied round.

The British Council played a key role for the United Kingdom in Indonesia, as in so much of the world. Language teaching was effective, a sound investment and a profitable 'invisible export' for Britain. That both Sir Martin Jacomb, chairman, and Director-General Sir John Hanson of the British Council came to Indonesia indicates the importance of the varied work done there, including by the energetic and able country director, Alan Webster. The British Council and the British Library organised an astutely curated exhibition named 'Surat Emas' – Golden Letters, of original illuminated letters from Sultans of Indonesian provinces to King James I in 1615, and later ones to Lieutenant Governor Stamford Raffles. Resource cuts, inevitably, have restricted the Council's impact around the world: there have been some sad closures and reductions in Indonesia.

There were many fine business operators among the British expatriates, who organised and ran so much, including for the Indonesian community. A cynic might say that absence from the United Kingdom makes the heart grow fonder of the home country, and there is certainly some truth in that. Yet the 'loyal societies' were more than mere nostalgic substitutes. The well-heeled and most successful St George's Society held Trafalgar Day celebrations and Guy Fawkes nights; and each year would fly a well-known and liked figure from the United Kingdom to speak at a major Jakarta dinner with cabaret to boot. Such guests included Johnny Morris (story-teller and star of BBC's *Animal Magic*), Rex Hunt (Falkland Islands governor at the time of the Argentine invasion) and actor and comedian Derek Nimmo. Sam Falle also spoke to the society. The guests would stay with us – a bonus we always enjoyed. The loyal societies were helpful with the embassy's warden system, designed so that we could be in touch with as many Britons as possible during times of crisis or emergency.

It is certainly invidious to single out any members of such a varied, talented and strong British community that even included a friendly former schoolmate of mine. I will, however, take that implicit risk by mentioning another: John Turnbull OBE with his always supportive wife, Anne. John was the head of BP in Indonesia. He had a wealth of expatriate experience around the world of oil; was a wise, thoughtful and sharp businessman; and a good man who helped others always. (In retirement he did much service for the charity Abbeyfield.) He needed to be sharp to manage BP's affairs in Indonesia so effectively – in such a complex and sometimes tense political environment. We became enduring friends. Two decades later, his funeral in England filled a large church and was attended by many who had known him in Indonesia and others from oil-important countries.

The diplomatic corps in Indonesia was good professional company. The Russian ambassador, Valeri V Malygin, was next to me in protocol order, so we waited together to greet the president at the Istana and in many other lines of heads of mission. There was an amusing edge of competition in the way we would exchange stories about Churchill. My Russian colleague had an impressive fund of such stories, but after a time we would inevitably both stray into the apocryphal; and we would interject to deliver each other's punch lines. The Russian invited us to a tennis party at his sumptuous residence, which recalled for me the mid-1960s when that house must have been the centre of Soviet Russia's manipulation of communist plots and disbursements of large sums of money. The whole story of putting down communist uprisings under Soeharto has probably yet to be told. During our time in Indonesia a ceremony was held every year to bewail the killing in 1965, allegedly by Indonesian communists, of six senior generals, their bodies thrown down a well, and to commemorate then General Soeharto's swift suppression of the apparent coup. Soeharto, by then in control of the army, followed up with an extensive purge of communists (and later plotted successfully to succeed Sukarno as president in 1968).

There is a rather grisly Indonesian museum to that time, which reveals something, but not all, of the killings. Estimates of the total of those killed vary widely among academics and apologists, but were probably in the hundreds of thousands. During my Russian colleague's tennis party, I admired his court and large swimming pool. He quietly led me to believe they were paid for with money left over from the mid-1960s. It was good of Valeri Malygin, thirty-odd years later, to give us a farewell luncheon.

We had close and productive working relations with the Australians and New Zealanders, the Americans, the Dutch and other European Union ambassadors. Personally, we were also friends with the Chileans. The Dutch ambassador, Jan Herman van Roijen, a fine European diplomat and good friend and colleague, later became ambassador in London. As representative of the former colonial power, Jan Herman had something of a special position and a sensitive role to play. The fact that he was the son of the foreign minister and chief Dutch negotiator with Indonesia of the 1949 agreement that ended Dutch military operations and Indonesian guerrilla activities and restored the republican government in Jogjakarta gave him a special status.

That advantage did not prevent President Soeharto from abruptly cancelling the extensive Dutch aid to Indonesia when he decided that the Netherlands were interfering too much in Indonesia's domestic policy. It was interesting that at the same time that Jan Herman was summoned early one morning to the Istana, the presidential palace, to hear this rather shocking decision from the president. I was called, also early, to see the wise and sensible minister of finance, Radius Prawiro, to receive the same news. Java being Java, it did not take long for Jan Herman and I to decide that the key Dutch aid programmes that were doing so much good should be quietly 'transferred' to British administration and to be confident that no objection would be raised by the Indonesian government.

Work with EU colleagues meant monthly meetings at ambassador level as well as at other levels on specific subjects. These were chaired by the ambassador from the member country then holding the EU presidency, which rotated every six months. Following the East Timor dispute and troubles, Portugal and Indonesia exchanged no resident diplomats; we British 'represented Portuguese interests' in Indonesia. Since the United Kingdom and Portugal happened to be next to each other in the then list of EU member states, we also held the 'local' presidency of the council of the EU in Indonesia for 12 consecutive months – the first half of 1992 in lieu of Portugal and the second half of the year in our own right. That continuity helped the EU locally, I thought, for example in making joint representations to the Indonesians, though that was not then a frequent practice. When we did make such representations, we were certainly taken seriously, and may well have been more effective than had we acted separately. Most of our embassy's work with the Indonesians, however, was bilateral, though also occasionally in concert with other close allies in pairs or, on one occasion, in an Anglo-Australian-American trio. Access for the British ambassador to cabinet ministers and indeed to Vice-President Tri Sutrisno and President Soeharto was never difficult to achieve, so polite and generous with their time were Indonesian senior officials. Such access is generally a very different matter in London.

While we were in Indonesia, Norway decided by referendum not to join the European Union. My Norwegian colleague, Torolf Raa, came to see me. He believed that his country had chosen the wrong course. That he was so evidently upset recalled for me the call made in Singapore in 1971 on my boss, Sam Falle, by the high commissioner for Pakistan in Singapore – to bring, close to tears, the message 'My country is torn in two' when Bangladesh was formed after the civil war in which India had intervened against West Pakistan. In Indonesia, as elsewhere, there was a little cooperation among embassies from Commonwealth countries. The Canadian ambassador was a lady, Ingrid Hall, for whom official life was occasionally difficult in this Muslim society where women were often, and apparently contentedly, segregated from the men.

My able and very professional French colleague for most of my time in Jakarta was another good friend. Dominique Girard and I worked together happily, and I was delighted when he later arrived in Canberra as ambassador. Problems he faced there are another story of diplomacy (see Chapter 11).

A little unusually for the United States, my first American colleague in Indonesia, John Monjo, was a professional diplomat rather than a political appointee, as several of his predecessors had been. John had an excellent command of Bahasa Indonesia, and used it to good effect. I found him a fine colleague – as was his successor, Bob Barry. During the 1990–91 Gulf War, there was initially popular support for Saddam Hussein, some in Jakarta and notably in North Sumatra and Aceh. Model Scud missiles and pro-Saddam T-shirts could be bought in the markets. Embassies of those providing troops to the Coalition force took security precautions. A bomb on his patio threatening John Monjo's house was made safe. An earlier attempt to plant the same or a similar bomb at our house had been foiled. As the short war proceeded, support for Saddam in Muslim Indonesia seemed to us to fade.

The recent troubled history of East Timor that culminated in a shooting war started for me in earnest with the massacre in the capital, Dili, in November 1991. It was a dreadful death for so many East Timorese. A small group of British journalists were among all those in the Santa Cruz cemetery in Dili where the Indonesian massacre took place that appalling day. Foreign journalists were, of course, the last people the Indonesians would want there. Communications with Dili from Jakarta were all but impossible. I had four difficult conversations with Indonesian minister of defence Benny Moerdani. They were difficult conversations for Benny Moerdani too. (Clearly understood between us was the unresolved incident of the 'Balibo Five' in which two Britons lost their lives during the 1975 Indonesian invasion of East Timor. 'Not again' was the vital message.) The British journalists, eventually, were all right, just. Despite the communications difficulties and the military's other preoccupations that night, Benny did eventually secure the right answer: in the last of our conversations, he told me that the Britons were now 'on the back of a truck ... they are covered in blood ... not their blood'. His answer to my question where the truck was bound was also satisfactory.

The Portuguese traded with and founded settlements on Timor in the sixteenth century. The Dutch came later and in 1859 reached four agreements with Portugal that established boundaries and thus split the island between Dutch (much later Indonesian) West Timor, and Portuguese (later Indonesian and now independent) East Timor. In August 1975, the Portuguese left, and the Indonesians, fearing a communist or at least an antipathetic regime in their midst, invaded in force in December 1975 and annexed East Timor. It was never a settled, stable territory, suffering dissension and many killings, and fostering independence movements.

Following the 1991 massacre, the subsequent years saw arguments, traumas, more repression and tragedies, and attempts at settlements (the then British foreign secretary, Douglas Hurd, sent me, one Christmas leave from Indonesia, to talk to the Portuguese in Lisbon, where I achieved almost nothing). Those years also saw British embassy hospitality given to a string of East Timorese seeking protection, culminating with Xanana Gusmáo.

A UN-supervised referendum in August 1999 found heavily in favour of independence. A militia sought retribution and wreaked much havoc. A UN peacekeeping force, the International Force for East Timor (INTERFET), arrived soon after and secured a good outcome. After all the killings, the arguments, the mistakes, the difficult decisions for Indonesia and strong and effective action by the international community, it was a good moment when, on 20 May 2002, East Timor became an independent country. East Timor in

Indonesian is Timor Timur, or 'Tim Tim'. Such jokey abbreviations are much liked: 'Timor' is the name and 'Timur' means east. The joke has been sacrificed in the new, less confusing and more official name of the independent country, Timor Leste ('leste' is Portuguese for east). It was a pleasure and a privilege for me in 2003 at the Royal Institute for International Affairs, Chatham House, in London, to chair a conference at which Xanana Gusmão, lawyer, freedom fighter, poet, prisoner and president of the Democratic Republic of Timor Leste, was the speaker. It was very good to hear Xanana Gusmão explain his philosophy: practical, cooperative, forgiving and hopeful. The country will surely remain dependent on external aid for some years yet, but there is real hope of eventual viability based largely on offshore oil.

The UN operations on the ground in East Timor were a prerequisite to East Timorese independence. The British contributed troops – Gurkhas, Royal Marines and others – under Australian command, to INTERFET. Military cooperation between the United Kingdom and Australia is longstanding, deep, operational, effective and continuing. Given that fact; given that the Australians were leading; given that Gurkhas were serving nearby in Brunei; given the political needs and the then human rights problems in East Timor and given the UN stand, it was not a difficult decision, in my view, for British ministers to commit British troops. This despite that our forces were even then stretched and that the logistic problems were considerable. Unsurprisingly, the British troops did very well.

Politically, it is worth noting that unlike Australia, the United Kingdom had never recognised the Indonesian annexation of East Timor in 1975–6. Neither had the United States, who did not send troops to East Timor in 1999. It is of political, but mainly humanitarian, importance and in all our interests that after further threats to instability in the small nation and help from Australia, Timor Leste has recently signed a memorandum of understanding with Indonesia designed to foster cooperation.

Fortunately for the pursuit of British interests, we had a rather larger share of senior official and business visitors to Indonesia than I had expected. Cabinet ministers came frequently – from Home Secretary David Waddington, via Chancellor of the Exchequer Ken

Clarke, Secretary of State for Energy John Wakeham, and Secretaries of State for Defence Tom King and (briefly) Malcolm Rifkind to Foreign Secretary Douglas Hurd. Richard Needham from the DTI was probably our most frequent ministerial visitor. These visits can often be the stuff of ambassadorial life, need much preparation and follow-up, and allow carefully planned (as well as unexpected) opportunities for advancing the cause of whatever is the leading or most relevant issue for the UK. They are also invaluable for bringing one up to date on the inside view of latest events and trends in Whitehall and Westminster.

These visits can throw up unexpected problems too. One such occurred when John Wakeham came to Jakarta, bearing the inevitable jet-lag. That was not the problem, however; rather the reverse. A busy ministerial programme included a helicopter ride to visit an oil operation based on a ship anchored in the Malacca Strait off Sumatra. The Indonesian helicopter, to my initial dismay not British-made, took off for a couple of hours' flight. Early on I noticed the smell of aviation fuel. I then noticed that recesses in the helicopter cabin floor were beginning to fill with fuel. While the secretary of state was still wisely sleeping off some of the jet-lag, I checked with the pilot. I had found that most Indonesians (not the tough-minded Batak) much dislike saying 'no': the language has a number of euphemisms for the negative, of varying proximity to 'no' and not excluding 'yes'. The pilot had all these at his ready command. He assured me that all would be well until we landed on the ship. While we were then conducting our oil business aboard, he would solve the problem. I asked if he had the necessary tools, or whether we should request these from the ship. He was fully equipped, he responded. We duly landed. John Wakeham awoke, and busied himself with the matters at hand, and with learning how this type of oil collection operation worked. A couple of hours later we rejoined the helicopter and a smiling pilot, and took off for Java. Soon after take-off, the same concerning odour and fuel appeared. I spoke again to the pilot, asking what repair he had made and with what tools. He pointed to a cloth, a screwdriver and some deodorant air spray. By the time we reached Jakarta, the recesses were full of aviation fuel and spilling across the cabin sole. John Wakeham was wisely back asleep. I later consulted air attaché Wing Commander Robert Manning, who spoke unsurprisingly and darkly of a fuel tank leak. He volunteered that he would not be caught flying in such a machine, which had been built (in neither Indonesia nor the UK) with its vertical rotating shaft two degrees out of true. I regretted that I had not been advised earlier of this professional view, but I regretted rather more that there had not been room aboard the helicopter for Robert to accompany us. On the other hand I was grateful to jet-lag, though it wore off quickly; and we had good meetings with Indonesian ministers and officials and valuable conversations among ourselves.

The energy sector in Indonesia was important to British industry, and both Colin (later Lord) Moynihan and his successor, Tim Eggar, visited as energy ministers. Both pursued British interests effectively. Colin later became minister of sport and has worked hard and well in that sphere, having been appointed chairman of the British Olympic Association in the run up to London 2012. I thought Tim a signal loss to the British government when he later resigned to pursue a successful business career.

Tom (later Lord) King and his wife stayed with us when he visited Indonesia as secretary of state for defence. As with other cabinet ministers, I took him to call on President Soeharto for a courtesy visit with a useful few substantive points. Such senior visits typically helped advance UK interests in a number of ways. That so many cabinet ministers did visit created new opportunities and good will that we could and did later exploit. Also in the defence field, ministers Lord Arran and his successor, the then Viscount Cranborne (later the Marquess of Salisbury), came too. I have seen a little more of Robert Salisbury since I retired and enjoy his company and thoughtful, knowledgeable and elegantly expressed views very much. Lord Jellicoe was another fun and effective visitor from defence.

Chancellor of the Exchequer Ken Clarke arrived just in time to celebrate New Year with us, bringing his splendid wife Gillian, his permanent secretary Terry (later Lord) Burns, and a bright presence from his Treasury Private Office. The chancellor did most useful work in support of a UK trade mission among much else. We visited the huge ninth-century Buddhist temple of Borobudur in Central Java. This vast monument had been covered by volcanic ash and jungle growth for centuries when Sir Thomas Raffles was lieutenant governor of Java. Made aware of it by Javanese, Raffles had some of it cleared and restored, and wrote of Borobudur in his *History of Java*. Further restoration work was done under the Dutch. Between 1975 and 1982 UNESCO and the Indonesians undertook a comprehensive restoration of what was thereafter designated a World Heritage site. There are nine platforms with shrines set in each, before the top platform with its many Buddhas set in perforated stone stupas.

Ken Clarke is the only visitor I ever took or saw there who looked outwards from the monument at each level rather than inwards to see the shrines: he knew where his priorities lay, and used binoculars to watch birds. That five-day visit, between the chancellor's visits to Hong Kong and Manila, was busy with bilateral business, but Ken fulfilled his home-based Treasury duties as well. Subjects discussed at our table included a decision needed immediately whether to revise the bank rate, and the arguments for and against the introduction of an airport tax. It was an unusual (and enjoyable) experience for a diplomat to be involved in such conversations, though the chancellor's chief support came, of course, from his Treasury officials. Given the time zone difference with London, Terry Burns worked at all hours. He had been a distinguished academic who came late to the Treasury and rose in its ranks with electric speed, and is a Treasury man whom I both much like and admire. Late one night I asked Terry what ambition he might have yet unfulfilled. His answer was 'to become a director of Queen's Park Rangers Football Club', a position, among many others even more elevated, to which he was indeed appointed.

The welcome visits to Indonesia by trade ministers involved much negotiation and other work, and were valued by both the British expatriate business community and the trade-related Indonesia-Britain Association. From the DTI (and formerly at the FCO) came Tim Sainsbury and his wife for a productive and interesting visit. From the FCO came Lord Caithness, with whom we had bilateral talks and memorably visited Sumatra to see British oil palm operations, among other interests. In that we were much helped by the fine honorary British consul in Medan, Geoffrey Brown, who, with George Ekanayake's help, constantly, calmly and effectively dealt with all manner of consular cases, many involving young, adventurous but sometimes ill-advised Britons. Geoff played wonderful Pavarotti CDs for us far into the tropical night. In Surabaya we had the good fortune to have the services of honorary consul Michael Page. Geoff was succeeded by J.P.C. Baskett, and Michael by the Standard Chartered Bank manager. In Bali, where there was quite a lot of consular work, the embassy had the benefit of reciprocal arrangements with the Australians, which in this case meant that the Australian consulate handled our cases in the first instance.

Importantly, Alistair (later Lord) Goodlad, the FCO minister who then covered the region, visited too, and did valuable bilateral work, which the embassy could pursue later to useful effect. I did not then think that Alistair would come to our next and last post too, nor that his wife, Cecilia, and he would become good and lasting friends. I did not then dream that, as a political appointee, Alistair would be a successor of mine in my last post – as high commissioner to Australia.

The secretary of state at the FCO, Douglas (now Lord) Hurd, paid a most valuable visit. His discussions with Foreign Minister Ali Alatas were particularly professional and fruitful. Douglas arrived by RAF Trident at the airport at the cultural capital Jogjakarta in Central Java to begin his visit with a briefing dinner. After leading him through the programme, I was not too surprised to hear him ask some penetrating questions about the press conference planned for Jakarta. In common with many (though not all) professional diplomats, I always thought that politicians in office worry excessively about the information media. I knew Douglas well enough to ask him, only half in joke, why he did not give up reading the press as a fortnight's experiment, and answer any awkward questions on press opinion by saying that he had not read the press. His answer, with a smile, was: 'Only a civil servant could offer that advice'. My response was: 'Only a politician could ...' but Douglas finished my sentence for me, humorously and accurately: '.... refuse to accept it'. The visit was off to a good start. It continued the next day, a Sunday, with a long walk in the rain up the mystic Mount Merapi. The volcano was not then active: it was a steep, wet climb, on which Douglas set a cracking pace.

We flew in the Trident together with Douglas's wife Judy from the cultural capital Jogjakarta to the seat of government, Jakarta. The captain warned us that a sharp climb would immediately follow take-off. The secretary of state and I, across a table from each other and busy rehearsing some points of substance, had to hang on to the table: no civilian aircraft would attempt such a take-off, save in emergency. The landing was tame, by comparison. The Hurds and two members of Douglas's FCO team stayed with us in Jakarta – an efficient and helpful arrangement. The two colleagues concerned were Head of the FCO News Department (and so Spokesman) Francis Cornish, and Private Secretary Richard Gozney. Coincidentally, both had earlier served in Jakarta, spoke Bahasa Indonesia and, I thought, might be candidates for my job there in due course. I was sorry that Francis was not, in the event, posted to Jakarta: he became senior British trade commissioner in Hong Kong, first consul-general there at the hand-over to China in 1997, and later ambassador to Israel. Some eight years later Richard, however, did serve as ambassador in Jakarta, and concluded his Diplomatic Service career as Sir Richard, governor of Bermuda. There were very pleasant relaxed aspects to that visit, including cooling off (a little) in the residence swimming pool after a hot tropical day's work and before a working dinner, and sharing the pool with Douglas's wife Judy and a journalist of the foreign secretary's party, Brian Hanrahan – he of later Falklands, Berlin Wall and *World at One* fame.

I met Brian again years later when we were colleague lecturers aboard a cruise ship in the western Pacific. He recalled the visit and the swim party fondly – the only one, he said, that he had experienced in an ambassadorial residence. We did a double act aboard the cruise ship, debating world affairs between us before a keen and participatory audience. Had Brian not died so sadly early he could have made a fine member or chairman of TV's *Question Time* panel. Also very sadly, I should record that Judy Hurd, too, died early, again far too early. Douglas turned to work (as some of us dared advise him) and produced yet another fine book – about eleven foreign secretaries.

That press conference in Jakarta did include, from a different, young, clever, but certainly opinionated British journalist, a couple of strange (and unclear) questions, one of which Douglas elegantly refused to answer. Some months later, when the journalist had infuriated Ali Alatas once too often, Ali telephoned me quietly to let me know the Indonesian government was about to deport the young correspondent. That action, certainly merited in the host country's mind, would have seriously threatened a possibly promising career, so I argued a contrary case. After some discussion, Ali kindly agreed to stay the government's hand, subject to some perfectly reasonable conditions. The journalist remained to complete his tour, and is evidently pursuing a good career.

The Duke of Edinburgh Award was considering establishing a scheme in Indonesia, so our Royal visitors included HRH Prince Edward, who came for several days, principally to advance this plan. Prince Edward was a particularly delightful house guest. The Duke of Edinburgh landed to refuel the aeroplane he was in part piloting on a World Wide Fund for Nature tour, but even that short time allowed a call to present a senior Indonesian to HRH and to discuss award matters. Other royal visitors who stayed longer included the Duchess of York, accompanied to our especial pleasure by her daughters, the two young princesses Beatrice and Eugenie.

Prince Michael of Kent brought an international team of businessmen whom we entertained to dinner one interesting hot tropical evening. The electricity in our part of Jakarta failed and, for the only time in its long life, our ancient stand-by British generator refused to start. The residence had a good supply of candelabra, and an abundance of candles, which provided both essential illumination and less than welcome extra heat. Hilary invited the men to dispense with their dinner jackets. All gratefully did so, save one who confessed that he was wearing a short sleeved shirt. I was glad to welcome Prince Michael: he had shared an office with me in the Washington embassy for a few days while he was serving in the Army.

Aid ministers came of course. The visit by former aid minister, and by then House of Lords front bench spokesman Frank Judd was especially useful and enjoyable, in part perhaps because he was so experienced and pleasant – and able to be more objective than most. The British aid programme in Indonesia was impressive both in its spread and focus, and was generally effective. 'Generally effective' is right, but an exception was a mini-project in which BP and their boron technology for solar photo-voltaic panels were involved. A small array was installed in a village in a Javanese jungle clearing to provide electric light and power for a radio where there had been no electricity at all. The villagers were delighted. A check a year later found no electricity at all. There had been no failure of the technology. Maintenance, rather than repair or replacement, was not a frequent practice in what Noël Coward called 'the sunny isle of Java': indeed the Indonesian word for the concept is a contrived one, and I have tried but found no word at all for it in Javanese. The jungle, once again, had simply reclaimed its own: thick growth had covered the array so that no light could reach it. The radical pruning solution was simple and quick. Once again the villagers were delighted – for how long I do not know.

Ministerial visits from Indonesia to the United Kingdom were fewer, unsurprisingly – but there were some in the foreign affairs field, and an interesting one by the kindly and studious minister for religion, Munawir Sjadzali. B.J. Habibie was another. I took him to call on Prime Minister John Major, not an easy meeting for the FCO to secure such is the pressure on the PM's diary. It was a good meeting that made a difference for British trade. Unusually perhaps for an ambassador, I was quite content that President Soeharto never showed any sign of wanting to repay the state visit that HM The Queen had paid in 1972. Had he done so, or had I suggested it, rather more problems would probably have been created for the bilateral relationship than advances made or the British interest served. We were better pursuing those interests on the ground in Indonesia. Later Soeharto history would, as I read it, support that view. That said, when the present president, Susilo Bambang Yudhoyono, visited London, some years and some welcome reforms later, real good was done.

There were many senior official and senior commercial visits, far too many to mention. All meant useful and nearly always productive work. Professor Alan Thomas, as head of defence sales in the Ministry of Defence was a good example. After I had retired, he paid me the compliment of asking me to join the court of the University of Westminster. (I had regretfully to decline, being far too busy at the time to do a good job.) Iain Dale, a lively and inventive chairman of the South-East Asia Trade Advisory Group, stayed with us during a helpful visit. So did Sir Derek and Lady Hornby, he of the British Overseas Trade Board. Also from BOTB came Peter Godwin and his wife (whom I was able to direct to the London surgeon who had operated so successfully on me). Peter was an accomplished organist, and played in the Catholic cathedral in Jakarta. Some visits provided unexpected diversions, such as when Sir Ralph Robins, chairman of Rolls-Royce plc (the aerospace company) came for an essential part of the campaign to persuade the Indonesians to buy the right aero-engines. During a break in the work, resident Rolls-Royce man Rod Williams took Ralph off for a game of golf. From the tee, Rod drove a ball very hard: it struck a tree, bounced off at a sharp angle and hit Ralph in the eye. I later saw Ralph in a darkened room after he had been treated, bandaged, and urged not to stir for several days. The work had to be completed: neither before nor since have I had a strategic planning discussion with someone I could barely see. Ralph recovered completely. I was a little surprised, and relieved, that the good Rod Williams also survived in his job. Lord Alexander, leading barrister, banker, politician and cricket enthusiast, led a mission of the British Invisibles Export Council, at whose opening seminar session the governor of the Bank of Indonesia relaxed rather too far in his chair and fell off the back of the stage. Despite this loss of both face and seat, the mission was a success.

All these visits naturally required a good deal of preparation and programme planning, and the British interest would never be served nor advanced without much embassy staff work. Apart from those already mentioned, Marcus Hope and his successor Peter Bacon as commercial counsellors were real operators and advisers. Marcus was already well ensconced and master of his brief when we arrived. With great speed, Peter became expert and invaluable in his judgments. He combined commercial and economic skills with fine political nous and an essential and unfailing sense of fun. He and his wife, Val, became good and lasting friends. Later in Australia, I hoped that Peter might become consul-general in Sydney – and the FCO were unusually kind in consulting me on the field of candidates. Sadly for us it was not to be, and Peter went on to do signally important work as consul-general in Houston, Texas. The redoubtable Jon Benjamin was succeeded by the also fluent and most able Ian Donaldson. Ian arranged some of our official visits to Indonesia's outer islands, on which he and his wife, Elspeth, accompanied us. He did first-class work.

Ian told me an excellent and true story about my predecessor of Confrontation time, Sir Andrew Gilchrist. Andrew, by now retired, living in his native Scotland and chairman of the Highlands and Islands Development Board, was the host at a Board cocktail party. A lady approached him to say that he was the only man in the room who would fully appreciate why she was that day especially happy: her son had just been accepted into the Diplomatic Service. She wanted to share her news and ask Sir Andrew if he could offer just one piece of advice for her son at the start of his diplomatic career. Andrew congratulated the proud mother, pulled his beard as he thought awhile and then said, in his fine Edinburgh tones, 'He must never lose an opportunity to empty his bladder'. I sometimes wonder if Mrs Donaldson, for the lady was Ian's mother, realised quite how sound was Andrew's advice.

Hilary and I went with the Donaldsons and Ann Douthwaite on a memorable official visit to Irian Jaya – or West Papua as it was later known. We flew in small aircraft, sailed in leaky boats and travelled well and excitingly around this extraordinary and in part primitive province. Jayapura, the capital, came first for necessary official calls. In Wamena in the interior, we called on the inevitably Javanese governor, who told us in effect that his heart, if not his head, was Irian Jayanese. Whether he expected to be believed is moot. We struck out further into the interior to see a small British hydro-electric energy scheme. There is much potential for 'hydro' in Papua, but in our time limited demand. That may change with resource development in offshore gas and oil. Outside a village we saw agricultural practices that we had glimpsed earlier from an aeroplane and that recalled for me diagrams and drawings of stone-age agriculture in a school geography text book. In the village, as in the tribal areas, men wore nothing but penis-gourds and the women loin-cloths. Yet, in a paradigm of Irian Jaya, there were also men in suits in the market-place. Further afield, a tribesman brought from his hut for us to admire – his mummified grandmother.

We were privileged to attend the felling of a huge sago palm tree, which would provide sustenance for the mini-village for months. As a guest, I was presented with a sago maggot the size of a farmer's thumb that crawled out of the palm. I was invited to eat it. Upper lip suitably stiffened, I did so. More maggots were then barbecued and offered to Hilary and the others. I assured them that the taste was merely that of fat bacon and that they should certainly consume the beasts. I was not believed about the bacon taste, but the grilled maggots were bravely eaten. My reward was to be presented with a used set of long, poisoned hunting arrows and a quiver, beautifully fashioned: they are now in the British Museum.

We flew to Merauke in the south-east of Irian Jaya, due south of Jayapura and near the north-south border with Papua New Guinea. We drove north into the interior towards the Equator and up to Freeport's Grasberg mine. Freeport was then reputedly, and credibly, Indonesia's largest taxpayer. The company mines, processes and exports vast quantities of copper ore along with gold and some molybdenum and silver. The mine is huge, and then constituted the hollowed out centre of a large mountain. Travel around the mine inside the mountain is by large four-by-four vehicles with extra headlights. (The vehicles were Japanese. I failed in a bid to interest the mine in Landrovers.) The mining machinery is the largest I have seen apart from at the biggest (open cast) mines in the world, in Australia. The scene inside Mount Grasberg was, I thought, a long thrilling sequence in a James Bond film waiting to be made. There are some problems with the local people, to whom we also spoke, though the US company work hard to make their operations acceptable, including culturally, in this remote region. There is danger, too and occasional death: again the company expend great effort to limit risk. By way of a treat and a little concentrated equatorial education, Freeport flew us in a helicopter to see a glacier among the highest mountain peaks anywhere west of the Andes or east of the Himalayas.

Our last visit in Irian Jaya was to the Bird's Head peninsula in the west of Irian Jaya. We flew to the town of Manokwari, and journeyed south by land and sea to the smaller town of Ransiki. Here we met Deirdre Cornish-Browne, an extraordinary, even saintly nurse from Northern Ireland. Deirdre provided medical services with total devotion and eventual wonderful success to tribal inhabitants of the dense jungle interior areas less than one degree south of the Equator. Deirdre operated nominally under the aegis of a bishop living hundreds of miles and almost inaccessibly away. Her medical supplies came from a small hospital in Ransiki, where the doctor we met thought her the best expert alive in leprosy and much else. With these supplies and her skills, Deirdre had been trekking the jungles, from village to village, for eight years, slowly gaining the confidence and cooperation of the tribespeople, who for long found it impossible to accept the notion of regular doses of medicine, let alone that offered by a woman – and a white woman at that. Deirdre learned local languages and painstakingly taught and demonstrated that medicine could work. To avoid her patients simply consuming the pills and other medicines all at once instead of over time, she kept trekking around her widespread jungle practice to deliver the medicine, often pill by pill, and to persuade her patients to take it. She gradually, so gradually, made converts to medicine. Deirdre cured lepers and prevented leprosy. It was a privilege to meet this marvellous lady. It was a shock when Hilary persuaded her to show us her legs, to find that they were covered in jungle sores. The Manokwari doctor clearly did his level best for her when, fairly infrequently, she returned to base to restock with medicines, but told us how determined and independent she was. Deirdre was a humbling inspiration.

Eight years was clearly more than long enough. Back in Jakarta I wrote to those I thought should be concerned. The honours committee in London said that Deirdre's was the finest MBE candidacy they had seen in living memory. In those days a higher honour was not on offer, but it was a wonderful recognition. Since Deirdre was paid only just a living wage, the British community in Jakarta rallied round and provided her with an outfit suitable for her investiture at Buckingham Palace and the wherewithal to stay in London. British Airways provided her flights. The distant bishop agreed that she had served long enough. (Sometimes, it felt especially good to be an ambassador.) After closing down and handing over her so successful medical operation in Irian Jaya, Deirdre returned whence she had come, to further service: as a nurse at the first hospice in England, St Christopher's at Sydenham in south-east London.

Indonesia is the world's third largest cocoa producer. Among other visits we paid was one to a British cocoa plantation, where we learned much about the economics of that industry – and saw a bird of paradise. We visited BP's one remaining coal mine, the rich and productive Kaltim Prima in Kalimantan. On the way there, a helicopter flight took us low over East Kalimantan north of Balikpapan and near Samarinda. We looked down on forests burning, clearly from combustion of coal seams at surface level or only just below it. This dramatic sight was the thought behind our later commissioning some batik panels for the new residence from the best regarded batik artist in Indonesia. The panels were for dining room windows and could be illuminated from outside at night, to splendid and tasteful effect inside.

A new residence was badly needed in Jakarta. The one we lived in was well over an hour from the office by car – the fastest means of transport other than walking, in a city choked with traffic. That house just about served its representational and operational purposes, but guests had to put up with long slow journeys. With a busy ministerial programme, that was inefficient – to put it mildly. The FCO were content to provide a new residence in a good location and to sell the old (asset recycling at work). Long negotiations, ending with a marathon session in my office one Christmas Eve, secured a good site close to the office in Menteng. A British firm of architects, Denton Corker Marshall, with a representative in Indonesia was commissioned. Director Steve Quinlan in London and Budiman Hendropurnomo in Jakarta did a fine job, despite the intricacies and obstacles of the Jakarta planning system. The new house was well located, good value, handsome but not ostentatious. Sadly for us, we did not live in it during our four years in Indonesia, largely because of building inefficiencies and delays that were inevitable at the time. I failed in an attempt to replace the tired, arguably even then insecure and poor-looking embassy office building. Money was an obvious major constraint and my thought was to work with a European bank to produce a largely self-financing, dual use, fairly low-rise smart tower block on our site on a major roundabout. The FCO were supportive, the bank was initially interested, but the effort came to naught. Years later, the FCO decided to build a new embassy in another quite good location.

The Indonesia Association of British Alumni (IABA) was established while we were serving at Jakarta. Impressively, the opening meeting attracted some 700 people. The Indonesian minister for religion, an alumnus of Exeter University, and I spoke. IABA has lasted. So have the FCO's world-wide Chevening scholarships. And I was impressed to see so many Indonesian students at the London School of Economics when the current Indonesian president, Susilo Bambang Yudhoyono, spoke there over a decade later.

A feature of diplomatic life in Jakarta was obligatory ambassadorial attendance at major weddings: for example, those of Indonesian ministers or their dependants. The wedding receptions were frequent, lavish and long; lovely and fragrant too in their jasmine and other floral and sartorial decoration. It was the custom to present gifts but also for guests to receive gifts. Quite often, at Chinese community weddings, these were of money: charities later benefited as, I imagine, the hosts often intended. Funerals seemed frequent too: one had to be quick, for in the Muslim tradition the bodies were on display for only a brief time very soon after death, and had to be saluted in person. The Indonesian generosity of hospitality was to the fore in all these and many other events. It was the tradition and general practice that if anyone called at a house, he or she had to be fed well. That applied at all levels of the social spectrum, notably the poorest.

Socially, I suppose, that kind of tradition has helped in a small way to keep the largest archipelago in the world together over the centuries. There were certainly profound cultural differences and inherent tensions both west to east and north to south. The consequential fissiparous tendencies of the islands were a constant preoccupation of the government, and helped explain President Soeharto's frequent travels to outer islands and nearly as frequent invitations to heads of diplomatic missions to join him there. On these occasions there would be a large gathering and a fluent and lengthy speech by Soeharto, much of it evidently learned by heart and by frequent repetition; but impressively so, since the recital of the basic statistics never varied during my four years of attendance at such gatherings.

After those four years, I wrote of Indonesia's social tensions in my mid-1994 valedictory despatch from Indonesia. Indonesia has been generally tolerant of the many religions practised there, and of ethnic differences, in this, the world's largest Muslim country. But intolerance always lurked at some level below the surface of Indonesian society, like hot lava in a dormant volcano. At irregular intervals it has burst through and caused dire problems.

Fewer than 3% of the population are Chinese Indonesians. The fact that in my time they controlled over 70% of the economy (and probably still do) was but one cause of dissent and racial tensions. Despite the recent welcome reforms in Indonesia – or, perhaps, as a price for those reforms – we have seen all too clearly such tensions erupt (or being fomented) in Jakarta in ugly and murderous fashion, and in sadly numerous places around the vast archipelago – even in normally gentle and tolerant Ambon, in far Ternate and Halmahera, in Sulawesi including lovely Makassar, as well as in the better known and more obvious centres of activism in Java, Sumatra, Aceh, Kalimantan and Irian Jaya.

In 1994, I believed that given the corruption and continuing problems of poor governance and management, Soeharto would probably leave the presidency unwillingly. Timing was problematical, but in that valedictory despatch I suggested 1998 was possible. As it turned out I was right about the timing, but I certainly did not predict the proximate cause of Soeharto's going, in essence that a financial crisis would ripple down the map from Japan and provoke the economic crisis that Indonesia's weak banking structure and political fragility could not withstand.

It was possible during the first four years of the nineties, to identify some of the seeds of the demise of President Soeharto. Here was a soldier turned shrewd and subtle politician and quasi Javanese prince who, many in Jakarta believed, did not eschew consultation with a dukun-buntut or shaman. Javanese mysticism, it seemed to me, was part of Soeharto's make-up. He did preside over steady, strong economic growth ever since his assumption of power from Sukarno in 1967. The economy grew at an average of 7% a year for nearly 30 years. Indonesia badly needed growth. When Soeharto took power,

GNP per capita was some $60 a year. By the time of his going in 1998 it was over $1,000. (The World Bank figure for 2010 was $4710.) When Soeharto took power, 60% of the population lived in absolute poverty. By 1994 when I left Indonesia it had fallen to 13.7% – still 27 million people. (In 2009 it was 15% – 36m). And the rich had become far richer far more quickly than the poor had become less poor. When Soeharto fell from power in1998, the economy collapsed. It has since recovered quickly and reasonably well, and in 2011 was doing pretty well.

I found President Soeharto difficult but eventually possible to penetrate as a man and a personality. Always, with me, smiling, polite and softly spoken, he gave me answers or messages with extreme subtlety, so debate was mostly gentle and subtle too. He was usually cooperative, whether on human rights, trade – civilian or defence, UN votes, economics or anything else. Rather rarely he was still indirect but uncompromising, at least apparently so.

The then foreign minister, Ali Alatas, was intellectually very able, easier to 'read' than Soeharto, and, even on the tough issues, a pleasure to deal with. My wife and I paid our farewell calls on Ali and his wife June at his bedside in a Jakarta hospital just after he suffered a nasty heart attack. Despite June's and our efforts to prevent him, he insisted on pursuing a long, detailed and complex discussion of some of the more intractable international issues between us or of mutual concern. We also spoke that day of the most impressive international statesman Ali had ever met, Nelson Mandela. I also met Mandela when he visited Jakarta as the newly elected president of South Africa. I recall President Soeharto standing next to Mandela, and the Javanese smiling mask slipping in shock and surprise at the warmth and gratitude with which Nelson Mandela grasped and embraced the British ambassador.

My farewell call in mid-1994 on President Soeharto was rather formal. We exchanged courtesies, presents and thanks, but it was clear that he did not, that last time, want a deep discussion. Perhaps he thought that since I was leaving, I was no longer relevant; or that because I was leaving for Australia, always sensitive for Soeharto, he preferred not to engage in serious conversation. By contrast, discussion was full of depth at my farewell call that same week on then minister of technology Habibie, who had become something of a friend. That call confirmed my private view that despite his lack of the qualifications generally then supposed to be essential for the presidency – Habibie was neither Javanese nor of the military, for example – and despite a less than well-judged and unsuccessful run at the vice-presidency, B.J. Habibie was even then, if secretly, a serious and eager candidate to succeed Soeharto. Privately, Habibie would readily accept then that he was a political neophyte. Intellectually brilliant, he was certainly by the time of that farewell call in 1994, also a swiftly and astutely calculating operator, learning fast. Notwithstanding his years of Western training and very senior management positions and influence, Habibie was also a real Indonesian patriot.

Among a long list, Soeharto, Alatas, Moerdani and Habibie were probably the most important figures for the pursuit of British interests in Indonesia during my time there. I liked many others, including two finance ministers, and the environment minister – a kind yet ruthless man. I nearly missed his oh so subtle signal to me during a speech that he planned an attack on a British company for polluting a river from its factory. In debate with the minister of justice I failed to right a legal wrong corruptly done to a British company.

Despite ready and friendly access to these and many other important figures in Indonesia, there were a few rare occasions on which ranks were closed against the embassy. The most regrettable was in the case of a piratical attack on a merchant ship in the Sunda Strait. The ship was crewed predominantly by Filipinos; the chief engineer was Spanish, but the captain was British. During the attack he was murdered. I was appalled. The seamen's union in the United Kingdom was justifiably outraged. The captain's family were devastated. The navigational and other evidence convinced my naval attaché and me of whence the attackers and the murderer must have come. We believed that the Indonesian Navy could help – if they were so minded. We went to the top, presented our case and requested that help and cooperation. I used all the diplomatic techniques I could think might serve in Indonesia. I failed miserably. At the instance of the owners, and for understandable reasons, the ship was conducted to nearby Singapore. That move, however, limited my freedom to manoeuvre and ability to act in Indonesia: I could do little more, although I sent my naval attaché to Singapore to ensure no stone was left unturned. I shall not forget that failure of diplomacy.

Our enduring impressions of Indonesia include astonishing variety and contrasts of geology and geography that range from the rice paddies of Java and many a rain forest to oil fields and mines; Lake Toba and orang-utans in Sumatra; the bird life of West Papua; barefoot children riding upright on water buffaloes; forest fires and unsafe timber processing in Kalimantan; so many islands, some to rival Thailand's and some with rare or even unique corals; so many volcanoes – a goodly number active; arid rocky islands and rich productive ones. Memories include sailing north away from Jakarta's polluted harbour of Tanjung Priok to lovely tropical islands and there eating freshly harvested sea cucumber. Among the wide cultural variety was the mixture of religions, Friday prayers and debates with Islamic scholars in Aceh ('Veranda of Mecca'); the Hindu temple at Prambanan; Buddhist Borobudur; the young embassy chaplain; and my diplomatic colleague, Monsignor the Apostolic Pro-Nuncio. The variety of languages and of peoples ranged from Javanese rice farmers and fisher-folk via Jakartan, jet-setting businesswomen and suave, rich, cultivated, internationally minded businessmen and academics to Irian Jayanese living and cultivating much as their forbears did in the Stone Age.

No doubt unwisely, I was invited to handle the skull of Java Man – *homo erectus*. I engaged in bio-diversity debates in Sulawesi. We thrilled to frenzied drumming in Bengkulu in Sumatra. We witnessed so many ethnic dances, from Jambi in Sumatra to Ternate in the Moluccas, that to this day we steer away from the risk of more. By the waterfront in Ujung Pandang, which, boringly, means Observation Point, we have steered away from mosquitoes that seemed the size of young ponies with appetites to match. I was rather pleased to learn that Ujung Pandang is now once again known by its older name Makassar. How else would we understand the origin of 'antimacassars', those protective cloths placed on chair backs from the early nineteenth century to protect them from hair treated with oil that our sailors had secured in trade with Makassar?

The Jakarta we lived in was a bustling international city with new skyscrapers changing the skyline every few months – but with open sewers and squalid shanty shacks that were determinedly, even ruthlessly, being ripped up. The consequential social problems were severe. The need for humanitarian and development aid was deep and wide across much of the economy. Great Britain was a leading aid donor to and a major trading as well as investing partner of Indonesia, its largest European investor. British trading and investment ranged from oil and gas through mining and civil engineering to consumer goods and financial and other services.

Britain thus had a serious and important interest in the Indonesian economy, with its strong growth potential and huge mineral reserves: oil galore (despite mismanagement producing a period as a net oil-importer), an untapped gas field five times the size of the North Sea fields, coal for 500 years, and much more. But, in 1994, banking stability was among the embassy's real concerns. Harsh regulation and control had been replaced, starting in the 1980s, by successive and eventually excessive deregulation. The number of banks had leapt from some 17 to 250. Sound banking practice and rules were widely flouted. The Indonesian finance ministers and Central Bank governors I knew did their best. Banks were warned, even censured. But while the economy grew well, serious underlying problems remained. Chief among these, and the common factor, was corruption – especially worrying because it was endemic in banks, bureaucracies, national industries and was at the centre of the presidential government system.

From mid-1997 in Australia, Hilary and I looked north and watched Australian relations with Indonesia improve and then worsen. We watched the Indonesian first family corruption grow, and grow more blatant and comprehensive. Among several causes of this rapid further deterioration, we thought, was the effect on the family of the absence, after her unexpected death, of Soeharto's wife, Ibu Tien, who used to be known in Jakarta as Ibu Ten Percent. Higher born than the powerful man she married, and a Catholic who later became a Muslim, Ibu Tien was intelligent and shrewd, and something of a matriarch. At one level she could tell Hilary how proud she was of her children's contribution to Indonesian economic growth, and then ask what our boys had done for Britain. At another level, within the Soeharto family counsels, we believed she could be a moderating, restraining influence on the pretty massive corruption. Certainly, after her death, any family restraint seemed to erode quite quickly.

More generally, the honesty and plain dealing that Stamford Raffles had found in Java had been altered – perhaps, as Raffles implicitly had warned, both by indulgence and oppression down the years, and by too much foreign influence.

In November 1997, seriously alarmed by the domino effect of the Japanese experience, the Indonesian Central Bank withdrew 16 operating licences. The inevitable runs on banks and bank failures followed helter-skelter. So did capital flight – out of the country. Soeharto took pretty strong economic action when the shock waves from Japan hit Thailand and then Indonesia that year. He may have believed that his 30 years of economic success and his genuine acceptance by the people as the father of Indonesian development (*Bapak Pembangunan*) would give him the authority and support needed for the austerity measures he took. Perhaps he believed that, with the help of the international community and notably the IMF, he would prevail. But the sheer size of the financial and economic tidal wave – some $200 billion of debt, combined with sharply rising inflation, sudden massive unemployment and, that particular Indonesian horror, contemporaneous shortages of both food and cooking fuel, was an overwhelming onslaught on both the economy and the people.

There was more. That onslaught came at a time not only of widespread and passionate resentment at the excesses of political and financial corruption in high places but also of stultified, undemocratic practices set apparently in the stone of a regime that had not moved sufficiently with the times to accommodate increasing political awareness and dissatisfaction at – and here's the key – grass roots level.

Powerful, unpalatable domestic economic medicine might have worked for a less corrupt regime. But too many Indonesians believed that both the regime and its system of government had to go. The regime went.

Though we had long left Indonesia, I dare suggest that it is a tribute both to the leaders of the passionate 1998 uprising who exercised calm common sense at its very height and to each of the successors to President Soeharto that the system of government was given a chance of reform, and is still reforming.

B.J. Habibie's year and a half as the next President was inevitably transitional. This former vice president of MBB in Germany, aeronautical engineer par excellence, was not a natural politician, yet made some particularly sound political decisions as president of Indonesia. I still wonder about Lady Thatcher's view that he was a genius: she may well have been right that he had genius in aeronautical science and engineering. In politics he may have applied his brain more than any political instinct: he did, I believe, lead Indonesia in some major steps of transition towards democracy. In Shakespeare's understatement, he did his state some service.

Habibie's successor, in 1999, another apparently unlikely candidate, and the first freely elected president, Abdurrahman Wahid, was a man I also knew quite well. Islamic scholar, intellectual, courageous leader of moral principle, purblind, fond of jazz and a lover of the music of Beethoven; he was also a man of humour. I once asked him, over dinner in our house during Soeharto's presidency, when *he* was going to become president. He roared with delighted and not really dismissive laughter. I had high hopes of Gus Dur, as Abdurrahman Wahid was known popularly. But eventually, and perhaps particularly after he suffered strokes, he was seen as too erratic in his decisions as president: in 2001 his political enemies ensured that he was impeached and removed. Pak Dur died on 30 December 2009.

I knew the fifth president, Megawati Sukarnoputri, only slightly. She is a daughter of Sukarno, which is what Sukarnoputri means, as well as 'Princess of Sukarno'. She was only just visible as a potential political figure in my time, and we knew a little better her younger sister – the one who spent time in a New York jail. Politically, Megawati grew considerably from an apparently biddable political figurehead to a president who made clear the need for democratic control over the armed forces yet commanded the forces' respect; who led some of the much needed political and administrative reform; but who also was a one-term president.

President Susilo Bambang Yudhoyono won the first ever direct presidential election in Indonesia in a second-round run-off with Megawati in October 2004. SBY, as he is popularly (and conveniently) known, is a former army general. He pledged to bring peace to the troubled provinces of Aceh and Papua, to fight corruption and to pursue prudent economic policies. SBY has made real progress on all those issues, even in Aceh, despite, and in part because of, the awful Boxing Day 2004 tsunami there. He has advanced considerably the cause of democracy in Indonesia, where the Bali Democracy Forum is now a well-established international institution. Corruption is being tackled, if too slowly and not radically enough for many in the West. It is clear that reform in Indonesia has made some real, even remarkable advances and will continue, though probably at a Javanese rather than a faster pace and by Javanese consensus.

Here I should just record President Soeharto's sickness, which was the principal reason, some would say excuse, why this wily, cleverly dominating, even inspiring but woefully corrupt president did not appear in court. His final illness and his death on 27 January 2008 came a decade after his fall from power. At his funeral, a protester illustrated a common feeling with a poster indicating that his epitaph should be no longer be 'Father of Development' – *Bapak Pembangunan* – but *Bapak Koruptor* – 'Father of Corruption'.

The threat from terrorism in Indonesia continues, even in Bali after those two major bombings, in a string of other much troubled islands, and in Jakarta. SBY has fought, and continues to fight, terrorism with skill and resolution.

So the story of Indonesia continues, as a long unfolding *wayang kulit* play, a play of leather puppets, shadows and gamelan orchestra, of quiet manoeuvring and sudden loud clashes so beloved of the Javanese and so deeply rooted in Indonesian politics, culture, consciousness. To the Western eye surprisingly, *wayang kulit* will continue to illustrate and influence the history of this vast and important Asian archipelago, this increasingly influential regional power, large and growing market for trade and investment, and beautiful and compellingly fascinating country.

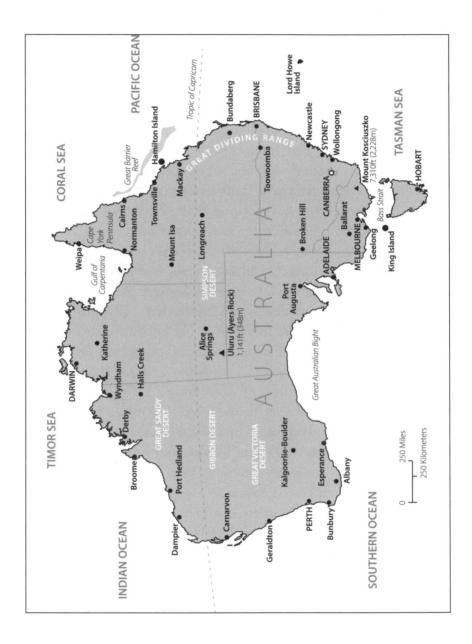

INDIAN OCEAN

TIMOR SEA

CORAL SEA

PACIFIC OCEAN

TASMAN SEA

SOUTHERN OCEAN

Tropic of Capricorn

Great Barrier Reef

Hamilton Island

Lord Howe Island

GREAT DIVIDING RANGE

Bundaberg

BRISBANE

Newcastle

SYDNEY

Wollongong

Mount Kosciuszko
7,310ft (2,228m)

CANBERRA

Bass Strait

HOBART

Toowoomba

Townsville

Mackay

Cairns

Normanton

Mount Isa

Longreach

Broken Hill

ADELAIDE

Ballarat

MELBOURNE

Geelong

King Island

Cape York Peninsula

Weipa

Gulf of Carpentaria

SIMPSON DESERT

Port Augusta

Great Australian Bight

Uluru (Ayers Rock)
1,141ft (348m)

Alice Springs

A U S T R A L I A

Katherine

DARWIN

Wyndham

Halls Creek

Derby

GREAT SANDY DESERT

GIBBON DESERT

GREAT VICTORIA DESERT

Kalgoorlie-Boulder

Esperance

Albany

Broome

Port Hedland

Dampier

Carnarvon

Geraldton

PERTH

Bunbury

0   250 Miles

250 Kilometers

CHAPTER 11

HIGH COMMISSIONER TO AUSTRALIA: MANAGING A FULL, FRIENDLY AND FRANK RELATIONSHIP

While serving as British high commissioner to Australia, I took a very senior British businessman to call on the then Australian minister of defence. The captain of British industry was very well dressed in an elegant dark suit, a crisp shirt and a fashionable tie with rows of animals or birds on it; these were ducks. He delivered a smooth, uninterrupted ten-minute peroration on why the Australian military should buy several hundreds of millions of pounds' worth of his famous company's world-class equipment. Much was at stake, including a significant number of jobs in the United Kingdom. At the end of the businessman's excellent and eloquent pitch, the Australian minister, still slumped in his chair, thought for a while, looked up and said: 'I do like your England cricket tie.'

There are countless true stories about Anglo-Australian cricket. There are almost as many myths. The same applies to Anglo- Australian history. I thought I should first learn some of the facts, in order to be able to deal with the myths that would surely arise in the course of my work both in the nation's capital, Canberra, and around Australia.

Forty thousand or more years after Aboriginal peoples probably began to live in Australia, Arab and Chinese sea captains may well have landed in northern Australia – in the first century AD. Western contacts followed fifteenth- and sixteenth-century mercantile expansion into Asia, notably by Portugal, Spain and the Netherlands. In 1606 a Spaniard, Luis Vaez de Torres, sailed through the strait later named for him, between the top of Australia, Cape York, and modern Papua New Guinea. Probably in the same year, a Dutch ship, the *Duyfken*, captained by Willem Jansz, touched at Cape York, and had some bloody encounters with Aborigines. In November 1642 the Dutchman, Abel Tasman, reached Tasmania but named it Van Diemen's Land – incidentally a repeat of the name given to part of the Northern Territory. The key date, however, is 19 April 1770, when then Lieutenant James Cook of the British Royal Navy sighted the fertile south-east coast from HM *Barque Endeavour*.

In Australia today, Cook is popularly – and in my view wrongly – believed to have sailed right past the Heads and therefore also what became Sydney Harbour, and to have missed it. However, skilled navigator as James Cook was, it is clear from his log that he identified the entrance; named it Port Jackson (after Sir George Jackson, then judge advocate of the Fleet); noted in his journal 'a bay or harbour wherein there appeared to be safe anchorage'; and added tidal details.

Having, with Joseph Banks, explored Botany Bay and recommended it for settlement, Cook had no pressing need to sail in past the Heads. Rather, he pressed on northwards to fulfil his priority task, his quest to claim the whole east coast for King George III and England. Cook's was an epic voyage, involving horrendously complex navigation and accurate re-charting of the Great Barrier Reef. Once, in adverse weather, *Endeavour* foundered badly on a sharp, hidden reef that ripped a very large hole in the ship's bottom. Captain Cook had the hole covered at sea temporarily with oakum on canvas – 'fotheringed' is the technical term – and then with great skill and resolve took the *Endeavour* into and up a river, where he careened the ship. The crew took some 40 days to repair her and make her fit for sea again, during which they had some interesting times eating turtles and debating right of access to this particular source of nourishment with the Aborigines. The place of *Endeavour*'s careening is today a small town called Cooktown.

It took another 17 years from Cook's voyage of discovery, during which time Britain's American colonies achieved independence, before Britain sent a fleet of 11 ships, under the command of then captain, governor-designate and later admiral, Arthur Phillip RN. I have written elsewhere of Arthur Phillip, a deeply impressive and acknowledged hero of Australia, yet an undersung British hero. That is until the recent plans to place a stone in the floor of Westminster Abbey and to erect a tribute sculpture in his retirement city of Bath. So here we will pass quickly over Phillip's establishment, against very considerable obstacles, of the first permanent settlement at Sydney Cove, New South Wales: a new colony with enlightened, humanitarian policies and practices.

After several austere, really tough years, the new colony found its economic feet, initially with whale oil, but more substantively with wool. By the middle of the nineteenth century and the discovery of gold, one Australian colony had become six and the continent was entirely in British hands. The colony's growing importance as a home for wealthy free settlers led to constitutional changes and to the popularisation of the name Australia, first formally recommended by Governor Macquarie in December 1817, and discussed earlier by others including Matthew Flinders. New South Wales was given a legislative council in 1823. In 1825 Van Diemen's Land became a separate colony. On the mainland, and despite privations and great physical obstacles, pioneers explored west and north. Legislative councils were granted to Western Australia in 1838 and South Australia in 1842. The Westminster Parliament's Australian Colonies Government Act of 1850 gave more constitutional powers to the colonies. Convict transportation ended to the mainland in 1840 and to Tasmania in 1853. Western Australia, a free settlers' colony with a labour shortage, chose to receive quotas of convicts between 1850 and 1868.

The gold rush began in 1851. Prospectors came from all over the world. Companies established by courageous Brits in the City of London financed large gold-mining operations in New South Wales, Victoria and later Queensland. In the following ten years, Australia exported more than £24 million worth of gold (a huge amount then). By 1861, the Australian population had reached almost 1.2 million, a three-fold increase in the 11 years since 1850. As the goldfields began to decline, wool exports kept the colonies viable. Railways were constructed. Colonies split over protectionism and free trade, which, together with jealousies, hindered attempts at co-operation and possible union among the six colonies and the Northern Territory until the 1890s.

The British government encouraged moves towards union. As early as 1847 the then British colonial secretary, the Earl Grey, issued proposals for unification; and ordered the closure of the convict settlement in New South Wales. Later a Scottish Presbyterian cleric in New South Wales formed the Australian League to campaign for a united Australia. But despite these efforts and those from London, it was not until 1891, at a convention sponsored by the premier of New South Wales, Sir Henry Parkes, that a federal constitution was drafted. It took a further six years of encouragement and persuasion before that draft was refined at another convention in 1897–98. The constitutional detail having been carefully negotiated, it was economic expansion and population growth that provided the motivation and the confidence for the colonies to call for self-government and to move towards federation.

On 9 July 1900, Queen Victoria gave royal assent to the Westminster parliament's Commonwealth of Australia Constitution Act, which led to federation itself, the birth of the Commonwealth of Australia, on 1 January 1901. Australia was now a nation.

In my view, the history of Australia as a new nation in the twentieth century is essentially the formation and development of an Australian identity and culture; of a national government and policies, notably in defence; and of a national economy. I do not believe federation in January 1901 carried with it any lurch or violent change in direction. Rather, federation marked the start of more identifiably national development on all these fronts, by and for Australians and at varying speeds, but also with a different and particular Anglo-Australian slant.

Underlying many of these developments is the classic pursuit of national interest – Australian national interest. During the twentieth century there were several swings away from, and some back towards, the connection with Britain, the former colonial power; but Australian national development has always been affected, and nearly always helped, by the continuing connection with the United Kingdom.

Perhaps the most traumatic, and the largest, step in the development of the Australian national identity we know today occurred in the First World War. The Australians had fought, and fought hard and well, alongside the Brits, in the Boer War. But it took the Great

War, far more than federation itself, to launch the transformation of an Australian national identity from that of six colonies to an independent commonwealth.

The first Allied shot of the First World War was fired in Australia on 5 August 1914 by Australian artillery as the German ship, *Pfalz*, attempted to leave Port Phillip. Australia responded to the Allied call for troops to fight in the defence of freedom readily, naturally and with no serious debate nor so far as I can judge any resentment. With a population then fewer than 5 million Australia sent more than 330,000 volunteers – more than three times the size of the British Army of today.

Those young Australians fought, half a world away, for values they shared with the British; and they suffered a casualty rate higher than most of the other participants. Australians who died in that war or as a result of their wounds are buried not only in Commonwealth war graves cemeteries right across northern France and in Belgium, but also in Britain. Wounded Australian soldiers were (and they would then have used the word) repatriated to England. Not all survived. There are nearly 1,000 Australian military graves in the Wylye valley in Wiltshire alone. There, at St John's Church, Sutton Veny, are 142 of those graves, including five of Australian nurses. At the wreath-laying after an annual Anzac service, the church's tenor bell is tolled 142 times – one for each dead Australian.

The much discussed Allied landings in the Dardanelles at Gallipoli in April 1915 and what followed are crucial to an understanding of the Australian national identity. The Allied operation was an unsuccessful attempt to force a passage through the Dardanelles in order to coerce Turkey out of the war and to open a safe route to Russia. The campaign lasted for months up and down the peninsula. Reinforcement on either side was massive. So was the slaughter.

The final dreadful tally of overall casualties (killed and wounded), according to the most objective sources I have found includes Canadians, Indians, New Zealanders, some 47,000 French, around 76,000 British, 25,800 Australians and over 250,000 Turks. Of Australia's casualties, the Imperial War Museum estimates that 8,587 were killed. Some authorities put that figure higher: at all events it was a huge number for a young country with such a small population.

The Gallipoli experience is seared into the soul – not too strong a phrase – of the Australian Defence Force, and of Australia today. Unsurprisingly, there is much myth in Australia about Gallipoli. The film 'Gallipoli', shown on Australian television every year on the eve of Anzac Day, bears only passing resemblance to the facts. But the myths – including the canard of bungling British officers putting the Anzacs first into the field as cannon fodder – live on as part of the background to an extremely traumatic national experience. Australia came of age, suddenly, terribly, as she was blooded. Australian 'mateship' was born and nurtured in the Dardanelles. 'Simpson and his donkey' is a legend: he brought his wounded comrades down the cliffs from the front lines to medical help time and time again, until he, too, inevitably, was shot and killed. Simpson is thought of as Australian but was English, a Merchant Navy seaman who jumped ship at Sydney. The scars of Gallipoli are still deep and visible today. Every Australian town commemorates Anzac Day, 25 April, every year in a dawn service and a later parade. The Returned Services League in Australia is stronger than in any other country I know or can imagine.

Every Anzac Day there is a dawn service in London: nowadays two or three thousand people, mostly young Australians, attend it. There is also a service at St Paul's Cathedral. The traffic is stopped for a service at the Whitehall Cenotaph, and there is a wonderful and overflowing service in Westminster Abbey. For me, on Anzac Day, the abbey becomes Australia's and New Zealand's parish church in England. A dozen or more separate Anzac Day services are held up and down England every year. The London annual dawn service nowadays alternates between the striking New Zealand War Memorial at Hyde Park Corner and the very close by and sublime Australian War Memorial that Her Majesty The Queen – of Australia – unveiled in a most moving ceremony with the Australian prime minister on 11 November 2003. The Memorial carries battlefield names composed of, incorporating and seeming to arise out of the carved names of all the villages and towns of Australia who sent their young to war and death.

The Second World War marked another quantum step in Australian national defence and strategic policy development, though arguably less seminally for the national identity than the Anzac experience. Immediately after Neville Chamberlain's broadcast in early September 1939 telling the United Kingdom that the country was now at war with Germany, Australian Prime Minister Robert Menzies announced that Australia was 'in consequence' also at war. Next day, the first Allied shot of the Second World War, just as in the First World War, was fired from Fort Nepean at Port Phillip.

Once again, there was deep co-operation with Britain and the other allies. Bob Menzies sat at meetings of the British war cabinet. But there were difficulties and disputes too. Among these was a serious policy difference between Prime Ministers Winston Churchill and John Curtin, Menzies' successor. This difference has also been distorted in the folklore, perhaps partly because people supposed the two would be at daggers drawn as one was Tory and one Labor, and partly because Australians blamed Churchill for Gallipoli: in April 1915, he was first lord of the Admiralty, and he did resign after the Dardanelles and join the army. The policy difference was about the deployment of half of one of the two divisions of Australian troops returning home from service in North Africa. Churchill needed that half-division to help the British defeat the Japanese in Burma. Curtin wanted the troops straight home, largely lest there be a Japanese attack on the Australian mainland.

I have read the exchange of lengthy telegrams between the two prime ministers. They are clearly written personally. They are well written and closely argued. All but one are written with genuine politeness and gentlemanly mutual respect: an honest difference, honestly discussed. The exception is one to Churchill drafted in Curtin's absence, by then foreign minister Herbert Evatt, whose style was perhaps less gentlemanly. The continuing myth of personal enmity between Churchill and Curtin should have been exploded with the memorial service Churchill ordered to be held in London for Curtin, a service described by a former leader of the Australian Labor Party, Kim Beazley, when he was deputy prime minister, as the best held anywhere for John Curtin.

Australia's Second World War effort was deep, intense and widespread. It was also unstinting. Until the start of that war and for the first part of it, the military history of Australia was mostly a long way from home, very much as the closest of allies with the British as the senior partner. This changed – with the threat of a Japanese attack on the Australian mainland and with American leadership in the war in the Far East.

The story is, of course, not quite that simple. For example, the British 14th Army action in Burma under General Sir William Slim (later governor-general of Australia) held down a significantly larger number of Japanese troops (385,000 of them), who might otherwise have been available for invasion duties further to the south-east. The Royal Air Force, having been decimated in the region following the fall of Singapore at the end of 1941, rebuilt – to the remarkable figure of 48 squadrons of Hurricanes in South East Asia Command by 1943, and by early 1944 to 93,000 personnel in the theatre. Even in early 1943, No. 54 RAF Squadron of Spitfires helped to defend Darwin against the 64 Japanese air-borne attacks on the city. And the British Royal Navy's contribution to the latter part of the war in the Pacific was both unsung and huge, involving over 600 ships of the British East Indies and Pacific Fleets, and much sacrifice of blood and treasure. These ships, in some of which Australians served, often worked in close concert with the Royal Australian Navy. When the commander-in-chief of the Japanese Southeast Army, General Hitoshi Imamura, surrendered on 6 September 1945, it was to an Australian army officer on board a British Royal Navy aircraft carrier, HMS *Glory*.

The Japanese bombed Darwin in February 1942. In March, they strafed flying boats at Broome in the north of Western Australia. In late May their midget submarines entered Sydney Harbour and torpedoed HMAS *Kuttabul*. Australia, as one Australian minister of defence put it, was 'shaken by the sense of its own vulnerability'. The Australian government sensibly then looked to the United States for major additional military support. In doing so, they made an historic shift in their alliance strategy. They welcomed the Americans into their midst, they joined in American military planning, and in American war-fighting. The United States became the senior partner and conducted the battle of the Coral Sea from an enormous base at Townsville in northern Queensland. The Australian effort in the

Asia-Pacific theatre against the Japanese was massive and, in Timor and Papua New Guinea, heroic and decisive.

The United States–Australia alliance persists and is vital today. In 1951 Australia, New Zealand and the United States signed a formal Pacific security treaty at San Francisco, the ANZUS Treaty, which became part of the fabric of Australia. So did the major shift of principal strategic partner, from the United Kingdom half a world away to the United States across the Pacific. Australia's now more forward defence policy posture reflects both a new view of Asia-Pacific regional and global realities, and enhanced national military confidence. That shift to a strong alliance with the United States was later demonstrated in Vietnam, where Australian forces joined Americans. Despite both this enduring alliance and Australia's own increasing military self-reliance, close co-operation with the British military has continued throughout the twentieth and into the twenty-first century. Fighting together successfully against President Sukarno's bloody Confrontation with Singapore and Malaysia in the early 1960s is but one example. Another is joint work in UN peace-keeping. Following budget cuts to UK forces, lengthy military exercises with Australia are far less frequent; but some 60 operational jobs in each defence force are still performed by members of the other. And today intelligence co-operation, which grew further during my time in Australia, is extraordinarily close, sophisticated and useful. Thus it is no surprise that British military personnel were the only European forces to take part in that Australian-led UN operation in East Timor in 1999. American forces did not take part.

Australia's alliance shift was not some deeply significant reversal of Anglo-Australian history: it was both sensible evolution and a positive, productive and mutually respectful exercise in cooperation with the friendly neighbourhood super-power in pursuit of shared objectives and values. More recently, in the twenty-first century, Australian forces, ship-borne, airborne, Special Forces and others, soldiered and are soldiering well in co-ordination with both American and British troops in, for example, Afghanistan.

The development of a national, federal government in Australia during the twentieth century is another study of its own. One of the key changes, this one due to the necessities of war, was from state to national, that is commonwealth, imposition of income taxes. The federal government has come a long way since the early days of federation, when Prime Minister Alfred Deakin established a protective tariff; procedures were designed for setting minimum wages; and a decision was taken to preserve the white immigration policy. Party politics apart, there is still plenty of (mostly healthy) argument both among the states, and with the Commonwealth of Australia. The late 1990s decision of the federal government, the government of South Australia and the administration in the Northern Territory to build the railway from Alice Springs to Darwin and thus complete the cross-continent link from Adelaide, is a good example of modern co-operation. However, it took over a century to fulfil the original federal government promise.

Britain played no direct role in the national governmental aspects of twentieth-century Australian history, beyond quiet encouragement early on. The Anglo-Australian slant in this context is a modern one: the designers and practitioners of the machinery of government in Britain today frequently consult Australian colleagues about such matters as devolution and other common interest policies such as in education and health.

The age-old debate, free trade versus protective tariffs, continues. To help internal development Australia was protectionist after federation in 1901, but has moved a long way since. Interestingly, only a decade or so ago a residue of protectionism became one area of dispute between the free trade oriented federal government of Australia and protectionist state governments. In my time in Australia there was a disagreement between, on the one hand, the British and Australian governments and, on the other, the New South Wales government. The United Kingdom failed to win a big contract because of a protectionist steel preference. When I left Australia, the then NSW premier had finally agreed to review the policy in response to my representations and arguments that he should abandon it. He has more recently told me that I was so much of a persistent nuisance that the policy was abandoned. But we had lost that one big contract. (Diplomacy uses many techniques. If one were silly enough to be seen as a nuisance in Indonesia, for instance, one would achieve nothing.)

In her national cultural development, from its first assumption of responsibility for foreign affairs, Australia was guided at least in good part by its cultural and political ties with Britain. From the middle of the twentieth century and probably for 30 years, Australians seeking fame, fortune, or even just a career, in the arts, typically headed for London. Actors often acquired an English accent. I first saw the late Leo McKern, later famous as 'Rumpole of the Bailey', play a small part in *A Midsummer Night's Dream* at Stratford-upon-Avon in the 1950s. He played it exquisitely well: I could not believe he was an Australian. The apparently magnetic attraction of England for Australian cultural practitioners was, eventually, criticised heavily in Australia. The cry was 'cultural cringe'. The development of Australia's own cultural endeavour in literature, film and theatre was perhaps a little closer to revolution than other national developments. Certainly by the last decade or so of the twentieth century, the cultural cringe had been replaced by a national cultural pride, even, some would say, an assertiveness – the phrase 'cultural strut' could be heard. And Australia continues to have enormous international cultural success in film, music, the stage generally and in arts administration.

Australian national cultural development has a nice Anglo-Australian twist, illustrated on our television screens. Humour crosses the huge distance between us far more readily in my experience than it crosses the Atlantic, the Channel or the North Sea. Only by the working of this Anglo-Australian cultural phenomenon can we explain the enormous success on British television screens of the Australian soap, 'Neighbours'. And only thus can we explain the extraordinary and continuing devotion of Australians to what they regard as among the very best of BBC factual documentaries, 'Yes Minister'!

The Commonwealth of Nations (as opposed to the Common-wealth of Australia) includes an arrangement that in third countries, the consular affairs of Commonwealth countries not represented by their own embassies or consulates may be looked after by embassies of other Commonwealth countries. As the pro-consul in Bulgaria, Hilary used to implement Australia's then 'white immigration' policy in Bulgaria. I mention this really to draw attention to the abandonment of that Australian national policy – though we did have some fun pointing out to Australians that Hilary had managed that particular policy for them. It lasted a little more than half the twentieth century, from 1901 to 1966. As in the United Kingdom, Asian and many other non-white immigrants in Australia now contribute significantly to social life, culture, sport, politics and the economy. The United Kingdom is once again the single largest source of immigration to Australia. New Zealand is a close second. China and India, who used to be nowhere, are not far behind.

The last 110 years have seen extraordinary family ties between our two countries. Over a million Australians of today were born in the United Kingdom. Another one and a half millions or so have parents who were born in Britain. Counting British visits to Australia and vice versa, there is a total of about a million visits every year.

The growth and successful development of the economy of Australia during these 110 years can be illustrated in part by population growth, from 3.8 million at federation in 1901 to almost 19 million at its centenary, and over 23 million in 2012. That some thinking Australians today argue that their country could successfully support nearly twice the present population is another. However climate change and events may be changing that view.

Australia started the twentieth century with a post-colonial economy that needed no subsidy. At the first federal elections in March 1901 Edmund Barton, among much else a cricketer, became the first prime minister of the Commonwealth of Australia. Parliament was opened in May 1901 in Melbourne by the then Duke of Cornwall and York, later King George V. In 1901 Barton and his Protectionist Party won most seats in the House of Representatives. In an early example of typically Aussie checks and balances, Free Traders dominated the Senate, but Labor held the balance of power. At federation, the Anglo-Australian economic relationship was based on the then standard model of inter-industry trade: raw materials from Australia to the United Kingdom, and manufactured goods the other way. The Australian economy, already a notable success after a very difficult start, was limited to a small number of sectors – based mainly on those raw materials and commodities, hence mining and agriculture.

Parliament continued to meet in Melbourne until it moved to Canberra in 1927, where it was opened by the then Duke of York, later King George VI. In Canberra, as many Australians still enjoy asserting, the construction of the national Parliament and all that went with it 'spoiled a good sheep run'. Soon after, the Depression in the 1930s hit Australia hard – some would argue even harder than they hit Britain. Australian accounts note that in those dark days national policy was mostly to follow Britain's leadership in seeking to cope with the Depression. Australia also sought to redirect more trade between Britain and Australia and with other former dominions. Britain certainly felt at the time not only fellow-feeling but some sense of remaining responsibility to help in hard times.

While I am on the Depression, I must pay tribute to a source of motivation for Australians struggling with all those economic and personal ills. The inspiration of his country at the time and, as former prime minister of Australia John Howard has said, 'a tremendous force for positivism and effort to overcome the Depression,' was a man who died in February 2001, Sir Donald Bradman; the greatest cricketer ever, and one of the greatest sporting gentlemen and inspirations of the twentieth century. One of countless Bradman stories occurred during the fourth Test match of the 1994–95 series played at the Adelaide (now Bradman) Oval. I was greatly privileged to sit next to Sir Don Bradman during part of the second day of the match. The England team, dispirited by a dreadful record in the tour thus far, were displaying classic signs of low morale. He and I were talking of his own extraordinary record against England teams much more successful than this one. I asked him what his score might be against this kind of England side. He thought for a bit and replied 'I might make about 65'. I remonstrated that he would surely do better than that. Sir Don responded: 'You have to understand, High Commissioner, I'm 86 years of age'!

Australian–UK bilateral trade declined after the Second World War, with the shift to intra-industry trade that drove expansion around the world, and with the movement in the terms of trade against commodities. This decline illustrated again, as the Depression had done so clearly, the limitations of Australia's then economy and her consequential vulnerability at difficult stages to external economic factors. Anglo-Australian economic history underwent another change when the United Kingdom joined the then European Common Market. Our economic relationship further evolved to become less special, less specialised. Australia and the United Kingdom began in some circles to be perceived as 'drifting apart'. But that perception of drift was false, and, I'm glad to say, died before it had established any durable life of its own. Indeed it lasted less time than the so-called 'cultural cringe'.

It is not only the British who are ambivalent about the United Kingdom's membership of the European Community and later the European Union. Australians are too. Australian exporters value the size and coherence of the European single market, yet I was sometimes attacked for the way Britain had 'treated' Australia in the negotiations for our membership. Among my answers was a reference to the comparative strength of the Australian economy before those negotiations and towards the end of the twentieth century. Australia was doing reasonably well at the time of our entry, but grew stronger through a testing time, and – a key to her later success – diversified out of necessity. The United Kingdom's accession to the EC may even have helped to inspire or accelerate this step in Australian economic evolution.

Australia's economy now is a modern, progressive, reforming, diverse, high tech economy, exporting not only raw materials and commodities but also modern manufactures and services, to remarkably profitable effect. Australia's economy now has a record of strong growth, including when her own region – and much of the world – has been economically weak.

Anglo-Australian economic and commercial relations have grown again, too, and remain strong, despite the post-credit crunch paucity of trade finance. This trading strength may have something to do with the fact that Britain has more real interest in an open trading system than most of our EU partners, and is a good base for European operations. Conversely, it also has something to do with the advantages of Australia as a base for our commercial operations in the Far Eastern region. Shared economic history helps too.

In two-way trade there is a balance in favour of the United Kingdom – though the way we in Britain are demonstrating our good taste and drinking more and more Australian sunshine in bottles may even things up a little. The United Kingdom today is Australia's third largest trading partner, her second largest source of both cumulative and direct foreign investment, as well as the second largest destination for Australian external investment. I was told in 1994 by a senior and powerful Australian businessman that he would still do business with the Brits, but only with the Brits, on a handshake. I was much struck by this, and for the next three and a half years was on the lookout for examples. I found plenty, including some large and surprising ones. One involved a score or so of expensive civil aeroplanes.

Further, on modern Australia's evolution, the constitutional debate, monarchy versus republic, was a major subject in our time in Australia, both before and in the aftermath of the republicans losing that debate in the referendum of November 1999. That result was the decisive end to a chapter in Australian constitutional history. More chapters will be written. While then prime minister, Kevin Rudd wrote what he may have thought was the foreword to the next chapter when in early 2010 he presaged another referendum in his second term. He has had, as yet, no second term; but in her election campaign later in 2010, his successor Julia Gillard proposed that Australia should become a republic after the Queen dies. Since then, a footnote to the 1999 chapter was written in May 2011, when a Morgan poll showed that support for the monarchy was at 55% (17% higher than in 1999), and that for a republic was at 34% (20% less than in 1999, and the lowest support polled for a republic since the 29% of 1988). This is not the place for a detailed discussion – partly because the most important point to this aspect of the Anglo-Australian story is simply that this debate is a national matter, for Australians alone. Whatever we may think, whatever view we may take, it is nothing to do with the United Kingdom, any more than it is do with any of the 'other realms and territories'.

The story, then, of Australia's history following federation in 1901 is of eventful evolution. These Anglo-Australian years were marked by management of change and development, achieved without rancour, if not without debate, and not without emotion (especially on the sporting fields). Australia and the United Kingdom have pursued shared values, often jointly; have defended those values at great cost in blood and treasure; and have advanced them to the good of both countries, and to the good of other countries too. Yet primarily those have been years in which Australia became her own independent and wonderful self. In that century-plus, Australia advanced from a brand spanking new ex-colonial federation with tough teething troubles, to one of the most successful countries of her region and one of the most respected and admired countries both in that region and right around the world.

As I began to work as high commissioner to Australia, the perceptions, however, of both Britons and Australians, differed often from the reality, sometimes starkly, and sometimes influentially for the pursuit of British relations. That was a problem I needed both to take account of and to address.

However, my diary for the first weeks was too crowded for there to be time to think much beyond calls in Canberra and Sydney on senior officials, politicians, the governor-general, the chief justice, military officers, the press, Australian and British captains of industry, other high commissioners and ambassadors, and many more. It was helpful that the diplomatic calls on colleagues, and indeed that on the governor-general, were shared with Hilary, who called on the wives – again no husbands: not quite yet. In the United Kingdom, Parliament was in recess, so there were British visitors aplenty, from ministers to the speaker of the House of Commons. There was a conference of British consuls-general from around Australia and there were official visits to Western Australia and to Victoria. A brisk baptism, during which we were based in an hotel, the residence being cleared of asbestos and refurbished. The first call on me in the hotel was by a former speaker of the Australian House of Representatives and high commissioner to the United Kingdom, Doug McClelland, as chairman of the Australian Political Exchange Council. Doug knew how best to lobby hard another diplomat; we did some good work together, later beating bureaucrats and establishing a useful Anglo-Australian exchange system for politicians. There was one treat during that industrious induction – to see Jayne Torvill and Christopher Dean, our Olympic and world ice-dancing champions, and to meet them after their show for a delightful chat.

The governor-general, Bill Hayden, a former foreign minister for Australia, I found always interesting, easy, open and helpfully instructive. In the Queen's absence, the governor-general is the *de facto* head of state. Since the Queen is head of state of both our countries, I had no credentials to present from one to the other monarch or to the governor-general. Rather, as for the other realms and territories, I carried a letter of introduction from the British head of government, then John Major, to his opposite number the Australian prime minister, then Paul Keating. When I handed John Major's letter to Paul Keating in his parliamentary office there was no ceremony, just the act and a good substantive discussion over coffee.

An important part of the high commissioner's job is to manage relations between the two heads of government. The party political differences between Paul Keating and John Major were clear and understood – and reminiscent of those expected between Churchill and Curtin. Modern communications, cooperation within the Commonwealth, important bilateral relations on so many governmental subjects, and Anglo-Australian history made for a particular relationship between the two leaders, which frequently became close and occasionally tense. Paul Keating, from New South Wales working-class origins, had grown up politically in a hard school. Also like his political hero Jack Lang, he was self-taught. Indeed he made himself a noted expert on English furniture and French and other silver. He was often tough and could be rough. I recall sitting in the balcony at a prime minister's questions session in Canberra when Paul Keating was being pilloried by the opposition. In the rough and tumble of debate (rougher than at Westminster) Keating was handing out the insults in characteristically vivid style and with free-flowing graphic language: the furious opposition howled. I was sitting next to Annita, Paul's (Dutch-born) wife, who, among the uproar, said into my ear with charm and loyal conviction that 'They may do that; but he is right'.

Perhaps in contrast was the Paul Keating on whom I called, among other things, to deliver an invitation to attend the London commemorations of the fiftieth anniversary of the end of the Second World War. To his evident disappointment, when he consulted his diary he had to decline: the budget demanded his presence in Canberra. He asked me to wait while he went into an anteroom and returned a minute or two later bearing CDs which he laid on the coffee table between us, saying: 'Tell them this is the music they should play in St Paul's'. I thought his choice spot on: the CDs included Elgar and Benjamin Britten's 'War Requiem'.

Certainly by way of further contrast was the strong disagreement between our two prime ministers when President Chirac of France decided in 1995 to hold a series of nuclear tests on the Pacific island of Mururoa in French Polynesia, 5,700kms east of Australia, some 3,250kms north-east of New Zealand and something over 900kms from the nearest British possession, Pitcairn. As I recall this sorry tale, the Australian foreign minister Gareth Evans, then visiting Japan, made a reasonable statement that was quickly superseded by one by Paul Keating strongly deploring the intention. The tests, of devices set deep into the atoll rock, would obviate the need for more, the French said. The British government took the firm view that objections by states which had benefited for so long from the Western nuclear umbrella to tests designed to ensure the safety of the Western weapons were not acceptable. Paul Keating had clearly judged the national mood aright: Australians, urged on by unions, boycotted French goods; blew up the French honorary consul's office in Perth (he was a doctor, whose patients' records were destroyed); committed similar, tasteless but less dramatic acts in Brisbane; refused sanitary and other services to the French ambassador's residence in Canberra; and mutilated important archive documents sent from the Louvre to the French ambassador's wife in connection with her work as curator of a Louvre exhibition. Dominique and Maud Girard, good friends from when we were ambassadors together in Indonesia, suffered badly, as did their two children at school, who had to be withdrawn and sent home to school in France. Diplomats expect to be in the firing line from time to time, certainly metaphorically, but this behaviour was disgraceful. Gareth Evans did try to help the French, and achieved a little, but the passion of the opposition to France won, hands down.

The British position was firmly in support of the French. I did what I could to help, both with representations and some practical assistance. The episode lasted too long. It did much harm to Australian-French and Australian-EU relations. The Girards behaved with elegant dignity. The only light moment in a distressing and unnecessarily bad-tempered Australian performance was when Dominique left Gareth Evans' office in parliament one day to be beset and immediately surrounded by many noisy journalists, pressing hard. In the throng, Dominique walked into an unseen but solid steel security bollard. His affronted yet aloof reaction and his splendid Gallic shrug were the basis of a cartoon next day that had Gareth Evans asking a member of his staff, 'Why can't I shrug like that?'

All this took place in the run-up to the Commonwealth Heads of Government Meeting (CHOGM) held in New Zealand in November 1995. The French eventually carried out a test in the month following both the CHOGM and a UN vote against testing. A few days before the CHOGM, Paul Keating telephoned to say that he did not want to have a row there 'with John', and to ask me to ensure that did not happen. I accepted that our interests could be argued to coincide on this specific aspect, though I certainly could not undertake in any way that John Major would not raise the subject, such was the strength and justification of his and British feeling. I did undertake to be in touch with Downing Street. I crafted and sent telegrams (the fastest means of classified communication at the time) to the FCO and No. 10. In the event the big press story at that CHOGM concerned Nigeria, and the two prime ministers had a frank and straightforward private exchange of views on Mururoa and all that.

The Mururoa story should also be seen against the background that Paul Keating's government wanted to alter the balance of Australia's international engagement in favour of Asia, and to the detriment of that with Europe. He and his ministers saw Australia's interests best served by becoming accepted as Asian, rather than a pseudo-European country in Asia. Hence Paul Keating's successful efforts to establish a friendship with Soeharto of Indonesia. Hilary and I watched with especial interest the further highs and lows of the Australian-Indonesian roller-coaster of relations; and the mixed success in practice of the pro-Asian policy.

With Keating's foreign minister, Gareth Evans, who came for a private lunch at the residence from time to time, I believe I developed a good understanding. There was often bilateral business with Paul Keating including some conducted while we sat together at the one-day cricket match at Manuka between Mike Atherton's England XI and the Australian Prime Minister's XI. Paul Keating seemed glad to talk business and politics: he is no cricketer. Indeed he had to check with me that Australia had won before he rose to make an impromptu speech linking that win with Australian Labor Party politics. By contrast, keen cricketer and very knowledgeable cricket enthusiast John Howard led the Liberal coalition with the National Party at the March elections, and succeeded Paul Keating as prime minister.

In the Australian Parliament in February 1992, Prime Minister Paul Keating had said that in 1942 Britain 'decided not to defend the Malayan peninsula, not to worry about Singapore, and not to give us our troops back to keep ourselves free from Japanese domination'. I had read the objective history while serving in Singapore, so Keating's inaccurate and distorted view of history had rankled with me ever since. In 1995, Australia organised an excellent year-long commemoration on the fiftieth anniversary of the end of the Second World War, known as 'Australia Remembers'. No Australian could have missed the fine events, which were held all across the country. Australian youth played a big part. Given the integrated and extraordinarily close nature of our wartime alliance and cooperation, I thought that Britain should play some small part in 'Australia Remembers'. A unit of the King's Own Scottish Borderers visited, won a rifle shooting competition, turned themselves into a pipe band and played at a string of events, including a moving performance at the Australian War Memorial. On a memorable and dark rainy night, they Beat Retreat, illuminated spectacularly on the suitably large patio at the rear of Westminster House before an audience, some under umbrellas, some crowding the windows of the residence, of many of the great, good and powerful of Australia.

My defence adviser, Commodore Brian Adams, RN and I took the salute. We were drenched but proud.

As a further British contribution to 'Australia Remembers', the matchless Imperial War Museum in London had prepared a superb photographic exhibition for us. Finely designed and presented, the multiple copies were dismountable, and moved among 20 venues around Australia. The photographs and their captions were thoroughly researched and provided an unchallengeable, objective and accurate account of Britain's deep involvement in and contribution to the war in the Far East and Pacific. The main exhibition was at the Australian War Memorial (AWM) in Canberra and did not move. My military adviser, Colonel Stephen Saunders, added carefully researched extra artefacts. The Australian minister of defence opened the exhibition with a well-judged and well-written speech. Margaret Thatcher attended the opening of the Sydney exhibition, held in the New South Wales Parliament. I did not invite Paul Keating to the exhibition in Canberra, but ensured that he knew of it, and that the chairman of the council of the AWM, Air Marshal Barry Gration, was briefed. Paul Keating twice visited the exhibition out of hours, privately and alone save for Barry Gration. He read all the captions. The close of 'Australia Remembers' was marked by parades and by a VIP lunch on 14 August 1995 in Townsville. At that lunch, leaving his prepared speech notes unopened, Prime Minister Paul Keating spoke at length, giving his history of the Second World War. He looked across at me a few times during his speech, notably when he came to the fall of Singapore: he then said the right things about Britain.

Colonel Stephen Saunders was a particularly fine soldier and Christian gentleman. He later served with distinction in Kuwait, and thereafter became military attaché at the embassy in Athens as a brigadier. In Athens, on 8 June 2000, Brigadier Saunders was killed as he drove to work by the terrorist organisation 17 November, in a misdirected murderous assault. We attended Stephen's funeral in Salisbury Cathedral, a magnificent, moving and memorable service. Among very many others, British secretary of state for defence Geoff Hoon, former Prime Minister Sir Edward Heath and the Greek foreign minister attended. I was glad that the Greek came, but after the service I could not resist remonstrating with him about his country's failure to deal effectively with 17 November since they began their many killings 25 years earlier. Heather Saunders, Stephen's widow, and their two daughters were splendid at the funeral but, of course, desolate. The day after the murder, Heather had made a most impressive television appeal outside the British embassy in Athens for witnesses and help. She and family members of other 17 November victims lobbied the Greek government effectively for stronger anti-terrorism legislation, which was passed the following year. Greek and British police worked together, with United States support. In 2003, Heather took part in the trial at which the murderers were sentenced to life imprisonment. Heather was awarded the OBE for her tireless and successful pursuit of justice.

Anglo-Australian defence cooperation was notably strong, despite financial and operational constraints. Under both the Australian governments to which I was accredited, Labor and Coalition, and both British governments, Conservative and New Labour, there were over 70 operational Australian military officers serving in the British forces, and vice-versa. An RN officer captained an RAN patrol boat working Australia's northern shore and did fine work, including in the drugs field. Major, extensive joint exercises were held right across Australia and involved serving British forces from all three arms. HMS *Gloucester* did fine service as a communications ship across northern Australia. Her Captain, quite reasonably, thought Derby in northern Western Australia the most remote, empty and grey port he had ever visited. HMS *Sheffield* came too – the successor to both the *Sheffield* in which I had served briefly in the Royal Navy in 1956 and to the stricken hero of the 1982 Falklands conflict. Hilary and I spent a night aboard *Sheffield*. We also joined the Type 23 frigate, HMS *Monmouth*, off New South Wales. We sailed aboard her over 500 nautical miles up the coast to Brisbane; but not before her crew demonstrated some of her kit to Australians, including grey-suited civil servants from the defence department. We were a good distance offshore, the weather was sporting, the ship was making high speed, and I shall never know whether the soaking those bureaucrats had from a huge and heavy wave over the bow was by RN design or maritime misfortune. Nor indeed shall I ever be sure that the naval equipment concerned was later bought despite the drenching of personnel and because of its intrinsic quality and reasonable price. But could the price have been higher if the suits had been drier? I do know that there is little more convincing to informed, even expert potential customers than the honest, salty comments offered and answers given by real front-line operators. The civil servants were put ashore back in Sydney to dry out and recover.

Our passage to Brisbane continued in the heavy weather. I suspected that certain naval persons aboard wanted to ensure that Lady Carrick, as by then she was, suffered from *mal de mer*. They had already seen success in the matter of the grey suits. However at dinner that evening in the wardroom, Hilary fared far better than the young officers, who had probably much enjoyed their shore leave before HMS *Monmouth* left Sydney Harbour. A visit to the heaving engine room was similarly unsuccessful, though I sometimes wonder what happened to the rather good pearl earring that a Rolls-Royce Spey engine appeared to have swallowed. The next day *Monmouth*'s Lynx helicopter was exercised. We were invited along for the ride. Hilary told me quietly, 'Yes – any motion but this!' We were briefed, signed on the line, donned life jackets, climbed aboard – and zoomed up to some 3,000 feet and well away from *Monmouth*. The pilots zoomed down again to buzz an unsuspecting cargo vessel making her own way through the heavy seas – and back up to 3,000 feet, where they proposed a '180-degree wing-over' to Hilary, who bravely, I thought, agreed. We were advised not to lose the horizon from sight lest we felt queasy and disoriented. The '180' was exciting and not too alarming. We were then told that if the helicopter were to ditch, it would immediately turn turtle and we would find it difficult to extract ourselves upside down. We were promptly offered a '360-degree wing-over'. I thought there could be no such thing short of a suicide attempt. The pilots quickly added that in practice it might be 270 degrees and we should watch that horizon. Over we went. Hilary did very well: I lost the horizon. I learned deep respect for the Lynx helicopter; and later also learned, not entirely to my surprise, that the pilots were among the best in the Navy.

I spent much of that night on the bridge, in the company of the navigating officer. There is a long careful passage into Brisbane, with a turn hard to port, leaving Moreton Island to starboard. This was before widespread GPS navigation. The chart informed us that an especially bright double navigation light aid should show at the head of the sharp bend in the channel. There was a tense wait as we neared the bend and should have seen the light. I was about to believe the light had failed when an officer on the bridge used the radio to ask the Australian authorities about the light. Almost instantly the light lit – brightly indeed. It is not only on the sports fields that Anglo-Australian friendship and joking rivalry is demonstrated (I also wondered what communications to the coastguard those dampened civil servants might have made).

It was during that visit to Brisbane that Paul Keating made what I think of as his corrective speech; that Hilary and I met Australian VCs; and that I learned, not for the first time, how sensitive Northern Ireland was for many Australians of Irish nationalist background. Paul Keating was tough but reasonable on the issue. Some Queensland officials were less reasonable and I found my first-hand knowledge of the troubles of help.

Defence sales was an important subject for us. The high commission had an able, respected and effective first secretary, David Richardson, from the MOD dedicated to defence sales work. The uniformed staff helped too, to good effect. Another eventually successful campaign, very different to that in Indonesia, was waged to sell very different Hawk aircraft. And there was much more besides. There was some stiff competition at several stages in the campaign and the Australian Ministry of Defence was good at its side of the negotiations. At one relatively low moment in this long-drawn out process, I learned that the Hawk-equipped Red Arrows were to be in the Far East. It took a good deal of work and cooperation from the MOD and British Aerospace (now BAe Systems), but they came down to Australia. They were, of course, magnificent. They performed in Adelaide, Canberra and Sydney. Weather conditions varied, so the performances did too. The Red Arrows really took Australia by storm. It was a delight that the Australians agreed that both the RAF Red Arrows and the RAAF Roulettes could perform over Sydney Harbour on a clear Australia Day. In Chicago I had learned the value of a short lecture before the Royal Navy went ashore. Perhaps unnecessarily, I thought it wise to warn the RAF Red Arrows not to fly under Sydney Harbour Bridge.

Hilary and I, together with the affable and able governor of New South Wales, Rear Admiral Peter Sinclair, his wife Shirley, and my air adviser, were guests aboard HMAS *Sydney*. She was anchored at the spot chosen as the centre-point of the Red Arrows display. We had an excellent view of a marvellous display. No pilot flew under Sydney Harbour Bridge, though one told me he had found it a most tempting target. However, after two red Hawks crossed each other low over the water, the lower one, a dual if I recall aright, upside down and with a rather senior officer in the back seat for the ride he may just not have been quite expecting, flew between two blocks of harbour-side apartments. I held my breath and looked at my air adviser. That Group Captain turned as white as the vapour trails emitted by the Red Arrows in part of their display. I therefore rehearsed what I might have to say by way of apology. Though I had not heard any breaking of glass, I later told the air adviser that I really did not want to know the size of the bill the MOD would have to pay.

Many British visiting companies had to be disabused, when they called at the High Commission or Consulates-General, of their evident assumption that the Australian market behaved just like the British. Even BAe had some people who thought the Australian specification of both heads-up cockpit displays and air conditioning in the Hawk cockpits were unnecessary: the RAF did not have them after all. Once such people had been to northern Australia, they were glad to accept the advice of our defence sales staff. There was a problem over the Rolls-Royce Adour engines. As I recall the story, the Royal New Zealand Air Force had them slung below the wings on aircraft that they evidently landed on gravel runways. Resultant damage persuaded some New Zealanders to distrust this excellent engine and to spread this distrust to Australians. It helped that good and longstanding friend Robert Alston was our high commissioner in Wellington. The problem of convinced perception seemed to me rather serious at an important time in our campaign. I asked Sir Ralph Robins (he of the golf-balled eye in Indonesia), then chairman of Rolls-Royce plc and a fine engineer, to visit New Zealand and Australia, to design and implement a recovery programme in the former and to talk to key decision-makers in the latter. Sir Ralph agreed, came, worked hard and solved the problem.

Defence sales apart, on which debates were held and decisions made in Canberra, commercial diplomatic work in Australia naturally centred on the commercial cities. Though as high commissioner I was ultimately responsible, the consul-general in Sydney had a large chunk of this work to direct. There were important market differences around the vast continent that is Australia, and the consuls-general in Melbourne, Perth and Brisbane played equally vital roles. In Adelaide we had a rightly well-respected and effective honorary consul-general, John Morphett, an accomplished architect. John retired on age grounds during our time there. The South Australia commercial scene was expanding, the market was growing and British firms were arriving there, so I was glad that John was succeeded by a full-time, locally engaged commercial consul, Vic Warrington. Vic worked to good effect to the experienced and helpful consul-general in Melbourne, George Finlayson (later appointed high commissioner in Malawi).

In Perth Tony Abbot was an excellent consul-general across the board. Tony was especially well supported by his wife, Margaret, herself formerly of the Diplomatic Service, and commanded respect at all levels that counted. Tony achieved his yearning ambition after Perth, to be governor of Montserrat, where Margaret and he did extraordinary work after the volcanic eruption of June 1997 that buried so much of the island. In retirement, Tony was head of the Pitcairn island logistics team overseeing the trials of child abuse – an extraordinary event in a remote and often inaccessible island. So Tony and Margaret were based in an Auckland hotel in 2002–03 and visited Pitcairn when they could: the Diplomatic Service inspires independence and versatility. Mike Horne succeeded Tony two months before I left Australia, and organised for Hilary and me a high-class farewell visit, of which I have written elsewhere. The Abbots returned to live in Perth in retirement, and have stayed good friends. Tony now runs the Western Australia branch of the Royal Over-Seas League.

Official travel in the high commissioner job meant we spent almost half our time in Australia away from Canberra. George and Pat Finlayson had a guest suite in their residence in Melbourne, of which we, visiting ministers and other VIPs took full advantage, so cost-conscious were we all and so hospitable were the Finlaysons. They gave a memorable dinner one evening at which the guests included two former governors-general of Australia, Sir Ninian Stephen and Sir Zelman Cohen. With Lady Cohen, Zelman stayed with us at Westminster House, and kindly gave his name to a flagship Chevening scholarship to the United Kingdom for an especially bright young Australian. With both these wise men I had enjoyable and helpful private conversations and correspondence. George Finlayson was a sound, able and thoughtful commercial and representational diplomat who made many friends in Victoria and could hold his own with Melbournians at all levels, in pursuit of the gamut of British interests.

In Brisbane our interests were also well served by John Durham and his wife Shan. They understood the different state politics, culture and history of Queensland, which has the only unicameral parliament in Australia, so were able to deliver whatever was required on the consular, commercial, representational and political fronts. They did so always cheerfully. The consul-general, as elsewhere, was supported by a notably strong locally engaged staff. Curiously, until the geography and distances are taken into account, the posts in Brisbane and Perth shared consular responsibilities for the enormous Northern Territory – and always had fast and good cooperation from Territory officials. Nonetheless, I was keen to find and appoint an honorary consul in Darwin, capital of the Northern Territory. Despite research and official visits, and some offers, I could not find anyone satisfactory both to me and to the chief minister in Darwin. For much of our time, following the able, experienced and thoughtful Marshall Perron, the excellent and politically feisty, hospitable and fun Shane Stone was chief minister. Happily we still see him and his wife, Josephine. That failure of mine to appoint an honorary consul has been rectified, I am glad to note.

The good Steve Hiscock succeeded John Durham in Brisbane at the end of 1996. It will be clear from Chapter 9 that to have Roy Reeve as consul-general in Sydney for a good stretch was a joy, professionally and personally. Until the 1980s there was a flat for the high commissioner at Point Piper in Sydney, which was mostly well used and cost-effective. While the consul-general's job is busy and productive, there is a multitude of British commercial, political and other interests to pursue there, and the high commissioner does need to visit and work in Sydney quite often. Members of the public accounts committee of the House of Commons, however, thought the flat was a luxury that should be sold. It was an easy target, notwithstanding the high cost of hotels. A smaller but equally well-used flat in Melbourne had been sold previously. The Sydney consul-general's residence had been acquired when the occupant was in a higher grade of the service, and was quite large. The decision to retain that house and to provide within it a self-contained, if very small, flat for the high commissioner's use was a sound one. It worked well in Roy Reeve's time. It was possible, just, for the high commissioner to entertain a couple of official guests there, provided that Hilary did the cooking. It was also possible and certainly cheaper than the hotel alternative to hold small meetings there.

Roy and Gill Reeve also became valued and lasting friends. Roy was not a stereotypical consul-general, and suited the job in New South Wales ideally. He refereed rugby matches. His relaxed easy competence delivered first-class results. He drove a Harley Davidson motorcycle. Once a year or so, a photograph of Roy driving the Harley to work would be published in the press – often with the official Jaguar following behind with the inevitable briefcase in chauffeur Bill Divall's care. That bright idea has evidently since been adopted, or adapted to the bicycle, by senior politicians in London.

One of the most loved figures in Sydney was Peter Doyle, who owned the famous Doyle's seafood restaurants, the one in Watson's Bay having opened five generations earlier in 1885 – early indeed for Australia. Peter was also a fan of Harley Davidsons and had a yen for one, but the nearest his family would permit was the ownership of a camel named Harley. Peter was diagnosed with throat cancer.

Sydney decided to celebrate Peter's sixtieth birthday in style with a large, black-tie reception in the fine National Maritime Museum at Darling Harbour. Peter was told that transport would collect his wife and him from his house in Vaucluse, not far from Watson's Bay. The consul-general's official Jaguar arrived at the appointed hour, but only for Peter's wife. Soon after, Roy arrived driving his Harley Davidson and accompanied by a Sydney Police Force motorcycle escort. Peter, in dinner suit, save for surgical collar rather than bow tie, donned a helmet and climbed on behind Roy. The escort set off, protecting the Harley, and cruised the 5 miles past Rose Bay, Point Piper, Darling Point, Rushcutters Bay, Potts Point and Woolloomooloo and on to Darling Harbour. Police outriders leapfrogged each other to stop traffic at junctions, so the motorcade crossed several red lights. At the entrance to the museum, the escort motorbikes stopped in front, forming a guard of honour, and the Harley drove up a specially installed ramp, along a hall and right into the reception. What an entrance! Roy told me that throughout the drive he could hear Peter Doyle, despite the throat cancer, singing for joy.

Roy went on to be ambassador to Ukraine. Later he left the Diplomatic Service to become the ambassador of the Organisation for Security and Cooperation in Europe (OSCE) to Armenia, and later to Georgia. There he must have enjoyed telling the president that in a previous existence as USSR foreign minister, he, Shevardnadze, had presided over Roy's blacklisting as part of the 1988 reciprocal expulsion of diplomats. Before returning to academia and conflict resolution, Roy did fine work as head of planning and deputy head of the EU rule of law mission in Kosovo.

The Australian National Maritime Museum is a national and international treasure. Dr Kevin Fewster was its dynamic director. It will surprise no one who knows him that after a later spell directing Australia's premier Power House Museum of Arts and Sciences, Kevin became the dynamic director of the British National Maritime Museum at Greenwich, where he is achieving great new things. I first met Kevin through Roy Reeve in connection with a then hoped-for exhibition in Australia of artefacts from the *Mary Rose*, Henry VIII's lost naval ship. The task and complications of arranging for these precious and delicate materials to travel from their damp climatically controlled quarters in Portsmouth were prodigious. The exhibition even travelled around Australia to four separate locations over 16 months in 1994 and 1995. I flew to the opening at Warrnambool in western Victoria from Melbourne in a small aircraft with the deputy premier of Australia, Pat McNamara, who kindly arranged that we flew low over the Twelve Apostles rocks off the coast as the sun was setting over them.

Tasmania often feels itself to be the poor relation among the states of Australia, with some justification economically, though it does not enjoy the indignity of sometimes being left off the bottom of the map of Australia. The good Paul Kemp, Commonwealth bank manager and honorary consul, looked after our interests there well. We visited fairly often, and stayed with the governor in his fabulous Scottish baronial official residence, whose royal suite has to be stayed in to be believed. Sir Guy Green was an excellent governor, the first Tasmanian-born governor and a former chief justice and university chancellor, worked tirelessly for his state. He and his wife, Rosslyn, were most hospitable. Hilary and I flew by helicopter with them down to Port Arthur after the mad massacre there in April 1996, when 35 people were killed and about the same number injured. We attended the sobering and powerful memorial service. Port Arthur, a prison colony and for twenty years from 1833 the destination for recidivist convicts, is a disturbing place for Britons to visit at the best of times. This was the worst of times. Later, we in the high commission arranged some joint work between Port Arthur and Dunblane in Scotland where, in the previous month another insane massacre, mostly of children at the primary school, had taken place. The mayor of Port Arthur and his team came to dinner at Westminster House on their way to visit Dunblane. The still brand new coalition government in Canberra led Australia-wide legislation to restrict private ownership of semi-automatic and pump-action weapons. The Conservative government in London took comparable action to ban high-calibre handguns.

In the months before we went to Australia, our two governments had reached agreement over the contentious issue of Maralinga, the site far into the outback where British nuclear tests had been conducted in the 1950s and early 1960s. Despite a 'clean-up' operation in 1967, radiation remained in some of the ground and might threaten wandering Aboriginal tribes and, particularly, their children. The 1994 agreement was for sharing the expertise and costs of a new and better 'clean-up'. My task in September 1995, with essential technical help, was to visit the site and to ensure both that work was proceeding well and the British taxpayer was receiving value for money. Hilary and I, with expert Murray McConnell from London, flew to Maralinga. The last leg was in a small aeroplane that landed on a barely used, high quality runway that had been designed to serve RAF heavy transports and bombers. During a fascinating couple of days we found that some material that had been at risk of radiation and marked as such, had been buried mistakenly in shallower pits intended for non-radiated material, and that there had been leaks. Remedial action included vitrifying equipment such as Landrovers in large cubic blocks, which neither degrade nor react over time. We saw finished blocks and found with Geiger counters no significant radiation from them. The blocks were then buried. Near the site, the radiation was less than that found in Sydney brownstone houses and by The Rocks at Circular Quay. The work was proceeding well and effectively, so our reports could be positive.

During the night after a starlit barbecue at Maralinga, we drove with two caretakers south to the railway line that runs from Adelaide through Port Augusta and Woomera and right across the Nullabor Plain. We pulled alongside the track and pointed the pick-up's headlights eastwards along it. Exactly on schedule the Tea and Sugar Train, with umpteen carriages, pulled to a precise halt with the grocery shop carriage next to the pick-up. We climbed aboard and bought supplies. It must have been about three or four in the morning. To our Australian companions, everything seemed mundane, except that they were almost as thrilled as we to see in the headlights on the way back the blood scarlet flowers of the iconic Sturt's desert pea, the floral emblem of South Australia. We stopped and warmly admired.

Victoria is an interesting state for many reasons. Politically, it was perhaps the only state or country whose general election was swung by a Standard and Poor's change in its rating. The premier for most of my time was the clever, quick-minded and likeable Jeff Kennett, with whom I did business happily. Melbourne, fascinating for its history, including as the first capital of Australia, for its architecture and its arts, is also distinguished by its fast-changing weather. I recall Jeff Kennett taking Margaret Thatcher one fine morning in a lift up a skyscraper on Collins Street, which then housed state government offices and the cabinet room. As we reached the top floor and the doors opened, Jeff stepped backwards into the cabinet room with its glass walls and splendid view. Arms stretched wide, he proudly said 'Welcome to Melbourne!' Something in Lady Thatcher's expression made him glance behind him and see pouring rain blotting out the view. Instantly, he added, 'We're just washing her down for you'. Later that day, over a meal, the two politically compatible leaders disagreed about casinos. Jeff had recently presided over the establishment of a large and profitable government-owned casino in Melbourne. Margaret Thatcher strongly disapproved, mainly on moral grounds, including harm to vulnerable minorities. Jeff defended his actions with the argument that the profits enabled his government to introduce large socially advantageous infrastructure and other state projects that could not be afforded from normal tax revenues. Both dug in, and I had to draw fire from each protagonist.

The state premiers and territory chief ministers I knew and worked with in Australia were people of high quality. Reformist Wayne Goss (Labor) in Queensland had a strong second-term majority reduced to one seat in 1995 in a close election in which, along with national politics, koalas played a part: their habitat was believed to be threatened by a planned new road. Wayne (whose chief of staff was former diplomat, later prime minister and then foreign minister, Kevin Rudd) lost his next election to friendly Rob Borbidge of the National Party, whose term in office was rocked by local and coalition issues and ended in his resignation the year after I left Australia. Richard Court (Liberal, broadly equivalent to UK Conservative) was Western Australia premier throughout our time. We had good conversations, including about United Kingdom–Western Australia business deals, which were large and growing. TV cameras were rolling when Consul-General Mike Horne and I called on Richard during Hilary's and my farewell tour of Australia by Rolls-Royce; Richard said he and his wife would have been more impressed had we driven the 17,400kms in a Morris Minor. Richard has an adopted Aboriginal daughter, whom we were delighted to meet by chance when we visited her school. Richard's father Sir Charles, whom we also knew and much liked, had also been premier. State, as well as federal, opposition leaders were also frequent contacts. Former Rhodes scholar at Oxford, Geoff Gallop of Western Australia (friend of Tony Blair and later premier) was always welcoming and both challenging and particularly rewarding in discussion. I recall talking to him about a bright British medical equipment company who exported to Indonesia hospital beds they manufactured in Western Australia – thoughtfully designed to meet particular Indonesian cultural needs.

In South Australia the two premiers in my time, Dean Brown and John Olsen, were political rivals within the Liberal Party. They were both most pleasant and helpful in United Kingdom–Australia commercial and political matters. John, whose premiership was probably the more controversial of the two, later became Australian consul-general in New York.

In Tasmania, where I was once much privileged to sit below the speaker's chair for a parliamentary debate, again both premiers in my time were of the Liberal Party: Ray Groom and Tony Rundle. The chief minister of the Australian Capital Territory during most of my time was the cheerfully helpful Kate Carnell, Liberal too, albeit initially in a minority government.

It was fun to take some British Labour parliamentarians to see New South Wales Labor premier, Bob Carr, the morning after he had defeated the Liberal incumbents. (The Conservatives of the visiting group had elected to do something else.) Bob's new office was crowded with men pushing trolleys of file boxes as he moved in. He asked cheerily what he could do for the visitors, who were then in opposition in the United Kingdom. One replied, 'A how-to-do-it kit would be helpful!' In March 2012, Bob Carr was made a senator for NSW and appointed by Prime Minister Julia Gillard to be foreign minister in succession to Kevin Rudd, who had resigned.

From retirement, Bob (who will be a mere 65 in 2012) fulfils an earlier frustrated ambition.

There is a vigorous rivalry over the qualities and attractions of those two marvellous cities, between Sydneysiders and Melbournians. It was good sport to tease the one about the other – until I debated Sydney's arguably more cosmopolitan, sailing and even culinary advantages over Melbourne with a Melbourne-based businessman. He acknowledged that I had a point or two, but asked if I knew what the real trouble was with Sydney. His answer was: 'It's just too far out of town'.

That attractive feature of Australian politics, checks and balances recurs. While Paul Keating was Labor prime minister, most of the states were under Liberal control. After Liberal success at federal level under John Howard in longstanding coalition with the National Party, that balance was largely reversed.

Hilary and I had visited Australia's delightful Lord Howe Island, so when Lord Howe of Aberavon, our much-liked former foreign secretary, Geoffrey Howe, came to Australia in May 1995, we were keen for him to go there too. So, he said, was his family, who had been wearing Lord Howe Island T-shirts since his elevation to the peerage. He enjoyed his trip there, evidently, in part because of the brief Hilary had written for him on the quirky politics of the island and its leaders. On his return to Melbourne and over drinks before a dinner George Finlayson gave for him, Geoffrey told me that it was a better brief than any he had read as foreign secretary. No doubt it was better than those I had written. He may, perhaps, have meant it was funnier, which it certainly was.

An interesting feature of Australian foreign and Commonwealth affairs is her relations with New Zealand. There are some parallels with the Anglo-Australian relationship, including fierce rivalry on the sporting field. I have illustrated above that Paul Keating is no great sports enthusiast. The Bledisloe Cup is the premier rugby union annual competition between Australia and New Zealand. It was played over two matches in 1995, the first in Auckland on 22 July, the same day as the launch in Williamstown, Victoria, of the first ANZAC frigate built for New Zealand, HMNZS *Te Kaha*. Rugby, of the highest national importance in both countries, has always seemed closer to an established church in New Zealand. Both prime ministers were to give speeches at the launch of the *Te Kaha*. Hilary and I, privileged to attend the launch (British equipment was involved) flew down to Williamstown in the vast cockpit of an RAAF Hercules. We were well ahead of schedule, so took the instinctive Australian action against a cold winter's early morning, and went into the nearest pub. There we found New Zealand Prime Minister Jim Bolger and joined in the informed and colourful conversation about the imminent Bledisloe Cup match. A couple of hours later we were in our seats on the podium, where Paul Keating stood waiting to make his launch-day speech. *Te Kaha* was poised, awaiting, no doubt, the right moment for man and tide. Paul Keating consulted his watch and aides and then asked the world around him where was Jim Bolger. I quietly left my seat and began a search of the quayside warehouses and offices. In a corner office on the first floor level, I found Jim Bolger and aides watching the game. They came and did their duty. Speeches, launch and essential photography accomplished, the New Zealand team disappeared: the game was still on. We mounted a bus to return to the aeroplane, with loudly cheering Aussies as they learned from the radio that Australia was leading in Auckland. The few Kiwis aboard were ritually ribbed. The game, however, was won by New Zealand before the bus ride ended. We congratulated the Kiwis. The Australians fell, equally ritually, silent, and remained thus. I presume the political damage to the Kiwi prime minister was minimised by the result and by no doubt the well-informed interviews he gave.

Per contra, I much enjoyed meeting John Eales, arguably the most successful Australian rugby captain ever, and learning that his nickname was 'Nobody' – because 'nobody's perfect'. I enjoyed even more Rob Andrew's last-second 1995 drop goal when England took Australia out of the World Cup, and hearing an Australian rugby union official at a reception next day argue that 'field goals' (as they call drop goals) should be abolished.

King Island lies between Victoria and Tasmania. On August 4th 1845, the emigrant ship *Cataraqui*, bound from Liverpool to Melbourne, was wrecked on the west coast of King Island in a storm.

Four hundred souls were eventually lost, of 409 aboard. The 150th anniversary of this, Australia's worst ever maritime civil disaster, was commemorated in a weekend of ecumenical service, ceremony, school projects and speeches, to which Hilary and I were invited. The dreadful tales abounded; the modern technical research impressed. In rain and wind, I read the lugubrious first lesson at the service by the memorial cairn on the shore nearest the rocks of the wreck. The service was memorable for civic involvement; for a fishing boat occasionally visible in the waves 100 metres off the shore near where the *Cataraqui* struck; and for a viticulturalist from Victoria. A descendant of a rare Cornish seaman-survivor, he broke down under the emotional strain of reading the second lesson.

Visits by FCO ministers to Australia could give useful impetus to bilateral work, and initiate more. Jeremy and Verna Hanley arrived at five o'clock one Sunday morning in September 1995 in Adelaide after an overnight flight from Singapore for a working visit that would also take us to Melbourne, Sydney and Brisbane. Among much else, Jeremy was to open our new trade-oriented consulate in Adelaide and new offices for the Brisbane consulate-general. A gentle first day of briefing seemed wise, and included lunch at a restaurant with a sense of humour and a menu with an entrée labelled 'Coat of Arms'. Jeremy learned from the waiter that the dish included a slice of emu and a slice of kangaroo (the two supporters on the Australian Coat of Arms). The minister chose the dish, saying that he couldn't get that at home. He and I have dined out ever since on the waiter's instant response: 'Too right you can't: you Poms have eaten all your flaming unicorns'! Work in Sydney allowed a brief visit to the iconic Sydney Cricket Ground and an imaginative performance by a 'ghost' of the ground: just right for the outgoing and positive Jeremy, who endeared himself to Australians in that visit.

Our next ministerial visitor the following week was the secretary of state for Northern Ireland, then Sir Patrick Mayhew, who came with Lady Mayhew. I had been keen for the secretary of state to visit: Irish nationalism in Australia had not died with Ned Kelly, and Sir Patrick delivered directly authoritative and corrective views to the press, government and other opinion formers in Canberra,

Melbourne, Brisbane and Sydney. I recall his particularly sterling and helpful performance at the National Press Club in Canberra. I left the secretary of state in Sydney with Roy Reeve (who had worked in Belfast) to return to Canberra to join Hilary in giving a dinner for a visiting UK Commonwealth Parliamentary Association delegation and Australians. In the next three days I had to prepare to lobby the relevant Australian minister on behalf of Scotch whisky; to brief a team from the Royal College of Defence Studies; to address the Australia-Britain Chamber of Commerce in Sydney; and to brief and accompany British Minister for Defence Procurement James Arbuthnot on ministerial and other calls in Melbourne, Adelaide, Canberra and Sydney. A signing ceremony and a dinner we gave for him closed that day. All good productive stuff.

Hilary and I were keen to call on Lowitja (Lois) O'Donoghue, an Aboriginal-born lady who was Paul Keating's appointee to the chair of the then Aboriginal and Torres Strait Islander Commission. Lois was known as a member of the 'stolen generation' – a reference to the practice under which children of, in her case, a mixed 'marriage', were removed from their families and provided with an education, often through church missions. In some cases, the children were given up by their parents. As we understood from her, Lois's parents lived in a remote part of northern South Australia, and took her to a mission for her education. From there she was removed to a children's care home in the Flinders Range. She did well, prospered and became a nurse. She did not like the word 'stolen', an emotional subject in Australian politics. We admired Lois's own later emotional public statement that had she not been 'removed' as she put it, she could never have achieved what she did for her people.

A visit to Western Australia focused on mining, and included Kalgoorlie, Meekathra, Kununurra and the Ord River Valley Irrigation Scheme (which has more water than Sydney Harbour), Hamersley iron operations and the Argyle diamond mine. We were especially glad to go underground to cool down from the 47 degree Centigrade temperature in the shade at ground level. In the following ten days, there was an Asia-Pacific security conference, and House of Commons select committee and more ministerial visits from Trade and ODA. Back in Canberra and Melbourne, there was a lengthy toast to Scotland to propose at a formal dinner of the Melbourne Scots; a speech to give and questions to answer at the Australian Institute of International Affairs; an export awards dinner in Sydney; and a three-day 1,300 delegate-strong national trade and investment outlook conference in Melbourne.

In late 1995, as the national debate about the future constitution of Australia was beginning to heat, I was inundated with requests and invitations to speak on the subject by both sides. I politely and resolutely declined them, needing to say on the matter only that it was nothing to do with the British government. However, I was beginning to be heckled on false assumptions in public, including once by a senior politician who should have known far better. I started to feel that there was so much misinformation and ignorance around Australia about the truth of the Anglo-Australian background to Australian constitutional developments that there was a need to put the facts on the record and to limit the risk of further distortion and of attacks on the United Kingdom. I had had (hardly necessary, I thought) oral instructions from the secretary of state before I left the United Kingdom for Australia to stay well clear of the debate. I thought that a clear, objective and unassailably accurate statement of the history might help to set the United Kingdom apart from the debate and demonstrate that there was no point in bringing Britain into the arguments. I therefore accepted two invitations to speak within three days to the Australians for Constitutional Monarchy and to the Australian Republican movement – both in Canberra. With the invaluable help of the excellent research department of the FCO, I wrote one 35-minute speech for both, arguably boringly entitled: 'The UK and Australia: close partners and sovereign independent countries'. It contained that objective statement of the history. It quoted Australian historians and politicians, argued why the Australia-Britain relationship was irrelevant to their debate and why it should grow still stronger in the interests of both countries. I recall being heard by both audiences perhaps attentively, but largely in silence, even through the obligatory sporting references, including one about the British military exchange officer who had been selected to play rugby for the Australian Army. I think the exercise paid off, though I may never know quite why I was never bothered with such invitations again.

Within a few days, I was giving a very different 'occasional address' in the Great Hall at the University of Sydney. Sometimes it is especially good to be a high commissioner.

A month earlier, in November 1995, Margaret Thatcher's visit to Australia as a former prime minister had posed some interesting problems of diplomatic management. John Howard had met Margaret Thatcher in 1988; but with an eye to longer term British interests, I thought it would be useful if, in 1995, Lady Thatcher were to meet leaders of the then Australian (Conservative) opposition. However, if the press were to learn anything of this, the results could easily be counter-productive. With the essential help of the consul-general in Sydney, we arranged a private dinner in a Sydney golf club house then closed for refurbishment. The golf club staff were wonderfully helpful and discreet. Denis Thatcher had not come on such a long visit, to my disappointment, but Hilary and I invited wives to the dinner party. The Howards, the Fischers, the Downers, Lady Thatcher and her private secretary all came. Lady Thatcher was in her element and usual fluent form, and offered advice that I privately thought a touch supererogatory on how best to win the Australian elections, then a few months away. I counted the evening an overall success, not least because the ruse worked, and there was no press coverage of the event.

By contrast a couple of days later, I took Lady Thatcher to call on Labor premier of New South Wales (and considerable historian) Bob Carr. We met him in his office overlooking – or looking down upon, as he made a jovial point of saying – the New South Wales governor's residence and domain. Within two months, Bob Carr announced that the new governor would neither live nor work at Government House. There is much history and local politics, including republican v. monarchist, in all this. A previous governor had dismissed an iconic NSW Labor premier in a constitutional crisis, and there was much protest. The use of Government House seems gradually to be changing.

Three months earlier, then leader of the opposition, Tony Blair and his family had visited Australia during the Christmas recess. The phrase 'Her Majesty's Most Loyal Opposition' had long fallen out of common parlance, but the British diplomatic practice of supporting the leader when abroad was natural and normal for us practitioners. Tony Blair visited old friends from Oxford – Geoff Gallop in Western Australia and Peter Thomson at his farm in Victoria – and flew to Hamilton Island at Rupert Murdoch's invitation. I spoke to Tony Blair several times on the telephone during his visit to offer various support and advice. Some advice he accepted; some he declined. I also spoke to members of the Australian government to help ensure that he met Paul Keating and others he did not know.

Paul Keating resigned his seat immediately on losing the elections in early March 1996. He was rewarded with a cartoon, most unusually in colour, in the *Canberra Times*. The cartoon depicted the slim Keating in uncharacteristic white tie and tails, taking a bow, Pavarotti-style, with, also Pavarotti-like, red roses strewn on the stage before him. Early that morning, I sought the original from the newspaper, only to be told that it had already been sold – no doubt to Paul Keating. I have a now much faded framed copy.

Paul disliked Canberra; Sydney was his place. Yet for the sake of his children's education, he stayed in Canberra for a couple of years. He was still there when I came to the end of my posting. I thought I should include him in my round of farewell calls. His response was firm: he would call on me. We put half an hour in our diaries. Paul was nearly half an hour late: his car had broken down while he was driving it, so he had walked. An hour and a quarter later we were still talking. He offered advice for retirement, including some he had learned from the iconic Jack Lang (like Paul, not a real socialist) to 'own something'. Paul Keating had owned a pig farm while prime minister, the management of which caused suggestions that he had misled parliament. But more interestingly, we had an engaging and instructive political conversation and he had sound comments on some of the (reproduction) furniture in the British residence and on some of the fine pictures owned by the British Government Art Collection. In his retirement Paul makes the occasional political intervention, his criticisms not sparing later leaders of his own party. He also pursues some business interests, collects antique French clocks and is a visiting professor in public policy at the University of New South Wales, where the audiences for his annual lectures are huge.

Hilary and I were in the tally room on 2 March 1996, the night of John Howard's convincing election win in Australia, a win that was no doubt applauded by John Major. Both Conservatives, they have a love of cricket in common too, and became and have remained good friends. Good cooperative work to the benefit of both countries followed. Hilary and I already knew John and Janette Howard, his fine foreign minister Alexander Downer and wife, Nicky, and a good number of other ministers well, and the high commission staff knew many others in the incoming government. This change of government in Australia meant a change of diplomacy for the high commission. That vital part of my job, managing relations between two heads of government, was suddenly bereft of inimical political undercurrents: the new and different task was now to make the best of calm seas and following winds. The bilateral party affinity provided a political background against which it was easy to develop useful exchanges. British and Australian ministers and officials quickly became used to exchanging ideas on public policy and practice with their opposite numbers, and to doing so with advantage to both countries.

Nineteen ninety-six was therefore another busy and different year in many ways. Work included planning the 'NewImages' campaign with the British Council, who, under Jim Potts and Jane Westbrook, did the bulk of the design and operation. NewImages was a major, year-long undertaking with many cultural, commercial and political aspects. The campaign spread right across Australia, including into schools, and tried to correct the false notions so many Australians had of modern Britain. The campaign hit home at a number of levels, did some real good and showed positive returns. Commercial sponsorship was effective and the sponsors were happy. We received many plaudits from thinking Australians. The federal government paid NewImages the compliment of mounting a parallel if smaller series of events in the United Kingdom under the same name; and an independent assessment was remarkably favourable. The more controversial later UK campaign, 'Cool Britannia', borrowed techniques and ideas from it. My only negative conclusion was that it might have to be repeated

– or bettered – in another ten or twenty years. But the financial resources will be lacking, no doubt.

The British high commission offices in Canberra were built in the 1950s at a time of exchange control constraints. The location is excellent. The building was rather uninspired and boring. By the 1990s it was also tired and worn. A new building was financially out of the question, but we made a case for some structural improvement and refitting and arranged temporarily to move out and rent offices in Canberra's nearby Old Parliament Annex. The FCO agreed and all concerned set to. Our Canberra architects worked with a will. They gladly accepted Hilary's brilliant idea for deepening the fenestration, which gave the whole building style and made the ordinary elegant. The architects designed a fine 'floating' staircase in Australian hardwood that splendidly solved a visual and practical problem, and a two storey atrium in glass that became the new entrance from the quieter garden side as well as a reception and even concert area. They barely flinched when deputy high commissioner David Fall, Hilary and I rejected all their first sets of proposals for internal furnishings. They started again and produced fine solutions. We moved back in ahead of schedule. Everyone was pleased. With the guidance and invaluable help of Dr Wendy Baron, Government Art Curator, we ran a limited competition for a porphyry sculpture that graces the garden and has inscribed around its base the words 'in tribute to shared sacrifice of British and Australian men and women in the defence of freedom'. The garden has an English oak grove. Concerned at the risk of damage by construction equipment or from building works upsetting the water table, we had surrounded the grove with substantial solid fencing, and kept the trees watered when necessary. When the fencing was removed, a healthy grove and a couple of hundred oak saplings greeted us. Hilary and a gardener potted them.

A pairing problem in the House of Commons prevented British ministerial attendance at the Canberra party in early February 1997, though Foreign and Commonwealth Secretary Malcolm Rifkind, whom I found particularly supportive of the campaign, and Prime Minister John Major attended a *New*Images event in London.

Despite the absence of a British minister – an absence the Australian politicians and press well understood – the Canberra party was a great success. Prime Minister John Howard spoke with characteristic verve, conviction, skill and evident pleasure. He made his important foreign policy statement that Australia does not have to choose between her geography and her history. He spoke warmly of the Australia–United Kingdom relationship, of its values and history shared, its traditions, its changing and developing nature, its modern characteristics, and its future. He noted that Australia and the United Kingdom are two of only eight countries in the world that remained continuously democratic throughout the entire twentieth century. But, recalling Dr Johnson's encouragement to keep our friendships in good repair, John Howard also urged that relationships between close friends, whether nations or people, should never be taken for granted, always be 'worked upon, refurbished, tended, and kept in the perspective of changing circumstances and changing times'. A rather good lesson for listening diplomats, I thought.

That evening, John Howard and I formally opened the newly refurbished building and launched *New*Images. Deputy Prime Minister Tim Fischer and I unveiled the sculpture. The band of the Australian Royal Military College, Duntroon played memorably. In a brilliantly professional venture by the Royal Australian Navy, at the extreme of refuelled range, single-handed British sailor Tony Bullimore had recently been rescued from his yacht, capsized while sailing (too far south in my view) in the Southern Ocean, in the Vendee Globe around-the-world race. As part of the Canberra party proceedings, I presented frost-bitten Tony in his wheelchair with a new passport – granted because it was too far to go back and retrieve his lost one. Hilary's potted English oaks, some 150 of them, were given as gifts to every couple and single guest as they left. Six saplings remained. They were cared for by a former air adviser at the high commission, Air Vice-Marshal Desmond Hall, who had made his retirement home in Canberra, and later by the National Parks people. The five surviving oaks were planted in Magna Carta Place near Parliament House. The Magna Carta monument there was erected by the fine Australia-Britain Society, in an initiative begun by splendid

British-Australians in our time. The site was dedicated on our last day in Canberra.

Among Australia's policy changes made after the March 1996 elections in Australia were some interesting shifts in foreign policy emphases, notably in the balance of attention to Asia and Europe. Paul Keating's government had stressed, with mixed results, Australia in Asia. Her relationship with China is vital economically and politically for Australia, but even that seemed beset for too long with more problems than success. John Howard and Alexander Downer rebalanced the policy. And, as I saw it, Australian relations with China improved quite quickly, to the benefit of both.

Ever since the Second World War, Australia-Indonesia relations have been on a roller-coaster. For many years, the war games and strategic planning studies in Australian defence establishments started with the assumption of an invasion from Indonesia – that huge archipelago arching its way like an inside-out umbrella or a threatening cloud across the northern spread of Australia, and lying between Australia and the rest of the world. Yet, by the mid-1990s, Australia was providing places for Indonesian officers at Australian staff college courses.

Between 1983 and early 1996 under Labor governments led by Bob Hawke, and particularly by Paul Keating, Australia saw a need to develop economic, commercial and political relations with the region to her north. Australia consciously sought convergence of interests, in pursuit of an aim the government then called 'economic complementarity'. Those policies certainly helped develop some of Australia's regional commercial relations, and hence her national interests. The surprise of the period, however, was a bilateral development: the sudden announcement of the signature of a security pact secretly negotiated in 1995 between Australia and Indonesia. That pact, in my view, contained some ambiguous wording (and arguably different meanings in the two languages) about the circumstances in which the provisions might be invoked, and when consultation, co-operation, even military involvement, would ensue, but it was nonetheless a major achievement for both governments and a contribution (for the rather short while it lasted) to regional stability.

From 1990 to 1997 in Jakarta and then in Canberra, Hilary and I watched at close quarters, with fascination and some concern, these two huge countries, so sensitive about each other, spar diplomatically, yet develop trade relations, begin some small measure of commercial interdependence, and even take some steps in military co-operation. This important roller-coaster of an international relationship declined steeply soon after 1997, but recovered pretty well again after a great deal of effort. Financial support, including intelligent intercession with the International Monetary Fund (IMF) by Alexander Downer and massive aid support after the Boxing Day 2004 tsunami, was important – and a good personal relationship between heads of government helped too, as always.

After March 1996, the Howard government returned to a broader internationalism, and to bilateralism in alliances and in strategies. Australian official spokesmen became more confident and positive about Australia's past, and criticised their predecessors for what they called 'the black arm-band school of Australian history'. John Howard and Alexander Downer not only led the development of closer ties with Europe and North America (there is now a free trade agreement between Australia and the United States), but also maintained and extended active engagement throughout Asia: Australia opened negotiations with ASEAN, which concluded in August 2008 in an ASEAN–Australia–New Zealand Free Trade Agreement.

Australia's change of international emphasis saw her world trade increase in absolute terms, her economy diversify, modernise, and grow well; and she was seen less in Asia as trying to be Asian without real Asian credentials. She also became rather more of a multiracial nation. In the first two years of the Howard government, 1996–98, Australia had paid off A$100 million of national debt, and turned an inherited A$96 billion deficit into a surplus. By the end in November 2007 of the nearly twelve years of that government, Australia had paid off all her national debt, balanced her budget and grown a substantial sovereign wealth fund. Thus she could face the global downturn in better state than many. A successful modern economy and democratic body politic, Australia came through the Asian financial crisis of the late 1990s in far better state than her regional neighbours. To the surprise of most commentators, Australian economic growth – rather low in the 1980s – accelerated through and after that crisis to almost 5% per annum. Commodity prices, as ever, will have helped, but are by no means the whole story.

The diplomatic convenience of like-minded parties in power in London and Canberra lasted from March 1996 until May 1997. The high commission took advantage of it to pursue and deliver a wider range of British objectives, including in trade and international politics. I felt we could emphasise the positive rather more. We failed, however, quite badly on climate change and the Kyoto protocol. The Australians argued that they were meeting what would be their Kyoto emissions obligations: we asked, 'Then why not ratify?' The reason, I concluded, was to do with higher costs and the risk of further investment in energy growth moving to lower cost countries, such as China, a huge and growing market for Australia. As we told Australians (as well as deploying more objective arguments), they risked being seen to shelter under the United States' capacious skirts. They were unmoved until much later, when the politics changed both within Australia and internationally. In his illuminating and important political autobiography *Lazarus Rising*, John Howard explains well these complex moves on the Australian federal and the global chess boards. I may dare to disagree with that finest of much published Australian historians Geoffrey Blainey on one detail of James Cook of the *Barque Endeavour* and Port Jackson, but everything else I have read of his I respectfully accept and support, including that John Howard will be seen by vast numbers of Australians as one of their great prime ministers.

Soon after Tony Blair became prime minister in May 1997, John Howard called on him in Downing Street. I sat on Tony Blair's right at the cabinet table that morning, and was thus well placed to see, in a young Blair face, signs of strain consequent, I felt sure, on his first experience of an almost all-night EU sitting in Brussels, from which he had just returned by air. There had been no time for a pre-meeting discussion. I wondered if Tony Blair had had a chance to absorb his written briefing, and how he felt about meeting a centre-right leader of a country he was very fond of but had seen through the eyes mostly of the intellectual left. John Howard was his usual pleasant and polite self. He briefly made his core values clear, and included his statement that Australia did not have to choose between her geography and her history. There was no immediate rapport, and I thought I detected some concern, too, in my opposite number the Australian high commissioner in London, Philip Flood, across the table. Both Philip and I intervened gently to try to help, and conversation flowed reasonably well. Tony Blair's intelligence was evident and sharp, despite his tiredness. Disagreement, polite but clear, on the then still vexed question of climate change entrenched positions rather than helped progress, and did not help this first meeting. It was clear to me that much work would once again be necessary to try to improve the relationship between prime ministers. Certainly, the two men worked well together at the CHOGM in Edinburgh in October 1997 (just after my retirement at the then mandatory age of 60) and thereafter on important world matters. They became friends. Tony Blair was the first British prime minister to address a joint sitting of the Australian Parliament. The Australian position on climate change did, eventually and with difficulty, alter.

Later that morning of the meeting in No. 10, John Howard called on Gordon Brown at the Treasury. We were an even smaller group, lacking, if I recall aright, any senior Treasury official. Once the conversation moved to rather abstruse tax theory, the rest of us became irrelevant. Former Australian Treasurer (= Chancellor) John Howard and Gordon Brown were on common home ground and much enjoyed the debate and each other's contribution to it.

I did think, during that cheerful exchange, how important the relationship was between the Bank of England and the (Sydney-based) Reserve Bank of Australia. It was a relationship I found it easy to help foster with the then governor, Ian Macfarlane, who conducted Australian monetary policy. An outstanding economist who had worked at Oxford and the OECD in Paris, he is rightly highly valued by politician, academic and civil servant alike. I needed to bother him rarely: when I did it was most rewarding.

Senior British visitors to Australia multiplied, both before and after the British general election. The trade mission flow further increased.

Chairman of the British Overseas Trade Board Sir Derek Hornby was welcomed around the country. Junior ministers and senior civil servants, such as that excellent permanent secretary at the Treasury, Sir Terry Burns, almost abounded. The chief of the general staff, all three service chiefs, the head of defence sales, captains of industry all came and advanced British interests, in co-operation with and to the advantage of Australian interests too. Industrialists included Sir Ralph Robins; Dick Evans; Sir John Egan, whom I had known when he led Jaguar Cars, and who now at BAA was looking for airports to buy and for advice on the relevant politics and best commercial approach; and, in connection with the acquisition of Qantas shares by British Airways, Sir Colin Marshall, the most effective and impressive chief executive of BA I have known (in retirement, Hilary and I drove for a day across New Zealand once to hear him speak). There are far too many more to mention: most did understand, or learn in time, that the Australian market place is a radically different place of business from the United Kingdom, and chock-full of opportunity.

The secretary of state for defence, Michael Portillo, visited in September 1996, the first holder of that office to visit Australia. He took a little persuading to do so: the Bosnian war was still raging, and NATO troops were by now heavily and crucially involved. That Canberra was one of perhaps only three capital cities in the world with the necessary classified real time communications capability helped. It was thus no surprise to be woken in the middle of the night by efficient telephone calls from the MOD, to bestir the defence secretary and to ensure he was swiftly at the Canberra end of those communications for urgent decision-making. Bilaterally the visit was most helpful across the range of defence (and some wider) interests: we covered high-level discussions on exchange officers, exercises, joint and overlapping policy matters, defence equipment sales and more. Hilary and I especially enjoyed Michael and his wife Carolyn's visit. So did senior Australians.

Another, earlier, ministerial visitor to Australia, from the other end of politics, had been a particularly able FCO minister of state, Derek Fatchett, who came with his wife, Anita. I thought Derek, too, was a serious loss to government as well as to all who knew him, when, tragically, he died in office at the age of 53.

On the far lighter side, the Melbourne Cup is the occasion for a public holiday in two Australian states. Attendance by the British high commissioner was as obligatory as top hat and tails. I recall completing a rather sensitive negotiation with the permanent secretary of a major Australian government department in Canberra while wearing most of that garb and using my mobile phone in a cubicle in the VIP 'stalls' at the Flemington Racecourse, Melbourne.

Lord mayoral visits abroad from the City of London are fairly frequent and can be useful in diplomacy. There is the problem of explaining why lords mayor serve only one year in office (then why should senior foreign officials bother to see them?), and, nowadays, the difference between the elected mayor of London and the lord mayor. The answer to both lies in the international importance for financial services and the apolitical leadership of the City. Thus we had a successful and productive visit by the personable and able Sir Alexander (Michael) Graham to Indonesia, which we could relate to a separate British Invisibles seminar there. Less explanation was, of course, necessary in Australia, where Sir Roger Cork visited, most ably supported by Judith Mayhew. Roy Reeve and I took the lord mayor to call on the premier of New South Wales at the parliament. Later that day, we learned that the lord mayor's jewelled badge of office had been lost. Even the travelling badge is of high value and iconic importance in the City. Only Roy could have known the hidden back way into the now closed and deserted Parliament. We persuaded the guards to let us in, and found the badge where we expected – down the back of a sofa.

There were important policy changes and developments under John Howard's new government to report to London. The high commission in my time was much blessed with a first-class team who relished their work and did it to high standards. None of us, nor his Australian colleagues, will forget Alastair Drummond, a fine analyst from the MOD, who had the very best of medical care and support in Canberra, but who so sadly died of a brain tumour, shortly after Hilary and I last saw him. Despite the predations of FCO inspectors during my predecessor's time, the private office was well staffed. Carol Dunnachie, wife of First Secretary (Economic) Hugh, upon whom I was much to rely, was my uncomplaining and always efficient personal assistant. When the Dunnachies left for retirement in Scotland, Ann Douthwaite arrived, also from Jakarta. Hilary and I counted ourselves fortunate and favoured indeed to be sent such a friend. Diplomatic Service senior secretaries are of the highest quality: Ann was among the very best of them. Hilary had a (busy) social secretary at the residence, but needed also to work with the PA in the office.

The deputy high commissioner position was key: on my arrival, it was occupied by the fast-thinking David Fall with his always bright and sound ideas, judgments and advice, and those vital qualities, a sparkling sense of humour and fine communication skills. Hilary and I hugely enjoyed his and his wife 'Dolyn's company. They had first met in Sydney as VSOs on their way to Papua New Guinea: the lineage of service shows. David was a forbearing and utterly reliable No. 2 in Canberra and more than deserved his immediate elevation to ambassador to Vietnam; and further promotion to Thailand (David is a fluent Thai-speaker) and contemporaneously Laos. In Bangkok, both David and 'Dolyn did and led towering and untiring work in the immediate and later aftermaths of the 2004 Boxing Day tsunami (and deserved the reverse of the pillorying David received at the hands of ill-informed journalists). The Falls were succeeded in Canberra in February 1997 by Andrew and Julie Pocock. It is no surprise that Andrew did very well in Canberra, was later ambassador in Harare in tough times and is now high commissioner to Canada.

All the staff throughout Australia, both Australian-engaged and UK-based, merit mention and gratitude. Lack of space also precludes mention of many other fine colleagues down the years in a Service that looks elitist from the outside but is a remarkable club of loyalists. But I should record that when I arrived in Canberra and called on Alexander Downer, one-time member of the Australian Foreign Service, then leader of the opposition and later a longstanding and distinguished foreign minister. His last remark to me at that first call was that I should know that the British high commission contained the single most effective diplomat in Australia, First Secretary (Political) Peter Beckingham. Peter later became head of the joint FCO/DTI export promotion directorate; consul-general in Sydney;

ambassador to the Philippines and deputy high commissioner in Mumbai.

David Fall quietly helped (he would say 'only at the margin') a wonderful and heroic British lady, Margaret Humphreys, a social worker from Nottingham who discovered the truth of the well-intentioned but in execution dreadful removal of many children from British (often unmarried, and often poor) parents by well-meaning organisations from the Second World War and on to 1970. With the apparent blessing of the Home Office, over 130,000 children were dispatched to Australia, and to (the then) Rhodesia, Canada and New Zealand, evidently to give them the chance of a better life. That children suffered physical, sexual and mental abuse; that many were told, untruly, that their mothers had died; that letters between them and their mothers were not sent on is a national disgrace. Apparently good, Christian, Australian organisations are also culpable. Statutes of litigation in some Australian states prevented redress. Margaret Humphreys established the Child Migrants Trust. She wrote *Empty Cradles* (which inspired a later British-Australian film, *Oranges and Sunshine*). She sacrificed family obligations to spend long months in Australia tracking down these people – and suffered in the process, including physical abuse herself. I recall a fruitless argument I had with the Home Office: I failed to stir any action there. Margaret was unflagging. She spent long hours with the former children in Australia, and, over time, reunited thousands of families. Hilary and I met some of the child migrants whom Margaret had tracked down at a gathering of them at Tony and Margaret Abbot's house in Perth. The Australian federal government recognised both the ills and Margaret's efforts earlier than did the British. Margaret was awarded the Order of Australia Medal years before she was made an OBE. I was thrilled when she was later promoted in the order to CBE. Her work, the work of the Child Migrant Trust, however, continues.

Our farewell tour of Australia by Rolls-Royce is described and explained in my book *RolleroundOz*, which also contains many more accounts of and thoughts about the unique, deep and mutually valuable Anglo-Australian relationship, which we should indeed always work upon and keep in good repair.

The tragic death of HRH The Princess of Wales occurred while Hilary and I were driving in the Northern Territory. We heard of it within an hour of the ghastly accident. The effects in Australia were remarkably similar to those in the United Kingdom; and although the royal family is Australia's in Australia, Hilary and I were deeply involved, as I have described in *RolleroundOz*.

To complete our farewell tour, we paid a particularly nostalgic visit to Tasmania. The list of formal farewell calls in the state and federal capitals, at nearly all of which some business was also done, included most of the Australian cabinet, premiers, opposition leaders and some leading industrialists. However, the final calls had to be truncated by unexpected and urgent work in Canberra and Adelaide on a consular matter – the Australian aspects of an alleged murder, allegedly by British citizens in the Middle East. This work involved long, late, complex negotiations with lawyers – especially Michael Abbott QC, one of the ablest in Australia, who was, as they say, against me, but whom I quickly learned to like as well as to respect. The task also included a free hand (avowedly with neither high cards nor trumps in it) from the FCO and some help from a British company. The outcome of this unusual diversion from winding down a diplomatic mission was more than satisfactory. It was made easier to achieve by strong support in research and drafting under pressure from First Secretary Rod Bunten. A fine officer, he was married to an Australian diplomat, Frances Adamson, now Australian ambassador to China. Rod is a sad loss to the British Service. The FCO employed him to good effect while Frances was deputy Australian high commissioner in London. Rod graced the groves of Australian academe when she was chief of staff to the foreign and the defence minister in Canberra. Rod too speaks Chinese: they constitute a notable Anglo-Australian success.

Consular work in Australia is unsurprisingly heavy. In my time the high commission had the largest passport-issuing operation outside the United Kingdom, widely and rightly admired as a well-run and cost-controlled production line. Hilary Dibble, then second secretary (consular), takes most credit.

The Anglo-Australian relationship certainly includes complexities and problems. One, the effect on the Australian exchequer of the fact that UK state pensions paid in Australia are not increased in line with inflation at home, was the source of much fierce debate with the Australian government as well as with 'frozen' pensioners. This problem is not restricted to Australia. The United Kingdom–Australia Social Security Agreement provided some help, including that emigrant British pensioners who passed means tests during their first ten years in Australia could receive benefits there. Successive Australian governments came to believe that the net effect was unfair and sought new arrangements. (Arrangements with the United States are different and more beneficial to British pensioners living there.) The rules are complicated. The issue is illuminated and distorted by hard cases and by sometimes emotional lobbying. We resisted the Australian arguments. When I paid a farewell call on the relevant minister, the argument was raised again with passion. I rehearsed the counter-arguments as coolly as possible, but left that 1997 meeting feeling that there was a risk of Australian abrogation of the social security agreement. I may just have helped hold the British government's line a little longer, but unilateral abrogation did happen: the agreement ended in 2001. It is typically Australian that the Canberra government also then passed its own legislation to protect the rights of some British migrants.

I have not dwelt on music and the arts. Sydney Opera House was extraordinarily welcoming to Hilary and me and, of course, thrilling. The Tallis Scholars sang divinely in concert, and later in our house. The Australian Chamber Orchestra under Richard Tognetti grew in reputation and thrilled us often, as it now thrills audiences around the world. I remember sitting next to my German colleague at one of their concerts: as we awaited a Beethoven piece, he whispered to me, '*Ah, echte Musik*' ('Ah, real music'). Later, I invited him especially to the Royal Shakespeare Company's (RSC) brilliant modern and new *A Midsummer Night's Dream* so that I could whisper to him, '*Ah, echte Literatur*'. The RSC, a young Frank Skinner and the Diversions Dance Company of Wales were among many British manifestations of the arts who contributed so well to the *New*Images campaign. They all helped our task of demonstrating the modern, high quality realities of the United Kingdom and of altering Australia's misperceptions.

Sports, broadcasting exchanges, technology, education, commerce, industry and science and much more joined them. A first-class *New*Images seminar on Anglo-Australian science exchanges was chaired by the then British government chief scientist, Sir Robert May – now Baron May of Oxford, a former president of the Royal Society and one of three Australian serving life peers. The other two are Baroness (Trixie) Gardner of Parkes and Baron (Alec) Broers of Cambridge. Bob May's seminar was crowned with a dazzling display of cosmic photography by David Malin, a British academic at the Anglo-Australian Observatory. The 180 other *New*Images events in Australia continued after our departure, which itself was marked for us most memorably when John and Janette Howard gave us a farewell dinner in their prime ministerial residence in Canberra.

By late 1997, I perhaps had something of an old image when I had to leave Australia at the then mandatory retirement age of 60. Well, not precisely: my longstanding bête noir, that institution called HM Treasury, required that one retire the day before reaching 60 – which was also the last day of salaried employment. We therefore left under our own steam, bound for a motel in the Sydney suburbs. A last, wonderful dinner followed with Sydney (and some Jakarta) friends at their harbourside house. Next morning we boarded a cheap flight to New Zealand. The compulsory fresh fields and pastures new beckoned, though the fresh fields were in practice waves. After a break, we sailed home non-stop as passengers aboard a container ship – not inappropriately pursuing her commercial business between Australia and Britain. That seemed right, as we left the Australia and the Service we loved to face retirement – for which I had not prepared in the least.

CHAPTER 12

REFLECTIONS *POST HOC*, AND A PARTIAL LOOK FORWARD

One foreign secretary sought to ban the use of Latin tags in the Diplomatic Service. Though I am by no means a classicist, in my case his instruction fell on incapable ears, so used was I to the trenchant and concise Latin tag way of conveying exact or convenient meanings. Hence the heading of this last chapter.

Our departure from Australia, albeit just over forty-one years after I had put my toe in the pre-Suez unhappy waters of the Foreign Office, made me sadder, and indeed angrier, than any other event in my career. Retirement at 60, when I thought I had learned how to do the job, seemed to me both absurd and a poor arrangement for the British taxpayer. I was fit; I had served in Australia for only three and a quarter years; there was so much more to do, and I thought I knew how to do most of it. But I had to make way for others. And I had had a fortunate career, with so much for which to be grateful, so little at which to complain and, I suppose, an average number of regrets – at that which I had failed to achieve or left undone. However, it is certainly right and good that members of the Service who are fit and able may now secure against the internal competition jobs which would allow, even compel, them to serve beyond 60. Would that that change had been allowed far earlier. Hilary and I would have relished at least another five years in the Service. And there is enormous advantage in spending a career doing work one enjoys and believes worthwhile.

At the age of 25 I might have favoured my seniors and betters retiring early, so that the rungs on the ladder were more accessible. But the only sound objection I can envisage to working past 60 is a reduction in physical or mental competence to continue to do the work well for an operationally reasonable period. The necessarily concomitant adjustments to recruitment and career planning can be made, and would overall be no bad thing as the excessively fast-spinning merry-go-round of postings could usefully be decelerated as part of the adjustment process.

As we put our bags into a taxi from the motel to Sydney airport, I told myself to cheer up. We were off for a month to New Zealand, which we had first visited during a journey back to Jakarta after mid-tour UK leave. We had the wit to visit Queenstown, and I the rare good sense to agree wholeheartedly with Hilary's impulse to buy a wooden holiday home some miles outside that dramatic town and adventure centre. The little house was half way up a mountainside with a 197-degree view from the mountains of the Remarkables Range to Lake Wakatipu and beyond. Within three days we had a mortgage and the keys. We were able to keep and enjoy the house quite frequently for nine years, until grandchildren needed some help with a roof over their heads: for that reason, we sold – the year before the film 'Lord of the Rings' was made across the valley and local house prices shot into space.

The Sydneysider taxi driver asked where we were bound. At our response, he said, 'New Zealand: I know what that is: that's a bloody great breakwater, way off Bondi.' Sublime, really, and a truly Australian send-off.

The Foreign Service that Hilary and I had joined and that had become the Diplomatic Service had changed a great deal in 40 years. Perhaps the most seminal changes in my time flowed from the Plowden Report, which led to the merger of the Foreign and Commonwealth Offices and Services, and to the finest, most radical and progressive reform of diplomatic work overseas ever. It was drafted for Lord Plowden by Donald Tebbit (later Sir Donald, ambassador, chief clerk, deputy permanent under-secretary of state and an enduringly effective high commissioner to Australia). Donald achieved where

I so often failed: he commanded the trust as well as the respect of those concerned in the Treasury, so the reforms were not opposed. They did great good for the United Kingdom and its diplomats. The much later information technology revolution could well have been the second most profound influence on the Service. It had many technical advantages, mostly in speed of operations; though initially at least, and arguably still, not in the security of the nation's classified information, where huge effort in skills, time and cost are needed to prevent serious damage to the public interest. The increased speed demanded quicker thinking: often, but not always, a salutary change. That quicker and more efficient conduct of diplomatic business has not been without disadvantage on the human and career planning fronts. For example, postings of diplomats used to be considered carefully against a detailed brief and personal knowledge. Nowadays, officers themselves bid for jobs on the computer screen. Their own skills and judgment in arguing for their preference will not be even. The results might include – and I suspect they have done so – the early promotion of the particularly bright and skilled in advocacy and lobbying, and the by-passing of less self-promoting yet able and experienced officers.

That of itself may not be entirely mistaken; though when combined with a political will to appoint younger heads of missions, it can risk performance abroad, especially in times of crisis such as political upheavals like the Arab Spring, major natural disasters and major rows with other governments. In these cases and more, experience is a valuable, even vital asset. If failures have occurred, is the officer solely to blame, or also the system? Too many early promotions can also have structural career disadvantage, and after an officer has had a few such senior appointments is there room, fairly, for more? That said, premature retirement is itself no bad thing if combined with extended service for the still able. That wise and brilliant permanent under-secretary of state and head of the Diplomatic Service, Sir Michael Palliser, tried to introduce progressive change in the 1970s. He proposed a system that would keep the best past 60 and retire others early in a civilised 'up or out' arrangement, but was defeated by ... the Treasury.

That the FCO, in common with other government departments, has a busy website is fine. But it will not impress or influence as much as it should, either abroad or at home (in what the Americans call public diplomacy) until its daily output is consistently written in far better English. So many formers of opinion abroad, not just, but notably, in Europe and the United States, to say nothing of Australia, write English well, convincingly and clearly. They abjure bad spelling, grocers' apostrophes and worse ills. It would be injurious to the pursuit of British interests abroad if the general decline in the standard of spoken and written English in Britain over the last decade or two were to have infected the FCO and Diplomatic Service to the extent I fear. FCO English may be at its worst on some of the websites, but it can be no excuse for British diplomats to argue, as some apologists do, that the means of communication are of less importance than the ideas and arguments communicated. In diplomacy above much else, accurate, precise, well-constructed and skilful communication is essential for the effective delivery of the message – and hence of British aims and objectives. A guide for new entrants written in the 1970s had much good, timeless advice, including 'do not eschew a dictionary'.

Resource cuts for the Diplomatic Service naturally grieve me. I doubt if, for many years, the Service has been as successful in negotiating on this front with the Treasury as it is overseas in negotiations on behalf of HM Government (though I shall never forget, after negotiations failed at officials' level, Lord Carrington simply saying 'no' repeatedly at a Star Chamber and thereby securing the resources the FCO needed). Then there are the necessary austerity measures of the present times. The concept of equality of misery that applied from the time the United Kingdom had to go cap in hand to the IMF has evidently been abandoned. The resources allocated to the FCO seem to me to have been limited disproportionately. The result is that in too many parts of the world the Diplomatic Service is less than able to fulfil its proper role in advancing British political, commercial, economic, consular and other interests. In my early days, the FO argued for the substance of what was needed: following agreement on that substance, the cash was provided. It is probably right that that system was changed from control of volume to control of cash – during, I think, Denis Healey's chancellorship.

Yet the removal by HM Treasury, without compensatory measures, of the overseas price mechanism under which the FCO could arrange some sensible hedging in currencies was surely a serious mistake. That the FCO could not find sufficient compensation for the falls in the value of the sterling it must use to buy currencies with which to pay its way and do its duty abroad was short-sighted and damaging to the national interest. It could be crippling. Secretary of State William Hague has presided over the wresting from HM Treasury of welcome positive change in this area. FCO battles with the Treasury are inevitable, and the history is too often a sorry one.

The 2011 decision to 'localise' some 400 UK-based jobs in posts abroad must have resulted from disproportionate resource cuts in London, and is surely another serious mistake. Thus to remove a large swath of jobs for junior and middle ranking UK-based diplomats is to deny essential training and experience to future senior representatives of the United Kingdom who need to have had that experience in order to do their jobs properly and effectively for Britain and British interests. The consequence that officers in the two junior grades of British diplomats may not now expect to serve abroad at all in those grades must have a deleterious effect on morale and eventually on recruitment, and distort the career badly. However able locally engaged officers abroad are – and I have worked with some excellent ones, British interests are bound further to suffer in the long run from this move. That wrong should also be righted, and as soon as possible. The British Diplomatic Service used to be judged by foreign governments as the best in the world. I am sure that the intelligence and ability of our diplomats is as high as ever; but if doubtful structural, personnel and financial decisions are made, I fear for the ultimate performance and reputation.

One current British foreign policy that was only a distant dream even when I left the Service is the commitment to spend 0.7% of our gross national income (GNI) on overseas development aid from 2013. In pursuit of that doubtless noble aim, our gross annual public expenditure on development (of which 85% is the DFID aid programme itself) increased by 16% between 2009–10 and 2010–11 to over £9 billion. We rank second (to the United States) among all the OECD-DAC (development assistance committee) aid donors, and in 2010 reached 0.57% of GNI. When I served as assistant under-secretary (economic) in the 1980s, we were striving and failing to reach 0.3% – but still held our heads high. We were restricted not only by budgetary constraints, like other government departments, but importantly also by the ability to spend aid money well, accountably to the taxpayer, and to deliver value for money. An apparently quick way to dispense (non-humanitarian disaster) aid was then, and perhaps is now, to give budgetary support aid direct to the governments of developing countries. Yet that way is fraught with risk, including of British taxpayers' money being siphoned off by corrupt governments: immense care and some cynicism in judgments (including by diplomats in the field, not just the 'aiders') along the way are required. Project aid carries complex risks, too, and needs commensurate care and attention.

The jury may be out on whether in practice it is possible for even an expanded DFID over time both to deliver good value for money to the taxpayer and to provide aid that defensibly sustains and delivers real development. However, I worry. The nobility of the aim and the ring-fencing of the aid budget may be argued to answer critics of the policy's affordability and to justify the risks, but risks I am convinced there are. I am sure I would be a lone voice in the modern wilderness were I to argue for the restoration of the aid for trade provision (ATP) of the 1980s and 1990s, abolished, unsurprisingly, against the advice of the Confederation of British Industries and others. My experience of ATP was favourable and showed that provision often to be spent wisely, well and directly on sustainable and sustained development projects abroad (e.g. electricity generation and water supply, even in Indonesia). The British companies who secured the contracts – and created and preserved jobs – may be seen as biased, but they had a healthy interest in ensuring value for money for the taxpayer; and an element of thus 'tied aid' (later a dirty pairing of words) did no harm to the British economy or reputation.

Our postings abroad were distinctly varied. Culture shock accompanied each change – shock which Hilary and I relished. Critics of the

Diplomatic Service sometimes argue that since we flit frequently from post to post and subject to subject, we are butterflies, lacking staying power and depth of experience. I usually respond that butterflies have sensitive antennae and make good use of the nectar they collect, that diplomats are versatile, and that versatility is a national requirement since the world changes fast and often. That said, the Diplomatic Service needs its specialists. Though I know that my Arabist colleagues nearly all enjoyed their specialism, I should not much, I think, have enjoyed being an Arabist, in large part because of the restrictions that would have imposed on Hilary, who had in any case to accept her own loss of career. I half expected to become a Soviet specialist, or at least a Slavist. The Cold War might easily have led in that direction, but timing, availability of jobs, one's superiors' views of where one might best be placed, and the operational demands on the Service at relevant times decreed otherwise.

Service at home in the Office was more in quantity than I had originally hoped for, but provided wonderful reliefs in that we could see so much more of our children. As for the decision to send them to boarding school, a *post hoc* judgment is not possible, because the experiment was not a controlled one. The boys pull our legs to this day, though they had some rare and wonderful holidays abroad with us. At all events, it was a joy to see something of them in the UK. I had a day off to join Hilary and watch our younger son Charles undertake a parachute jump for charity. He had trained well for two full days before the jump, which was from some 3,000 feet, high above Kent. Charles told us that he would be jumping from the aeroplane in fifth position. We watched, avidly, and 'counted them out'. To our utter horror, number five jumped but no parachute unfurled. Another figure then dived in free fall down to meet number five, whom he grabbed, sorted out what was evidently a reserve parachute, and two parachutes opened as the two men separated. Later, Charles came strolling towards us carrying a bundled parachute, and wearing a broad grin. It was only then that we learned that number five was not Charles! He had been moved to number six, had been in no extra danger, and enjoyed the experience hugely. We had watched someone else. Our relief became a mixed emotion of concern for the other man and his frightening escapade, and delight as Charles told us that he had been so thrilled that on the way down he had been singing (something, mercifully, he does not do on the ground) and reciting poetry he was not aware he knew. Much later, the reason for the change in order of jumping was revealed. As Charles put it, 'the others were all firemen, big, burly and brave – until it came to jumping'. One had evidently needed a deal of physical encouragement to leave the aeroplane.

Partly because we then lived in Kent and partly due to my service in OED, the FCO asked me, after retirement, if I would become a member of the board of trustees of the Chevening Estate. After a meeting with the then lord privy seal and leader of the House of Lords, Ivor Richard, I was appointed. The appointment was later extended by the prime minister. The estate includes an especially fine country house. Its owner arranged by Act of Parliament that it should be available to 'nominated persons' on a list he provided. The owner was the last Lord Stanhope (who, among many other fine services to the nation, was a member of the cabinet, including as lord president of the council, and established the National Maritime Museum). The nominated persons have included the Prince of Wales, but have mostly been foreign secretaries. It was a pleasure to serve, with fine co-trustees, for five years until we moved house to Exmoor, and a bonus to visit Chevening since.

The Britain-Australia Society and the Cook Society also took, and still take, some time and happy effort, mostly now in the West Country. The Cook Society was founded in 1969 by prime ministers Alec Douglas-Home and Bob Menzies. I have believed for years that this was after we diplomats had not achieved enough. The society was formed primarily of senior businessmen and charged with improving relations, notably in trade and investment. It did well and continues to do so.

However, after a couple of failed attempts, the 'real world of commerce' allowed me past its portals to engage with a number of companies. I chaired a few, and for eleven years was deputy chairman of the D Group, a leading networking group with an international emphasis, founded by its presiding genius for many years, Paul

Cautley CMG DL. Paul's skills in lateral thinking and operating are legendary. At the D Group I was constantly reminded that most of government and business do not understand each other well. They have to be brought together, helped and the one explained to the other as each generation takes office.

Hilary and I have delightedly returned often to Australia, mostly by virtue of lecturing aboard cruise-ships. It was also a joy to be invited to return to Chicago, twice. We marvelled in awe at the Chicago Shakespeare Theater and at Barbara Gaines' superb work. I was asked to lecture at the University of Wisconsin, Milwaukee. At the university's request, one lecture was about the United Kingdom and Europe. I entitled it 'Britain and Europe: one foot in and one foot out'. *Plus ça change.* The title of the other lecture a few years later was given to me by the university: 'The Cost of Conflict and the Value of Peace-Building'. Perhaps that title is something of a *pièce justificative* for much diplomacy.

There are, of course, myriad definitions of diplomacy. Among the most common is that attributed to Sir Henry Wotton (1568–1639): an ambassador or diplomat 'is an honest man sent to lie abroad for his country'. The most believable explanation is that Wotton, a diplomat himself, wrote those words in an ambassadorial visiting book in rather sharp jest: the word 'lie' in his time also meant 'stay' or 'live'. In my view and experience, a diplomat who lies fails. I rather enjoy the ideal definition which none of us quite achieves: to tell someone to go to hell and make him look forward to the journey. However, mine own recalls, and is about as misleading as that defining a lady: 'when she says no she means perhaps; when she says perhaps she means yes; and if she says yes, she is no lady'. Mine is: 'when a diplomat says yes he means perhaps; when he says perhaps he means no; and if he says no he is no diplomat'.

One British minister used to be habitually awkward about officials. He wrote that he used to ask British ambassadors what their job was, and never received a satisfactory answer. He was, I suppose, mostly making a point about commercial diplomacy. I wish he had asked me. I hope I would have replied that an ambassador's job is to pursue the interests and business of his government, of his country's economy and its people, and to do so in the government, body politic, culture and, crucially, the market place of the country to which he is accredited. As mentioned in Chapter 9, there is new hope for commercial diplomacy: let us hope sufficient resources of sufficient quality are devoted to its success.

In these days of instant communications I am occasionally asked why we need a Diplomatic Service at all. Why do not home civil servants and ministers do the work in direct contact with their opposite numbers abroad? I am told that only two countries operate, or operated, without distinct and separate Diplomatic Services: the small Seychelles Islands and Qadhafi's Libya. It is hard to contest that a body of people who are flexible, able, willing and equipped to spend most of their working life operating overseas in different cultures is necessary for the proper conduct of a country's business in the world. It would be wrong for such a service to exclude, for example, some secondments to posts abroad from academia, industry and home departments, especially where particular sectorial expertise would help the work. Crucially, a diplomatic service represents not its own headquarters, be it foreign office, state department or department for foreign affairs, but its whole government, from treasury to national archives. It thus has a responsibility to rise above all too frequent turf wars, to ensure coherence as far as possible, and to pursue national above departmental policy and interests. Absence of that coherence produces exploitable weaknesses.

It is worth adding that the British usually do, or did in my day, their major bilateral work through their own embassies, rather than with the foreign embassies in London. This is seen by some as a factor of the quality of the Diplomatic Service and of the access its members have abroad to those foreign officials who count. I think it rather more a matter of the history of the conduct of foreign affairs and secure communications, and of recognition that the man or woman on the spot understands how most effectively to conduct Britain's business in the culture in which he or she lives. That is not to deny that modern communications do allow some technical bilateral work to be done efficiently through direct contacts between officials in the two capitals. Yet there are dangers. I well recall how essential it was for British and American diplomats, properly and officially, to listen to the important, sometimes crucial telephone conversations between Prime Minister Margaret Thatcher and President Ronald Reagan. The diplomats had to agree between them exactly what had passed and what had been decided. Each head of government often had a different view from the other of those conversations. In this field, as in many others, the more the world is 'globalised', the more it demonstrates that it remains a world of separate states.

When I wrote my valedictory despatch from Jakarta in mid-1994, such despatches were, to the regret of many, no longer compulsory. Valedictory telegrams succeeded them but were abolished by ministerial decision in 2006 following some arguably excessive publicity for one valedictory that contained some thoroughly justified criticism of the Whitehall management culture of the day and of the application of too much political correctness. I very much share that regret, not only for the loss to diplomacy of frank, experienced views and advice, even that which may later prove ill-advised, but also for the serious loss to history of sometimes newly enlightening and valuable original source material in the public archive. Matthew Parris (whom I just recall when he was a young desk officer in the FCO and met again when he spoke to the D Group) and Andrew Bryson have done the British body politic and wider public good service in their book *Parting Shots* by editing and reproducing a selection of the genre available at the National Archives. I agree with many, though not all, of the book's conclusions; and was much relieved that my own valedictory efforts were either not available or not selected by the editors. Perhaps this longer anecdotal valedictory may be of some use.

It is time to return to advanced training for old bufferdom.

ACKNOWLEDGMENTS

Hilary, for inspiration, corrections and excellent editorial suggestions.

Sir Nicholas Bayne, Mark Bertram, David Montgomery, Roy Reeve, and Sir Derek Thomas for facts, corrections, advice and encouragement.

Dr Ronald Hyam of Magdalene College Cambridge, for finding the ambassadorial telegram of 18 September 1963 from Jakarta to the FCO and the prime minister's comments thereon, and for writing to me about it.

Colonel Ian Ker, former military attaché in Jakarta, for his most helpful reading, comments on and additions to the section in Chapter 10 about Corporal Collins of the Royal Marines.

A variety of cruise ships, and their staffs in Far Eastern and Pacific seas and the Danube, and the time between lectures allowing work on this book.

Colleagues and protagonists, and all who made real people-to-people diplomacy work. In particular a good number of people, unnamed or insufficiently praised, and especially some of the greats in Australia, whose friendship and fellowship made for such fruitfulness and fun.

Olivia Bays, for fine editorial understanding and wisdom.

BIBLIOGRAPHY

Bayne, Nicholas. *Economic Diplomat: The Memoirs of Sir Nicholas Bayne KCMG*. Durham: The Memoir Club, 2010.

Bertram, Mark. *Room for Diplomacy.* Reading: Spire Books, 2011.

Carrick, Roger. *Admiral Arthur Phillip RN, Founder & First Governor of Australia: A British View*. London Papers in Australian Studies No. 17. Menzies Centre for Australian Studies, King's College, London, 2011.

Carrick, Roger. *RolleroundOz: Reflections on a Journey Around Australia*. St Leonards NSW: Allen & Unwin, 1998.

Carrick, Roger. *East–West Technology Transfer in Perspective*. Policy Papers in International Affairs. Institute of International Studies, University of California, Berkeley, 1978.

Falle, Sam. *My Lucky Life: In War, Revolution, Peace and Diplomacy.* Lewes: Book Guild, 1996.

Hall Brierley, Joanna. *Spices, The Story of Indonesia's Spice Trade*. Oxford: Oxford University Press, 1994.

Howard, John. *Lazarus Rising*. Pymble NSW: HarperCollins, 2010.

Humphreys, Margaret. *Empty Cradles*. London: Corgi Books. 1995.

Parris, Matthew and Bryson, Andrew. *Parting Shots*. London: Penguin, 2011

INDEX

VISAS

ambassador

IMMIGRATION CONTROL
LARNACA AIRPORT

2 - ARRIVAL -
- 1 FEB 1985

T.R.(EMPLOYMENT)
T.R.(BUSINESS)
T.R.(PUPIL)
T.R.(TRANSIT)

EMBASSY OF THE REPUBLIC OF IRAQ
CONSULAR SECTION LONDON

AUG 17 1983
ST. VINCENT, W.I.

HOLDER IS A MEMBER OF

HER BRITANNIC MAJESTY'S

DIPLOMATIC SERVICE

IMMIGRATION
SERVICE

20 JUL 198

HONG KONG

NAIROBI AIRPORT
KENYA

REPUBLIC OF K_
IMMIGRATION OFFICER
- 9 MAR 1983

115

NAIROBI AIRPORT

上陸許可
ADMITTED

17 FEB. 1985

DURING
MISSION

DEPARTED
22 FEB. 1985

NARITA(1)

PASSPORT OFFICE

18 MAY 1990

187
LONDON